PROBLEM SOLVING:
Research, Method, and Theory

PROBLEM SOLVING:

Research, Method, and Theory

Benjamin Kleinmuntz, *Editor*

Contributors for This Volume

D. E. Berlyne, *University of Toronto*
Garlie A. Forehand, *Carnegie Institute of Technology*
Robert M. Gagné, *American Institutes for Research*
Israel Goldiamond, *Institute for Behavioral Research*
Bert F. Green, Jr., *Carnegie Institute of Technology*
Adriaan D. de Groot, *University of Amsterdam*
John R. Hayes, *Harvard University*
Allen Newell, *Carnegie Institute of Technology*
Jeffery M. Paige, *University of Michigan*
Herbert A. Simon, *Carnegie Institute of Technology*
B. F. Skinner, *Harvard University*
Arthur W. Staats, *University of Wisconsin*
Donald W. Taylor, *Yale University*

The First of an annual series of symposia in the area of cognition under the sponsorship of Carnegie Institute of Technology

John Wiley & Sons, Inc.
New York • London • Sydney

Library of Congress Catalog Card Number: 66-14136
Printed in the United States of America

Preface

The papers in this volume were prepared for and delivered at the first annual symposium on cognition held at the Carnegie Institute of Technology on April 15 and 16, 1965. Each annual symposium for the next several years will focus on different facets of topics that could come under the heading of cognition. This year's topic was problem solving, and judging from the group of eminent psychologists we were able to obtain to participate, and the enthusiastic reception given these scientists, the choice of topic appears to have been a timely one. Problem solving is an area of much current interest; however, work in this area has lagged considerably behind the interest. It was the major purpose of the symposium, and of this book, to stimulate further interest in and disseminate information about the work that is being planned and done on problem solving.

The symposium was conducted as follows: On the morning of April 15, Professors Adriaan D. de Groot and Herbert A. Simon presented their papers and these were discussed by Professor Donald W. Taylor. During the afternoon Professors

Robert M. Gagné and John R. Hayes spoke about their work and this was discussed by Professor Allen Newell. On the following day, Professors Israel Goldiamond, B. F. Skinner and Arthur W. Staats made their presentations. Professor D. E. Berlyne's discussion of these papers concluded the symposium.

The order of the paper presentations has been preserved; and the papers themselves, with minor editorial modification, are essentially the same. The discussants' remarks can be found immediately following the relevant papers; but rather than publish these in their transcribed and possibly rough forms, Professors Taylor, Newell and Berlyne prepared written versions of their comments. Additionally, for purposes of providing the readers of this volume with a cohesive and integrated presentation, Professor Bert F. Green, Jr., has written an introductory chapter which describes and evaluates some current trends in the research, method, and theory of problem solving. And Professor Garlie A. Forehand, in the epilogue of this book, has written a carefully considered critique and synthesis of the various and diverse points of view presented during the symposium.

Of course the vibrant vitality of the symposium, attended by some 300 interested persons, cannot be preserved entirely between the covers of a book. The reader is therefore deprived from experiencing the lively exchanges that occurred during and following each session. Among other things the reader will have to conjure an image of the consternation on Skinner's face when the information processing group spoke of internal representations and of information storage. Moreover, the reader will have missed being a "pigeon" in Goldiamond's experiment which required audience participation. Finally the reader cannot possibly reconstruct the comic situation that occurred when one of our speakers inadvertantly wrecked the reading lamp on the podium and then calmly announced, "there will be a fire shortly." But if he has been denied some of the benefits that are derived from attending one of these symposia, the reader has nevertheless an advantage in that he can skim and skip and is free to select those portions of some papers that seem to him to have most relevance to the major points being made. This gives the reader many more degrees of freedom than the 180° afforded the person who must sit through some of this.

The publication of this and future volumes within this series on cognition, has been made possible by grants from the Carnegie Corporation, and the National Science Foundation; and the time spent by me in organizing the symposium and editing this volume was supported in part by a grant from the National Institutes of Health (GM 11734-02). On behalf of the Department of Psychology, I should like to express my indebtedness to these foundations. Royalties that accrue from the sale of this and future volumes in the series will be used to defray the costs of future symposia, and possibly for other graduate training purposes.

Special gratitude is due the symposium participants whose total and cheerful cooperation has made this event and publication a meaningful learning experience for all concerned. I also gratefully acknowledge the assistance given by the Administration of Carnegie Institute of Technology, especially that of Dean Richard M. Cyert. Thanks are due to Mrs. Betty H. Boal for her efficient handling of many of the administrative and secretarial details without which symposia cannot be held. And finally, it would be unjust not to express my fondest appreciation to my wife, Dalia, for her innumerable intangible contributions.

Benjamin Kleinmuntz

Pittsburgh, 1965

Contents

1 BERT F. GREEN, JR.
Carnegie Institute of Technology

Introduction:
Current Trends in Problem Solving *

Problem solving has always been easier to talk about than to investigate. Until about ten years ago, psychological research on problem solving could best be described as sporadic. A few lonely scientists worked consistently in the area but there was no major point of view or technique to bring this work into focus, as Hull's stimulus-response (S-R) theories and Skinner's operant techniques had done for learning. Then, Newell, Simon, and Shaw (1958) introduced a new theory of problem solving, based on concepts of information processing and computer programming. They were primarily interested in the process of solving problems and argued that computer programs could serve as exact, unambiguous theories about the way humans process information to arrive at solutions. Their approach has spawned a number of experimental and theoretical studies, but its main

*This work was supported by Grant MH 07722 from the National Institutes of Health, United States Public Health Service.

3

importance is in providing a theoretical position for students to acclaim or assail. The resulting arguments have been lively and fruitful; controversy often begets progress in science.

At about the time that information processing theories were being introduced, some (S-R) theorists and operant-behavior analysts were turning their attention to the complex behavior exhibited in problem-solving situations. Arguing that complex behavior is not different in kind from simple discrimination learning, they proceeded to analyze problem solving in the language of operants, habit family hierarchies, and chains of association. (See, for example, the following, all reprinted in Anderson & Ausubel, 1965: Staats, 1961; Kendler, 1963; Cofer, 1957; Maltzman, 1955; Schultz, 1960.) Generally, these researchers have disavowed any interest in process, preferring either "mediating responses" or nothing at all intervening between stimulus and response in the problem-solving situation.

The trouble with problem solving and other behavior we call thinking is that a simple S-R contingency or a chain of such contingencies does not provide an adequate account of the behavior. Hierarchies of S-R contingencies are needed. Staats provides an example in this volume when he tries to show that S-R chains can be used to explain verbal behavior. The resulting argument is so totally unconvincing and unreasonable that it implicitly demonstrates the need for something else. Studies of grammar by Miller, Chomsky, and others (see Miller, 1962), strongly indicate that some kind of hierarchical organization is crucial in any adequate theory of verbal behavior. Organized hierarchies of activity are the

substance of computer programs so the language of programming (flow diagrams, subroutines, list structures, and the like)
provides a convenient way of talking about complex behavior.
In fact, Millenson (1964) has pointed out that a hierarchy of
S-R contingencies can readily be translated into a hierarchy
of TOTE units (Miller, Galanter, & Pribram, 1960), or into
other programming representations. Nevertheless, the behaviorists focus their interest on the S-R units, whereas the
information processors attend mainly to the organization of
units into hierarchies.

The emphasis on organization is not new. Gestalt psychologists such as Köhler (1925), and Wertheimer (1945) had
seen problem solving as a matter of integrating previously
learned responses. For them, true problem solving was insightful, meaning that the organization occurred relatively
suddenly (the "aha" experience) and that the organization of
responses was both enduring and readily generalizable. But
Gestalt psychology had little to say about the structure of insightful organization, and the research springing from this
tradition was concerned mainly with establishing insight as a
phenomenon.

The research strategies of the behaviorists and the information processors correspond with their differing attitudes
toward organization. The behaviorists press for simplicity,
wanting clear relationships and unencumbered theories. They
view the organism as an inaccessible black box, and they seek
the relationships between the inputs and the outputs of that box
by choosing appropriate stimuli and recording appropriate responses, so that the contingencies are manifestly clear. The

information processors prefer complex, or as they say, "rich" experimental situations so that the complex structure of man's behavior can be displayed. Evidence for the processes intervening between input and output are sought usually by obtaining "thinking aloud" protocols from the subjects.

Another suggestive difference between these schools of thought is in the interpretation of the close relationships between learning and problem solving. One school feels that problem solving is but an extension of learning; the other believes that learning is often problem solving in disguise. As Shepard (1964) puts it: "Human subjects who are certainly capable of problem solving and thought do not abandon this faculty when they enter the learning laboratory. On the contrary, in order to deal with the welter of unfamiliar material with which they are suddenly beset in the usual rote learning task, human subjects will resort to any strategy or heuristic device at their disposal." For example, in the familiar binary choice experiment human subjects are asked to predict on each trial whether a red light or a green light will go on. When a subject has made his prediction, one of the two lights is turned on according to a prearranged random sequence in which each light has a certain chance of being selected, for example, 75% red, 25% green. Human subjects cannot easily be convinced that the alternative stimuli are governed by random processes and are not serially dependent. Feldman (1961) used this observation as the basis for a problem-solving theory of behavior in the binary choice experiment. He found that subjects clearly formed hypotheses about the sequence and kept trying to find some basis for prediction.

In rote learning experiments, it is necessary for subjects
to take an active role in the experiment if they are to learn something. They must *try* to learn, whatever that means. I once had
a subject in a finger maze learning experiment who, unfortunately,
had read and believed the theories of incremental learning. He
passively ran his finger up the maze, trial after trial, confident-
ly expecting his finger finally to learn the maze. After his
finger had had four times as many trials as the other subjects
had needed, I persuaded him to take a more active role in the
proceedings. In this experiment the subject must symbolize the
information in some way, and must choose some representation
of the information—presumably as a sequence, such as right,
right, left, right, left . . . . Then on successive trials he must
find the correct symbols for each position in the sequence and
learn the sequence. This activity seems to qualify as problem
solving. There is less of it in verbal experiments because the
experimenter has done everything he can to eliminate it. The
typical rote learning experiment uses nonsense syllables of low
association value in an attempt to keep the subject from solving
the problem by using meaningful associations and other "mne-
monic devices." How hard it is to suppress problem solving!

The author's bias must now be clear to the reader. Information processing models seem the best way of explaining
complex behavior. No attempt will be made here to present
the behaviorist's position. Goldiamond has done that very well
in his paper in this volume, and certain aspects of this approach have been amplified by Skinner and Staats. The information processing approach does not fare so well because its
representatives (de Groot, Simon, and Hayes) have discussed

particular problems and experiments but have provided very little background. Consequently, this paper attempts to provide the necessary background.

First, however, some of the major findings in research on problem solving will be reviewed. Gagné provides a thorough analysis of problem solving, and he and the other authors refer to most of the relevant literature, so only a few selected findings will be discussed here to indicate the nature of past research in the area.

THE CONDITIONS FOR PROBLEM SOLVING

Traditional research on problem solving has examined the conditions for the occurrence of problem solutions with major emphasis on the previous learning of the problem solver, perhaps interacting with the structure of the problem. Köhler (1925) observed that his apes needed to have previously learned the relevant responses before they could put these responses together into a complete problem solution. Thus, the ape who · fit the two sticks together to reach a banana beyond the reach of either stick, had first to learn that a banana outside the cage can be brought in with a stick. Then, when the ape fit the two sticks into one, more or less by chance, the solution to the problem occurred swiftly.

Both "functional fixedness" and the "atmosphere effect" show that learned associations of some elements in a problem can affect problem solving. In the famous two-string problem, two strings are hanging from the ceiling and the subject is required to tie the ends together. However, the strings are too far apart and too high for the subject to hold one, walk over to the other, and tie them together. The solution is to tie a weight on one string and set it in motion as a pendulum, then hold the other string and wait until the swinging string comes within reach. The only object in the room available to serve as a weight is a pair of pliers on a nearby table, but the pliers are not easily seen as a pendulum bob because they normally function as a tool rather than as a weight. This has been called functional fixedness. Presumably, if pliers were replaced by a lead weight, the solution would be quicker.

The atmosphere effect refers to Sells' observation (1936) that syllogisms are easier to comprehend if presented in a concrete form consonant with experience. For example, the premises *all members of fraternities are students* and *all freshmen are students* will not lead many people to conclude that *all fraternity members are freshmen*. But the same premises in the form *all A are C* and *all B are C* more readily engender the conclusion that *all A are B*. And, for a certain set of people, the form *all democrats are leftists* and *all communists are leftists* leads rather naturally to the conclusion that *all democrats are communists*. Here the solution is conditioned by associated information about the objects in the problem.

Previously learned associations may also be the basis for the assumed, but unstated, restrictions that make some problems impossible. One cannot pass a set of four connected straight lines through all nine points in a square three-by-three array without extending the line beyond the boundaries of the array. The problem states no constraints, but subjects typically work within the boundary of the array. Perhaps the word "connected" in the presence of the dots calls forth the association that dots can be connected by lines, and that lines run between dots, with the dots as end points. But many other interpretations are possible, and evidence is weak.

Experience in solving similar problems may either help or harm. In an experiment by Luchins (1942), the problem is to measure a certain volume of water given three jars of known capacity. The first problem might be to measure 100 quarts of water with jars holding 21, 127, and 3 quarts respectively. The solution is to measure out 127 quarts, subtract 21 quarts, and then subtract 3 quarts twice. If the subject is given five successive problems, all of which can be solved by the same formula $(B - A - 2C)$ he typically solves them faster and faster. When he is then presented with two problems that can be solved either by that formula, or in a much simpler way, he continues to use the original formula. For example, to measure 20 quarts with jars of 23, 49, and 3 quarts respectively, he is much more likely to subtract 23 and twice 3 from 49, than simply to subtract 3 from 23 to get the result. A more dramatic effect occurs when the subject is asked to measure 25 quarts with jars holding 28, 76, and 3 quarts respectively. Here, the formula will not work, and many subjects fail to find the correct solution although subjects who have not had the experience of solving the preceding problems will easily subtract 3 from 28 to get 25. Luchins calls the strong positive transfer of methods of solution the Einstellung effect. When the method succeeds, as in the early problems, the transfer has a positive effect, but when the method fails the effect is disastrous.

The Einstellung effect can also be shown with anagram problems. After correctly unscrambling *lecam, nelin, nedoz,* and *sdlen,* subjects are much more likely to rearrange *pache* into *cheap* than into *peach*.

THE PROCESS OF PROBLEM SOLVING

Studies of the conditions for problem solving tell us little about how people actually go about solving problems. The information-processing approach focuses attention on process by building a theory of problem-solving behavior that describes the process. There was some interest in process before computers, especially in the work of Selz and de Groot, reviewed by de Groot below, but their theories and investigations were largely ignored by American scientists.

It is plain that American psychologists feel the need to say something about the problem-solving process because most introductory psychology texts preserve the sterile stages model. There are said to be four stages in problem solving: *preparation,* in which the elements of the problem are studied and the implications are investigated; *incubation,* in which the frustrated problem solver turns to other tasks without having solved the problem; *inspiration,* in which the solution suddenly appears in consciousness either spontaneously or when the subject intentionally returns to the problem; and finally, *verification,* in which the subject checks that his bright idea is in fact a solution to the problem. This model has come largely from the descriptions of scientists working on difficult problems. The model is relevant only to such special cases and says nothing about the problem-solving behavior of an ordinary high school student on an ordinary algebra examination. The salient feature of the model is incubation followed by inspiration. If a problem is solved in a straightforward manner by the solver, there is neither incubation nor inspiration, and the model is empty. Further, the nature of incubation is obscure. If incubation is merely leaving the problem, we have all incubated many problems that have never hatched. Probably the subject must return to the problem intentionally, and cases of unconscious inspiration are exaggerated. Perhaps the Einstellung effect weakens in the incubation period or some implicit assumptions about constraints in the problem may be forgotten. Whatever its interpretation, research on incubation seems difficult. The stages model has been accepted passively but has led nowhere.

A more sophisticated stages model could be constructed in terms of human abilities. We might consider problem solving to involve first, assimilation of the problem statement, then perception of relations among the problem elements, and then production of the proper arrangement of elements. Bunderson (1965) has some evidence supporting such a view, but it is not clear whether these stages must occur serially; in many situations all of these activities could be happening simultaneously. And, the model has still failed to describe the problem-solving process in any detail.

The general theory of problem solving proposed by Newell, Shaw, and Simon (1958) considers a problem-solving situation in which the subject proceeds through the problem from start to finish without passing through stages. The situation they consider is one in which the subject is to produce a given result from a given initial situation using a given set of operations. Proving a mathematical theorem poses such a problem. Many riddles are also of this form. As a simple example, consider the well-known riddle of the missionaries and the cannibals (Simon & Newell, 1961). Three missionaries and three cannibals must cross a wide river using a boat that will hold no more than two persons. All six know how to row the boat, but the problem is to get the entire party ferried across the river without ever allowing fewer missionaries than cannibals on either side, since those missionaries would be eaten by the cannibals. The theory, written as a computer program called *The General Problem Solver* (GPS), uses a means-ends analysis in solving such problems. Proceeding in a stepwise fashion, GPS compares the current status of the solution (the initial conditions to begin with) and the desired result, and determines some differences. In order to do this, GPS must be able to characterize the required result and the current status by the values of several attributes. Differences in corresponding values of the two situations are noted. Thus, in solving the missionaries and cannibals problem GPS might recognize the difference that there are too few missionaries on the left bank of the river. Having noticed a difference, GPS tries to take action to reduce the difference. The program has available a number of processes (the transformation rules) for altering the current status, for example, to move two missionaries and the boat from the left to the right side of the river. Some operations are relevant only to some differences, so there is a table of connections indicating which operations are relevant to which differences.

When an operation is selected GPS checks whether it can be applied. If it cannot, a subproblem is created, namely to change the current status so that the operator can be applied. For the subproblem, the program notices differences, selects appropriate operations, and so the process continues. If at any stage GPS reaches a dead end it backs up and selects a different operator or focuses on another difference. Plainly, it will matter which differences get noticed first and which operations are used first to reduce a particular difference. By noticing differences in the right order and using methods in the right order GPS can become a very efficient problem solver. The noticing order and the methods order are said to be heuristics, or rules of thumb, that will generally lead to an efficient solution. They constitute the main parameters for adjusting the program to match human performance.

Theories such as the general problem solver are assailed by radical behaviorists for talking about what goes on inside the organism. The business of science, they claim, is to describe relationships between stimuli and responses, and not to make guesses about intervening processes. But it can be argued that the theory is simply a particular codification of the observed relationships between stimuli and responses. To the extent that the theory fits the data, it is in fact a description of the stimulus-response relationships. An information-processing theory can be judged solely on its merit as a codification of the input-output transformation rules.

As a matter of fact, the theory has many other implications which may or may not correspond to some observable behavior. Thus, GPS asserts that the subject will go through a certain series of steps to achieve his solution. To check such

assertions, Newell, Simon, and Shaw found it necessary to have
subjects think aloud as they solved the problems, and to compare
the subject protocols with the equivalent protocol of the theory.
The problems they used were theorems to be proved in that
branch of logic known as sentential calculus. Of course, subjects were not told that this was what they were doing—they were
simply presented with a puzzle: How to transform one expression
into another expression following a given set of rules. Although
no subject does precisely what the theory predicts, there are
long stretches of behavior from each subject that are very well
matched by the theory. Moreover, the responses of the subjects
make it clear that they are performing an analysis of the GPS
sort even when not following the theory step by step.

The theory describes processes at the level of symbolic
information processing. There is no attempt to consider analysis at the neurological level. Eventually, perhaps, all behavior
can be related to corresponding neural events, but the current
knowledge about the nervous system precludes meaningful
neural theories of complex phenomena. And when our knowledge
expands, we shall still need intermediate levels of explanation.
An automobile is a complex collection of atoms but cannot con-
veniently be described in atomic terms. Likewise, human behavior can best be described in successive levels of detail.
The information processing level seems especially useful as
a potential bridge between organized behavior and neural activity.

Game playing is closely allied with problem solving. The
game of chess is a popular subject of study (de Groot, 1965;
Newell and Simon, 1964; Baylor, 1965). Here the problem is to
select a particular chess move rather than to play an entire

game. The way human players consider a chess position in order to select a move can be compared with the process of a machine programmed to play the game. It has been found that subjects consider many fewer moves than a machine is likely to, even when the machine has powerful heuristics for selecting useful moves so that it does not simply run down all of the legal moves. Further, humans do not investigate possibilities in a systematic way, but rather jump back and forth among the salient move sequences, considering variations in a manner that de Groot calls progressive deepening. The ability of human players to single out the most likely move possibilities without extensive analysis provides the human's current advantage over the computer chess programs.

Several studies of problem solving have been done with problems that can be classed as concept learning: Gregg and Laughery (1962), Laughery (1961), and Hunt (1962). Here the task is inductive rather than deductive—the subject must find the general rules from specific instances. Because concept learning is such a large area of investigation, it will be omitted here, and with a few exceptions, is not treated in the papers that follow. Concept learning deserves separate treatment at another symposium.

PROBLEM SOLVING AND COMPUTERS

Although information-processing theories of problem solving grew out of attempts to program digital computers to solve problems, it is important to treat the theories as descriptions of human behavior apart from the computers that spawned them.

The theories are stated as computer programs because the program serves as a useful notation and the computer serves as a useful mechanism for testing the implications of the theory. But the theory is evaluated by its success in describing human behavior. Having said this, we must also emphasize that there are many computer scientists whose main objective is to build clever programs that can solve intricate problems. They too are interested in human problem solving, but only in order to find better ways of programming computers. They have written programs that can prove theorems in sentential calculus, do problems in plane geometry and integral calculus, and do algebra word problems, as well as play a number of games from tic-tac-toe and nim to checkers and chess. Research activity in this field of "artificial intelligence" is increasing and is progressing somewhat independently of studies of human problem solving.

As the science of computing develops we can expect to see general theories of computer problem solving corresponding to our current theories of human problem solving. Someone has already suggested the possibility of a general theory that encompasses both human and machine problem solving. At present, computer simulation models of human problem solving are very similar to the problem-solving programs produced in the pursuit of artificial intelligence. But the two lines of inquiry might well diverge in the future. Whether human problem solving will turn out to be sufficiently like machine problem solving to permit such a general theory remains an open question.

CONCLUSION

The stark contrasts drawn in this paper between advocates of the behavioristic and the information processing approaches have obscured the differences of opinion within each group, and in fact, the identification of two opposing schools of thought has perhaps been premature. Plainly, there are many points of agreement—some kind of organization of single units into hierarchies is essential in discussing complex behavior. Disagreements about language and research strategy provide a useful diversity in studying a poorly understood area. The diversity, disagreements, and incongruities of the papers that follow will give the reader a good look at the current ferment in the psychological analysis of an ubiquitous kind of human behavior—problem solving.

2 ADRIAAN D. de GROOT
University of Amsterdam

Perception and Memory Versus Thought: Some Old Ideas and Recent Findings*

The present paper is primarily intended to give you a glimpse of the kind of work we are doing in Amsterdam, the kind of ideas we have (many of them old), the kind of methods we use and the kind of findings we have obtained (some of them recent). In a number of respects, both our research goals and methods differ from those of most others. First, the research is directed toward systematic description of cognitive phenomena rather than to strict hypothesis testing. Second, we keep machine simulation in mind but we hardly do it as yet. Third, the experimental settings often are more like real-life than the strictly controlled artificial conditions of the lab-

*The project "Denken en Geheugen" (Thought and Memory) is supported by the Netherlands Foundation for Pure Scientific Research and is being carried out by The Research Institute for Applied Psychology, in cooperation with the Psychological Laboratory of the University of Amsterdam. The principal investigators on this project are Nico H. Frijda and the author; and the graduate co-workers are Jan Elshout and Riekent Jongman. There are three subprojects in "Denken en Geheugen": (1) "Operational Thinking"; (2) "Perception"; and (3) "Memory."

19

oratory. Fourth, extensive use is made of introspective techniques of various kinds. Fifth, as a result, protocol coding and interpretation are of crucial importance (and consume a large part of our time). Sixth, prospective outcomes are expected to be primarily valuable to the extent we succeed in providing adequate, systematic process descriptions, possibly to be used as a basis for simulation.

What exactly is meant by each of these characteristics will, I hope, become clear in the course of this paper.

Let us start with the old ideas mentioned in the subtitle. They are a number of general statements, opinions, and convictions that I held at the time I worked on *"Het denken van den schaker,"* in the late thirties and early forties. Some of these ideas were new at the time, others were not so new; some were then accepted by, or at least acceptable to many, others to a few only while they were strongly contended. There is no particular system to the following list of statements except that it provides the framework for my paper.

> I. It is worthwhile and scientifically important to try one's hand at a descriptive analysis of high level, complex, cognitive processes on the basis of experimentation in a real-life-like setting.
> —A statement of *valuation*.

Comment: In fact, this was—and is—rarely done. One example of an earlier comparable study: Julius Bahle's analyses of the process of musical composition. Another: Geza Révész' analysis of the work of blind sculptors. In the thirties, studies of this type appeared for some time to announce a new look in European psychology—a trend away from strict, artificial, simplifying laboratory experimentation. However, this trend was (if it ever really existed) broken off by the second world war.

> II. It is worthwhile and scientifically legitimate
> practice to collect data by means of introspective experi-
> mentation: "systematic introspection," "thinking aloud"
> and the like.
> —A statement of *methodology*.

Comment: Although in European psychology introspective
techniques have never been as suspect as they used to be in the
United States, the early enthusiasm of, for instance, the Würz-
burg School had been overflooded by the strong appeal of other
movements, such as Gestalt theory, and *Ganzheits*-psychologies
of various types. On the other hand, European psychologists
were acquainted with the behaviorist critique of introspection*.
As a result, only a few investigators ventured to base their
work on systematically collected protocol statements of subjects.
Even Duncker, although certainly one of the few, apparently preferred not to be too explicit about his use of introspective data.
In general, many psychologists have a bad conscience about
using introspective data; as a result, they often use them poorly.

> III. A process of directed thought (for example, in
> problem solving) can be conceived as a linear sequence of
> operations that are actively carried out by the subject
> according to a system of linkings governed by laws.
> —A statement on the theoretical *model* used.

Comment: Nowadays we call such a system the subject's
(personal) program. Thirty years ago, this position (obviously
the position taken by Otto Selz) was highly unpopular. Selz's con-

---

*In Europe itself, for that matter, Selz's methods of experimen-
tation and inference, for instance, had been strongly criticized, among
others by G. E. Muller (1919)—see also Wundt (1907).

ception was considered terribly mechanistic and one-sided; it left no room for "true" creativity, nor for simultaneously functioning "layers" of the mind, nor for inspiration and irrationality. In particular, the alleged miracles of unconscious functioning in the conception of great ideas were supposedly not given their proper place. Generally, it was somewhat of a shame even to try and reduce the productivity of the human mind to a chain of mechanically linked operations.

> IV. The system, mentioned in III, is characterized by a hierarchical structure of operation dispositions— "solving methods," "typical problem transformations," "heuristics"—ordered by co- and subordination, priority rules, outcome (or decision) criteria, etc.
> —A statement on the *model,* again.

Comment is superfluous here. Obviously, this is again Selz.

> V. From experimental evidence and analysis, it must be possible to develop an ordered classification of human mental operations to cover every method, trick, heuristic, transformation that may be instrumental in productive thinking (problem solving, creativity included).
> —An expectation of *sufficiency.*

Comment: Here again, Selz is the *auctor intellectualis.* Although he did not pretend to have completed such a comprehensive taxonomy, he contributed many solving methods of primary importance as well as a useful division into a number of main types.

> VI. It must be possible systematically to relate the taxonomy (V), as derived from largely introspective experimentation, to the outcomes of statistical analyses of cognitive achievements such as factor analytical studies of mental test performance.
> —An expectation of a *correspondence* between two systems.

Comment: Curiously enough, it was again Selz, who first suggested this possibility. A lawyer by primary training, he knew little about statistics but he had heard of the work of the British factorists. In one passage (1935), he mentioned Spearman's general and specific factors and expressed the expectation (rather loosely and implicitly, it is true) that, in future research, the two approaches would appear to be compatible and become mutually fertile.

> VII. Selz's general conception of the thought process, while extremely important and generally useful, has some limitations of a fundamental nature; its descriptive (explanatory) limitations become particularly apparent whenever problem-solving processes involve many perceptual and abstractive subject activities.
> —A statement on *theoretical gaps*.

Comment: This was certainly not Selz's point of view but rather my own problem when I tried to apply and accommodate his *Denk-psychologie* to chess thinking. There are certain gaps in his analyses of perceptual methods, their description is rather shallow compared to the complexity of the processing we must suppose to occur.

The problem is paradigmatically implied in two of the main conclusions of my chess study: (1) Although it is very difficult to show that chess masters are superior to lesser players in the structural qualities of their operational thinking they are easily superior in *perceptual* achievement; and (2) the basis of chess mastership (that is, again, the superiority of the master over lesser players) is to a very large extent a matter of *memory* (the "highly differentiated system of immediately available, specific playing methods," and other problem trans-

formation dispositions). So, the questions remain: How does
(chess) perception work; to what extent is it instrumental to
(chess) achievement generally; how is (chess) memory built up;
what structure has it and how does it function?

> VIII. If the main cognitive functions are ordered
> (a) according to their supposed social or human "values,"
> the resulting order is (from low to high): perception-
> memory-thought-creativity; if ordered (b) according to
> complexity, the result is the same.
> —An expectation of *correlation*.

Comment: This is not a statement of psychological theory
but rather an implicit assumption of some sociological (or philosophical) interest. According to this assumption, thinking (problem solving), for instance, is not only more exclusively human
and socially of a higher order than is perception, but also more
"interesting" and more complex. It is difficult to estimate how
many people worked on this assumption; but it used to be a
strong prejudice for me. At the time, I found perception and
memory rather dull subjects and thinking and creativity to be
the *real thing* psychological—in every respect.

The leading question for the rest of this paper is: What
happened to these ideas; (1) during the last 25 years generally,
(2) in the opinion of psychologists, (3) in our recent work in
Amsterdam, (4) in my personal opinion? The following answers
are necessarily brief and incomplete. I shall emphasize (3):
the relation to our present work.

Re Statement I
     This is a statement of valuation I am still prepared to de-
fend with complete conviction. The mainstream in psychological

research of cognitive processes still is in favor of: artificial problem-solving situations; atomized experimental materials and units; exclusive trust in experimental evidence, both in theory testing and (worse) in theory formation; staying within the laboratory walls; etc. Although the situation has changed, systematic (that is, non-"impressionistic") straightforwardly descriptive studies have remained rare.

One problem is, of course, that the methodology of a good, systematically analytic, descriptive investigation in a real-life-like setting is much more difficult to pin down than the methodology of experimental hypothesis testing. But, this difficulty should not prevent us from trying to fill the gap between real life and the Lab culture. Even now, a plea for comprehensive descriptive studies is not superfluous—present company perhaps excepted.

Re Statement II

This is a statement on methodology which I have somewhat elaborated in Chapter 9 of *Thought and Choice in Chess*. One of the things we are at present trying to do (and this is a matter of primary concern to all three subprojects of "Denken en Geheugen") is to evolve a somewhat more detailed general methodology of protocol interpretation.

In the three subprojects of "Denken en Geheugen" (see Appendix 2), the experimental tasks subjects have to carry out are quite different. In subproject 1, tasks consist in the main of traditional problem solving; subjects are required to think aloud. In 2, one of the main tasks is to reproduce a chess position after an exposition of 5 seconds; the subject's retro-

spective comments on "what happened" are recorded. In 3, we
ask, among other things, informal definitions of concepts such
as: "What does 'lucidity' mean?" or: "What is a cigarette?"
Again, subjects are required to think aloud.

In spite of differences in tasks and introspective method,
the problems of coding and interpreting the ensuing protocols
are fundamentally the same. There is always a protocol proper,
containing statements of various types; there is always a record of the subject's explanatory comments made in the inquiry
after the experiment. And there is a number of standard problems to be solved: (1) translating subject statements into subject activities; (2) reconstructing the chronology of the events;
(3) coding subject activities in terms of a limited set of "methods," that is, roughly defined problem transformation subroutines; (4) trying to design, to fit, to test, or to improve a
program-like conception of the process corresponding to the
data.

All this is analogous to what Laughery and Gregg (1962)
have done and to other work in this Institute. However, the
methodological problems are sufficiently fundamental and
difficult to justify parallel efforts to try and master them.
At present, we feel that proper distinctions between the
various interpretive steps in protocol analysis are of crucial
importance; but it is hard adequately to define and maintain
them.

By far the most unruly protocols are those produced by
the experiments in perception (subproject 2). We have now set
our hopes, therefore, on registering parallel behavior, namely
eye movement tracing, but this work is not yet beyond the pre-

Example of Protocol

"eh, what is a cigarette . . . that is a long, . . . thin object with white paper
around it, and with tobacco in it . . . no, not always white, and not always,
. . . well, with something like tobacco in it, used to . . . be smoked for
pleasure. Boy what a complicated statement. I just saw it, a vague kind
of image. After saying that about white paper I thought about cigarettes
with maize paper in France after the war, and then thought of marihuana
cigarettes. I had to search for the expression "for pleasure," I tried to
classify things which you have just for fun. Also, after describing the shape,
I thought, now I should classify the function."

(Protocol continues with attempt at more fluent verbal description.)

Protocol text	Comment	Methods	Ref. to 1b
"eh, what is a cigarette		search-signal into memory	1
. . .		actualization of knowledge?	2
that is a long	I just saw it, a vague kind of	successive selection of aspects	3,5,8
. . .	image	tests of aspects?	6,7?
thin object with		selection of aspects	3,5,8
white paper around it		same	3,5,8
and with tobacco in it		same	3,5,8
	I thought about cig. with maize	relevance test	4
. . .	paper, etc.		
no, not always white and not always, . . .		correction	(11,12,5)
	and about marihuana		
. . .		relevance test	4
well, with something like tobacco in it,		correction, corrected output	(11,12,5, 8)
used to	I thought now I should classify the function	test against over-all goal	8
. . .		search for verbal descr.	3,5
be smoked for pleasure.	I had to search for the expression		8
Boy what a complicated statement		verbal control process	10

Fig. 1a: Analysis of Protocol.

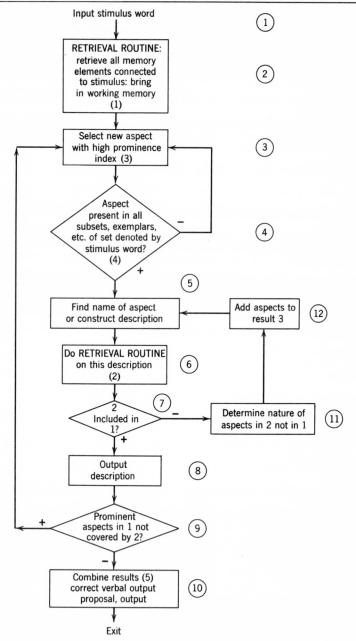

Fig. 1b: Block diagram for "defining word meanings."

liminaries of equipment development and testing. An important
advantage of the registration of eye movements should be that
the reliability of, at least, chronological statements and interpretations can be checked—and possibly improved. Even so,
our experiments in perception are not likely to get very near to
the stage of simulation. As a statement of principle, I would
like to add that this fact in no way diminishes their importance.

Somewhat nearer to the programming stage are Nico
Frijda's protocol analyses in subproject 3 ("Memory"). As a
simple example, one protocol analysis and the corresponding
block diagram are presented in Figures 1a and 1b.

Obviously, the "lore" of introspective experimentation and
protocol interpretation is of crucial importance whenever, for
instance, the likeness of a machine-simulated problem-solving
protocol to a human protocol must be judged. Both theory
formation and theory testing hinge on the experimental requirements and on the rules of coding and decoding of protocols. So,
if we want to simulate at all, if we want to try out program
models of cognitive processes, we need good, old-fashioned
introspection along with a modern methodology of protocol
analysis. Speaking personally, my conscience about using these
techniques is in good shape—even better than it was in the old
days.

Re Statements III and IV

With regard to these two statements on the theoretical
model, the situation has drastically changed over the years. As
a result of the progress in the field of artificial intelligence and
simulation of cognitive processes, the old (European) criticism

of Selz and others that their models were "mechanistic" has become obsolete. The argument has not been completely silenced, it is true, but it has no serious influence any more on the discussion of the real issues, let alone on the progress of research itself. At present, program models are highly "in." Their hierarchical structure is taken for granted and the controversy of process linearity versus simultaneously active "layers" has lost its acuity since it is realized that the issue is hardly empirically decidable—or, at least, hardly decidable by psychological experimentation. Except for some reservations, the victory of what is fundamentally Selz's conception is almost complete.

Re Statements V and VI

I treat these statements together because they are the two main expectations underlying Subproject 1 of "Denken en Geheugen." The idea to combine the two in one investigation rests on a very simple argument. First, both the introspective analysis of problem solving activities in terms of methods, and the factorial analysis of cognitive (test) performance, claim to be able to detect resemblances and differences between various types of cognitive functioning. Second, the more the two systems approach complete coverage or "sufficiency," for which a criterion is difficult to define, for that matter, the more promising ought to be an endeavor to find out how they are or can be related.

Selz himself has never worked this out, but I have personally been cherishing the idea for a long time. In the early fifties I was ready to start a pertinent research project except

for the organizational facilities. This shortage prevented it
from becoming anything important at the time. But, in our
present project (1), the idea has been taken up anew and is
materialising in the work of Jan Elshout. I borrow the following remarks largely from his progress reports.

From the point of view of the factor analyst, a well constructed, reproducible common factor in the intellectual domain should correspond to a "capacity"; that is, a capacity of
the subjects to carry out a certain type of activities. These
activities are supposed to be homogeneous in some important
ways. Now, what we would like to be able to do is to predict
the factor composition of any kind of complex cognitive process on the basis of an independent, systematic analysis of the
way it is performed by experimental subjects. If, and insofar
as, the prediction of factorial structures (loadings, correlations) from introspective protocols is feasible, the existence
of relationships between the two systems would appear to be
warranted.

The first experimental step was to collect thinking-aloud
protocols of subjects solving typical items of some forty tests
such as are commonly used in factorial analyses in the cognitive domain (Guilford's, for example). If it is possible at all
to relate "methods" of problem solving to "factors" of intelligence test performance, these carefully edited, purposefully
simplified problems ought to provide the correct material for
a pertinent two-way analysis.

Second, provided some correspondence is found, it should
now be possible to predict the correlations between the (40)
test scores, on the one hand, and performance on an independent

"criterion task," on the other—on the sole basis of a qualitative analysis of thinking-aloud protocols of subjects performing the criterion task.

As a criterion task, Elshout has devised a complex problem of a well-known type—a concept attainment task. From a series of case presentations, subjects are to discover a principle (a simple formula, in fact) whereby the value of an outcome variable can be predicted from three easily observable, variable, uncorrelated cues (see Fig. 2). Apart from the serial presentation of cases (with subjects first guessing, then being informed about the right answer) another condition was also used: subjects had to construct their own stimuli, that is, their own test cases for their own hypotheses.

At present, the data (1200 test scores and 270 thinking-aloud protocols) are all there, and the analysis is on its way.

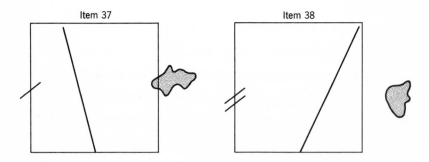

Fig. 2: How long will the amoeba live? Cues are: the position of the bar, the position of the amoeba, the number of marks on the left border, each attribute having five values. The range of life durations (1-30 hrs.) is given.

So far, the leader of Subproject 1 has little reason to be op-
timistic about the results from the viewpoint of relating factors to methods (Re Statement VI). However, he expects a good
payoff in terms of descriptive concepts (Re Statement V)
whether they have much to do with factors or not.

Re Statement VII

The statement on gaps in the Selzian model can be easily
generalized. Our understanding of problem-solving processes
(as demonstrated, for instance, in our skill and success in
simulation) is at its weakest where perceptual and complex
memory functioning enter the picture.

Our ignorance in this respect can be succinctly expressed
in the following statements.

(1) In trying to understand problem solving, we know we
cannot do without a large group of operations usually called
abstraction or abstractive operations, but we do not know very
well how they work. The problem situation from which a property, a cue, a means is abstracted (cf. for Selz's method of
(immediate) "means abstraction," de Groot, 1965) may either be per-
ceptually given (a chess position on the board) or in some way
represented from memory (a chess position in your mind). The
dynamics of both cases are obscure.

(2) We know that increasing experience and knowledge in
a specific field (chess, for instance) has the effect that things
(properties, etc.) which, at the earlier stages, had to be abstracted, or even inferred, are apt to be immediately perceived at later stages. To a rather large extent, *abstraction*

is replaced by perception, but we do not know much about how this works, nor where the borderline lies.

(3) Albeit, we know more from daily experience than from experiments, that as an effect of this replacement, a so-called "given" problem situation is not really given since *it is seen differently* by an expert than it is perceived by an unexperienced person, but we do not know much about those differences.

(4) In general, we suppose that perceptual differences of this kind must be explained in terms of *different codings*, but we do not know those codings.

These are crucial problems. They are taken up in Subproject 2, for the case of chess. Roughly, we are trying to do with regard to chess *perception* what, in the old days, I tried to do with regard to chess *thinking*. I shall now briefly discuss some of our experiments.

If the experimental problem is to find a good move in a chess position the subject has not seen before, the process of problem solving starts with a perceptual intake: finding out how things stand, and what the position is like. At this point, my 1946 results suggest an enormous advantage of the master over the lesser player. Within the very first five to ten seconds, the master subject is apt to have more relevant information about the position available to him than the lesser player can accumulate in, say, a quarter of an hour of analysis. Part of the former's superiority is quite tangible: to him, a *five second exposition of a complicated middle game position is sufficient to be able to reproduce it with only very few errors*—often with no errors at all. A lesser player, even one of expert level, cannot do this.

This more or less amazing fact of mastership has been
taken as the starting point for Subproject 2. How is this type of
perceptual achievement* to be explained? What happens within
those five seconds?

As early as 1927, a group of Russian investigators
(Djakow, Petrovsky, and Rudik, 1927) demonstrated that chess
masters are *not generally* superior to control subjects in visual
memory achievement. By their *specialty*, therefore, masters
must have a superior coding system immediately available.
What they "see" must be something quite different from what
lesser players see. The crucial question is how this coding system works; and on what it is based. My 1946 study contained
a few suggestions (both findings and hypotheses) which, by continued experimentation in the same vein, could quite well be
followed up. This is in fact what we are doing.

But, there was a preliminary problem, namely: *How much
is there to be explained?* The specific achievement of master
subjects (well validated by now) may appear unbelievable to the
layman, but is it really that exceptional? Is it possible to measure the achievement, that is, to measure the amount of information the master subject is able to take in, to process, to store
and to reproduce? It is easy to see that the uncertainty of chess
positions must be very much smaller than numbers (such as up
to 32 pieces of 12 different kinds scattered over 64 squares) are
likely to suggest. How much smaller?

---

*Compare, e.g., the "amazing" ability of musical score reading
in a master-composer or director or, for that matter, the amazing
ability of every literate person to read a text (a field in which nearly
everybody is a "master")!

This question leads to a number of other questions. For instance: how restrictive are the rules; and how does the number of possible "random positions" compare to the number of possible *legitimate* positions? Apart from the rules, we must take into account that experimental positions are taken from master games. That is, the positions must be of a kind, likely to have occurred in a well played game. This is known to be a necessary condition for superior achievement: bizarre, problem-like, possible but highly improbable positions are not so well reproduced (see discussion of Djakow, Petrovsky, and Rudik, de Groot, 1965). This condition of "master level likelihood" should amount to an enormous reduction of uncertainty. Is it possible to estimate how much?

We tried at least to get some partial or approximate answers, by calculating varieties, by trying out coding methods and calculating master game statistics (on the computer, for a set of 192 positions after Black's 20th move) and, finally, by experimenting with masters as subjects.

Table 1 shows, first, the variety of all possible random positions, that is, positions of two kings and any number of other pieces, up to 30, located at random on the board. The outcome, 143 bits, can be considered exact (1).

Square by square coding with an optimal binary code for expected piece-frequency leads to a maximal total length of 164 (for 32 pieces). On the average, random positions would require a code length of 161 digits (2). However, if applied to the collection of 192 positions (after Black's 20th move) from master games, the average length is about 140 (3)*.

The next entry (4) shows the uncertainty reduction resulting from one simple consequence of the rules of chess,

TABLE 1

Information in a Chess Position (Binary Code Length)

		Info Reduction	Total
1.	Variety of random positions (min 2 kings; max 32 pieces)	—	143
2.	Given piece frequencies $H_{max}(32)$ (optimal code) $\bar{H}$(random)	— —	164 161
3.	Empirical code length (192 positions; 21st move), $\underline{\bar{H}}$	—	140.3
4.	No pawns on first rows	5.6	—
5.	White-black separation (first 3 rows)	18.1	(116.6)
6.	Given occupation probabilities (192 positions; h; square by square), $\bar{H}$	—	90.3
7.	Given location probabilities (192 positions; (1) material, (2) piece by piece), $\bar{H}$	—	60*
8.	Number of one bit questions (W-Ss.)	—	85†
9.	Number of one bit questions (M-Ss.)	—	80†
10.	Complete master game guessing (M-Ss.) (21st move; 2 good moves per position†)	—	40*
		100 bits	

*) Estimated.
†) Preliminary average.

*The reduction results from the fact that pieces have been ex-
changed (the code for "unoccupied" requiring one digit as against five
for, say, a black knight).

namely that no pawns can be on the first rows: 5.6 bits.

Much larger is the reduction in average code length (5) if a simple empirical fact is exploited, namely the fact, that in middle game positions, generally, the white pieces are at one side of the board and the black pieces at the other. If, in coding the occupancy of squares within the first three rows on either side, one color is primarily presupposed, the gain in efficiency appears to be substantial: 18.1.

The next two entries (6 and 7) are based on first order probabilities, of two kinds. They are both derived from the statistics of the set of 192 positions (compare Fig. 2 and Tables 2, 3, 4). By far the most efficient way of coding appears to be the piece-by-piece method, according to location probabilities. The average code length is about 60—an enormous reduction compared to the 140 for random positions. Emmanuel Lasker was right when he said that chess is a highly stereotyped game.

Entries 8 and 9 are preliminary outcomes (averages for some 10 experimental sessions so far) of position guessing experiments by means of one-bit questions only. The expectation was that masters would be able to apply an experience-based strategy of well-considered questioning that would enable them, first, to do much better than weak players, second, to beat the mechanical method of first-order location probabilities (7). Although the results are not yet definitive, they already show quite convincingly, first, that the superiority of M over W is slight, second, that in this type of experiment, experience and knowledge do not pay. Master subjects do make use of higher order probabilities the coding program (7) does not know; they often do so quite cunningly but to the detriment of their over-all achievement.

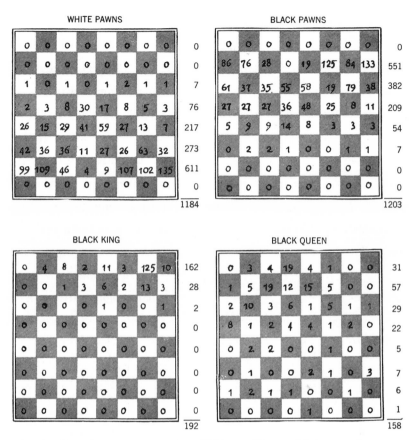

Fig. 3: Location Frequencies (192 positions; 21st move)

This negative result shows that the superior achievement of masters in perceptual experiments can not be explained by a supposed *general* knowledge of chess possibilities and probabilities. Their superior performance in perception experiments is not based on the availability of (first-order) "probability tables" in the backs of their minds.

Finally, the entry sub 10 is simply based on empirical estimates of the number of good moves in any position, that is,

moves a master could possibly play. In my 1946 study I came
(for one tournament game played by myself) to an average number of playable alternatives of less than two. This estimate was,
again, nicely validated by our new data. One session was devoted to an analysis by international chessmaster Kick Langeweg
of the game in which he had recently beaten grandmaster Geller.
In this game the frequency of positions in which only one move
could possibly be played by a master was quite high. As a result, the average number of good alternatives was even nearer
to one than to two.

TABLE 2

Occupation Uncertainty Per Square
(192 positions; 21st move)

	QR	QN	QB	Q	K	KB	KN	KR
8	1.07	.87	1.50	1.28	1.40	1.50	1.03	.85
7	1.13	1.82	1.50	1.57	1.98	1.34	1.87	1.19
6	1.33	1.35	1.73	1.60	1.65	1.63	1.49	1.08
5	1.27	1.17	1.62	2.09	2.05	1.33	.94	.94
4	.99	1.33	1.68	2.03	1.69	1.35	.82	.80
3	1.20	1.61	2.00	1.34	1.90	1.71	1.46	1.13
2	1.36	1.61	1.56	1.66	1.68	1.53	1.70	1.17
1	1.06	.82	1.57	1.32	1.45	1.28	1.10	1.21
	QR	QN	QB	Q	K	KB	KN	KR

Since master-game positions after Black's 20th move can
only result from a sequence of moves "a master could possibly
play," with 2 as an upper bound for the average number of alternatives in each position, the total number of master-game
positions after 20 moves should not exceed 2^{40} (or 10^{12}). This
explains the variety estimate of 40 bits. The difference between
60 (7) and 40 (10) appears to point to the fact that there is more

to "master-level likelihood" than location probabilities. What this is, remains to be explained.

The following few figures and tables show some of the empirical data underlying the uncertainty estimates of Table 1. They are, in the main, self-explanatory, and they give a concrete picture of how "stereotyped" the game of chess is.

TABLE 3

Location Uncertainty Per Piece
(192 positions; 21st move)

	White	Black
K	2.21	2.16
Q	4.58	4.59
KR	3.16	3.11
QR	3.16	3.14
KB	3.19	2.91
QB	3.40	3.37
KN	2.99	3.18
QN	2.95	2.96
QRP	1.85	1.94
QNP	1.98	2.27
QBP	2.26	2.20
QP	1.77	1.93
KP	2.02	2.21
KPB	1.93	1.92
KNP	1.86	1.81
KRP	1.39	1.44

Figure 3 shows empirical frequency distributions of some pieces over the board. Tables 2 and 3 give piece location with square occupation uncertainties. In Table 4, the somewhat lower presence frequencies for White are nothing mysterious: by his last move, Black may just have taken (ex-

TABLE 4

Presence Frequencies of Pieces
(192 positions; 21st move)

	K	Q	KR	QR	KB	QB	KN	QN	P	Totals
White	192	152	176	174	124	125	98	98	1184	2323
Black	192	158	176	180	131	123	105	90	1203	2358

changed) a white piece that, in White's next move, will be re-
captured.

Figure 4 is quite interesting. It shows the results of, first,
selecting the most probable material situation (two pawns, one
Bishop, and one Knight being exchanged) and, second, combining
the highest location probabilities for pieces to one "average
position." So, this is the stereotyped chess position *par excellence*.

After this preliminary walk through the bits-shop of chess,
let us now turn to the perception experiments proper.

Fig. 4: "Average" position (192 positions; 21st move).
Most likely: (a) material (b) location

188: White on (21st) move

from: Janosevic-Krisnik;
Zenica 1964

27: White on (21st) move

from: Bannik-Geller;
Moskou 1961

Fig. 5: Examples of experimental positions (out
of 192; used in guessing and reproducing exp. s)

Figure 5 shows two of the series of experimental positions—again selected from the set of 192.

In these experiments, a regular chess set is used for
showing the positions. The situation is as natural as possible.
The subject sits at a table, is required, during the preparation,
to close his eyes and to open and close them again on the experimenter's signals. After the (5 seconds) exposition, the subject is free to concentrate for some time (with eyes closed) on
what he has seen, that is, to pin it down: to order, to code, to
relate, and to "integrate" his data. Next he is given the pieces
that were on the board and asked to put them down as he thinks
the position was. When he is ready, the experimenter removes
the pieces which were wrongly located and asks him to try those
again. Trials (without ever showing the position again) are repeated until either the position is correct or 12 trials are com-

pleted. Meanwhile, all subject (and experimenter) remarks are
tape-recorded. As soon as the position is correct which, with
master subjects, is a matter of a few minutes at the most, the
subject is asked (1) to try and reproduce the perception process and (2) to comment on what he did during his concentration
pause and on his considerations during reproduction. Protocols
are apt to be rather long and difficult to code but often highly
informative regarding process details.

So far, only the *quantitative results* are available to me.

TABLE 5

Masters Versus Weak Players;
Blind Position Guessing Versus Reproducing:
Percentage correctly located pieces after one
and more trials (5 positions per S per condition)

Number of trials	Blind Guessing $W(N=5)$	$M(N=5)$	"Average" Position	Reproduction W (N = 5)	(5 sec exp) M (N = 5)
1	34.5	37.3	44.5	41.2	91.4
2	55.9	65.0		67.6	96.7
3	69.8	80.5		80.9	98.0
4	79.8	88.0		85.5	99.0
5	85.9	91.8		91.9	99.2
6	88.3	94.6		93.7	99.7
7	90.5	96.2		96.0	99.8
8	92.4	97.0		96.7	100
9	93.7	97.3		96.8	
10	94.5	97.6		97.0	
11	95.5	98.0		97.5	
12	95.9	98.6		97.7	

Table 5 shows, first, how well the old finding of superior
achievement of master subjects in this type of experiment is
confirmed. As in the experiments reported in "Het denken van

den schaker," the average number of hits is well over 90 percent. In contrast, weak players (although selected on superior
intellectual level) do not even score 40 percent. Their results
are only slightly better than those of M-subjects who did not see
the position. Most curious of all, both are beaten by the percentage of hits a consistent use of the "average position" for
the given material would yield—this percentage being no less
than 44 percent.

Furthermore, the data of Table 5 enable us to compare
the results of position *reproduction* with position *guessing;* that
is, with the results of an identically organized series of recon-
struction trials except that *no* perceptual information is offered
at all.

The way in which the four resulting curves approach the
100 percent level is shown in Fig. 6.

Apparently, W-subjects benefit little from the five second exposition, the distance between the two W-curves being
slight. After a few trials, the guessing results of M-subjects
even become superior to the reproduction results of W-sub-
jects. The latter are not able to retain much of the perceptual
information offered.

As to the M-subjects, the contrast between the results of
the guessing and the reproduction condition is striking. This
means, for one thing, that general prior chess knowledge is of
no importance; we have to do with specific perceptual achievement, to be explained by the chessmaster's *coding system*. In
view of our findings about the comparatively limited variety of
legitimate and master-level-likely positions, an explanation of
the "amazing" performance of master subjects in terms of a

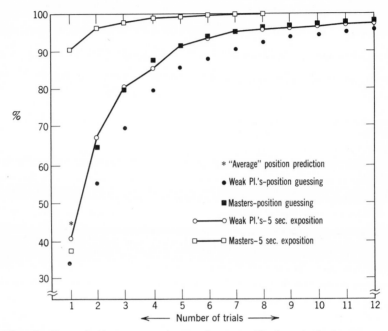

Fig. 6: Cumulative percentage of correctly located pieces.
(data from Table 5)
* "Average" Position Prediction
● Weak Pl.'s—Position Guessing
□ Masters—Position Guessing
⊙ —— ⊙ Weak Pl.'s—5 Sec. Exposition
□ —— □ Masters—5 Sec. Exposition

coding system and, hopefully, in terms of a program does not
seem to be beyond reach.

I cannot now enter upon a discussion of what is the real
core of Subproject 2, namely the protocol analysis, except to
say that it is in progress. Only a few remarks are due, namely
on our plans and on some preliminary findings.

Some plans are shown in Table 6. This table gives an

TABLE 6

Experiments and Subjects
(Cell entries are numbers of Ss, so far.)

Experiments in progress:	M	**E	W	N
Reproduction experiments, 1 sec*	4	4	4	4
" " 2 sec*	4	4	4	4
" " 5 sec†	8	8	8	-
Blind position guessing†	8	8	8	-
One bit questions‡ (pos guessing)	3	1	2	1
Move guessing‡ (given positions)	2	1	3	-
Predicting error probabilities ‡	1	-	-	-

* Preliminary series; data and analysis completed.
† Part of main series; data completed, analysis in progress.
‡ Part of main series; experimentation in progress.
**M = Master; E = Expert; W = Weak; N = Non-player.

Experiments Planned:
— Reproduction experiments, S-decided time limit.
— Interrupted exposition: series of 1 sec expositions.
— Eye movement tracing during 5 sec exposition.
— "Free association" with chess stimuli: "Tell everything (knowledge, experience, feelings, memories) of which this reminds you."

overview of experiments (in progress and planned) and subjects. As stated before, we expect much benefit from experiments with eye movement tracing.

The "association" experiments are meant to provide some descriptive information on the structure, the organization and the the degree of complexity of a chessmaster's memory. Both perceptual and playing (problem solving) achievements of masters must be based on an extensive and highly flexible memory organization. (I have, for that matter, become very skeptical about the possibility of writing a skillful chess program without trying one's hand at the express simulation of a chessmaster's memory organization.)

TABLE 7

Predictability of Reproduction Errors
(5 sec expositions; 4 M-subjects, 5 positions each)

| Frequency | Error probability (estim by de Groot.) | | | Total |
	Low	Medium	High	
Correct	293	91	61	445
Error	10	14	11	35
Total	303	105	72	480
Error, %	3.3%	13.3%	15.3%	7.3%

Trying to predict reproduction errors (so far by one sub-ject, namely myself) is expected to be useful as a rough test for hypotheses on the processes of perception, coding and reproduc-tion. Typical errors may be quite informative, but, again, some check on the legitimacy of error interpretations is badly needed. Table 7 shows at least that reproductive errors are not com-pletely unpredictable, so we have some reason to continue hy-pothesizing on them.

Finally, a few remarks on the problems of pinning down the chessmaster's coding system. What is immediately per-ceived as perceptual units or aspects, what is abstracted, what is inferred?

To show the complexity of the pertinent borderline prob-lems, let me relate what happened one day when grandmaster Reuben Fine was in Amsterdam. Walking together in the street, we came by the well-known chess cafe at the Leidseplein. Through the window, we saw, first, two chess players sitting at the nearest table, and then the position on the board between them. Said Fine (and this was after an "exposition" of hardly two seconds): "Hm, they are good players."

Even if there was an element of showing off in his behavior, the question is: What did he actually *see*, and what did
he infer? Is it possible that he immediately saw an acceptable
"master-level-likely" position? Or was this an inference? I
only raise the question.

In our experiments, such problems of perception versus
abstraction (inference) (or problems of determining the primary
units of perception) are certain to arise. A case in point is the
question of what I have called "dynamic perception" in chess.
Is "seeing" a move possibility, as some of my old subjects in
short exposition experiments have reported on, really seeing
or is it an inference? From our experimental protocols, we
have come to the preliminary conclusion that the occurrence of
real dynamic perception in chess is dependent upon the instruction, that is, on the subject's resulting set: either correctly to
reproduce or, also and finally, to *play* a move. One subject, at
least, distinguished introspectively between: "seeing that a
pawn is for the taking" (non-dynamic?) and "seeing the move:
take the pawn" (dynamic). Questions of this type are of some
importance for the construction of an adequate coding model
for the perceptual process. For example, given the empirical
fact that a chess position is perceived and temporarily stored
in terms of primary perceptual parts or "units" (piece configurations) must we allow for primary dynamic units? Are the
dynamics of the position (possible captures, threats) "seen" or
"inferred"? Units of the Gestalt type and various stereotyped
configurations, such as a King's side castling position, are
quite obviously of importance. But, must we distinguish func-
tional-dynamic primary units as well?

From the foregoing, it will be clear that my attitude toward the phenomena of perception, and toward those of memory functioning, has become one of deep respect. These phenomena are highly complex, often ambiguous and very difficult to pin down in terms of a code, a model, or a program.

Re Statement VIII

With regard to this statement my position has radically changed over the years: one could speak of an *Umwertung aller Werte,* a revaluation, if not a reversal of all values.

Animals can perceive very well and they can remember to some degree, but they cannot think as humans can, let alone create. As an implication, one would expect the resulting hierarchy of values to correspond to the degree to which these functions can be theoretically understood and imitated. But in actual fact, the order is the reverse. Although it is comparatively easy to make a machine create and difficult but not impossible to make it think, the simulation of memory functioning and, even more so, of perception has remained quite primitive compared to what humans or, for that matter, animals can do.

However, I had better resist the temptation to get involved in this pretty paradox and leave it to the discussion.

JEFFERY M. PAIGE
University of Michigan

HERBERT A. SIMON
Carnegie Institute of Technology

3

Cognitive Processes in Solving Algebra Word Problems *

Almost all the thinking and problem solving that people
do requires that they handle natural language. Often they must
perform tasks that also require simple arithmetic or even
algebraic manipulations. The study of information processing
systems, using computer languages as research tools, has
reached the point where programs can now be constructed
(indeed, have been constructed) that are capable of interpreting
simple natural-language expressions and simple mathematical
questions. In this paper we shall use one such computer program, which is capable of solving algebra word problems, as
a point of reference and departure for investigating the processes that humans use in solving such problems.

The two following parts of this introduction describe the
task environment (algebra word problems) for the human

*This investigation was supported in part by the Public Health
Service Research Grant MH-07722 from the National Institute of Mental Health. We are indebted to David Klahr and Allen Newell for comments on an earlier draft of this paper.

behavior we wish to explain, and comment on the methods of inquiry we shall use. Following the Introduction, Section I sets out a theory, due primarily to Daniel G. Bobrow, that explains the behavior of subjects solving word problems, to at least a reasonable first approximation, in simple situations. Section II presents empirical data of human behavior to illustrate some modifications in the basic theory that are required to accommodate individual differences in performance, and identifies some processes, visible in the human behavior, that are treated inadequately in the theory.

Section III introduces a distinction between "direct" and "auxiliary" translations of natural-language expressions, and presents data to show that human subjects often make use of auxiliary processes that are absent from the original form of the theory of Section I. Section IV shows how auxiliary representations permit the problem solver to use physical assumptions that are not explicit in the problem statement, but that are essential to its solution. Section V summarizes the empirical findings, and sketches the extensions of the theory that are required to encompass them. This summary section also discusses the relation of problem solving in algebra with the processes that have been identified in theoretical and empirical explorations of other task domains—proving theorems, for example, and playing chess. Our aim is not merely to account for human performance in solving algebra word problems but to do so in a way that will make apparent the relation of this performance to performance on other cognitive tasks.

Algebra Word Problems

The tasks of manipulating natural-language and mathematical symbols are both combined in answering the questions
posed in simple algebra word problems:

> If the number of customers Tom gets is
> twice the square of 20 per cent of the number of
> advertisements he runs, and the number of adver-
> tisements he runs is 45, what is the number of
> customers Tom gets?

At a common-sense level, it seems plausible that a person solves such problems by, first, translating the problem
sentences into algebraic equations and, second, solving the
equations. In fact, that is exactly what textbooks instruct students to do. The following example is typical (Hawkes, Luby
and Touton, 1929):

> In the solution of problems involving the use of
> simple equations, the following steps are necessary:
> 1. Read the problem carefully and find the state-
>   ment which will later be expressed in an equa-
>   tion.
> 2. Represent the unknown numbers by means of
>   numerals and letters.
> 3. Express the conditions stated in the problem as
>   an equation involving these symbols.
> 4. Solve the equation.
> 5. Check, by substituting in the problem the values
>   found for the unknowns.

Assuming that these recommendations describe at least
roughly what equation solvers actually do, we postulate two
main subprocesses, corresponding respectively to the first
three, and the last two, of the steps listed above:

TRANSFORM INPUT TEXT INTO EQUATIONS

SOLVE EQUATIONS

In this paper we shall be concerned almost exclusively with the first of these two subprocesses—with exploring how problem solvers set up an algebraic equation to correspond to a problem stated in English prose.

Information Processing Theories

The explanations we shall propose for the behavior belong to the class of theories known as *information processing theories*. An information processing theory, usually stated as a computer program in a formal programming language, postulates in detail a precise set of mechanisms to account for the observed behavior. In a problem-solving task, the behavior to be explained consists of what human subjects do, in writing or orally, under specified experimental conditions, while solving the problems.

An information processing theory is tested, as all theories are tested, by comparing its predictions with the observed behavior. The test can be extremely detailed and severe, for, using a computer programmed to behave in accordance with the information processing theory, the program can be confronted with exactly the same problems that are given to the human subjects, and either the broad outlines or the minutiae of its behavior, or both, can be compared with the corresponding aspects of the human behavior. This paper will provide a number of examples of such comparisons.

The theory must first pass a gross test of sufficiency. That is to say, since human beings who have had some training in algebra can solve simple algebra word problems, we would consider a theory of this performance unsatisfactory if its processes were not sufficiently powerful to solve simple problems of the same kind. The theory to be described in Section I passes the test of sufficiency; in solving algebra word problems it is roughly comparable with a human being having better-than-average manipulative skill in algebra but possessing a rather limited knowledge of English grammar and vocabulary.

Of course the flight of airplanes does not much resemble the flight of birds, except in the fact that both can sometimes stay aloft. Having satisfied ourselves of the sufficiency of the theory in the limited sense just indicated, additional evidence is needed to determine to what extent the problem-solving processes used in the theory resemble, or differ from, the processes used by humans when they handle the same tasks.

Sections II through IV carry out such comparisons for the theory introduced in Section I. We shall see that the main mechanisms postulated in the theory appear to be present in the behavior of most of the human subjects, but additional mechanisms have to be postulated to account for some aspects of the human behavior. Hence, the theory may be regarded as a first approximation that explains some of the broad outlines of the human behavior, and, by allowing us to abstract from these, brings into sharp focus additional phenomena that might otherwise escape our gaze. A next task (carried out only informally here) is to enlarge the theory into a second approximation so that still finer detail of the behavior can then be detected as deviations from this more accurate model.

The procedure just outlined has become a standard

method for testing information processing theories. To be worthy of consideration, such a theory must pass the test of sufficiency. It must be able to handle cognitive tasks comparable to those handled by human subjects at some level of skill. If it passes the sufficiency test, it is tested in more detail by comparing its behavior with human behavior on sets of identical or similar tasks. The differences between predicted and actual behavior then provide the basis for a new round of theory modification and testing. If fortune smiles, the cycle of theory construction and testing will show forward motion—its path will be helical rather than circular, producing successively more adequate explanations of behavior.*

I. DIRECT PROCESSES FOR SOLVING WORD PROBLEMS

Fortunately, the work of constructing a sufficient system of processes for solving algebra word problems has already largely been done for us. During 1958-60, Sylvia Garfinkel (1960) developed and hand-simulated a program for solving such problems. More recently, the work has been carried further by Daniel G. Bobrow (1964a, 1964b) who, in his M.I.T. doctoral dissertation, constructed a running computer program that solves a considerable range of algebra word problems. Miss Garfinkel's and Mr. Bobrow's programs differ in one

---

*For a survey of information processing theories of cognition see Allen Newell and Herbert A. Simon, "Computers in Psychology," Chapter 7, in Luce, Bush, Galanter (eds.), Handbook of Mathematical Psychology, Vol. I, John Wiley and Sons, New York (1963), pp. 361–428.

important respect: the former translates all problems using a single unknown, whereas the latter allows more than one unknown and simultaneous equations. Because it is more specific, and embodied in an actual running computer program, we shall in general take Bobrow's program, called STUDENT, as our base of reference. In fact, however, the task given our subjects resembles more closely the one handled by Miss Garfinkel's program, since we restricted the subjects to using a single unknown.

In proposing the STUDENT program as a theory of human problem solving, we are departing from the intent of its author. STUDENT was constructed in an investigation of artificial intelligence—"to discover how one could build a computer program which could communicate with people in a natural language within some problem domain." (See p. 7, 1964a.) The author did not intend to simulate human problem solving, nor does he make claims in this respect for the program. Hence, our analysis is in no sense an "evaluation" of the STUDENT program, but rather an inquiry into its relevance to a question quite different from the one it was designed to answer. Since the processes in the program do, as we shall see, parallel human processes in important respects, the fact that its author had other goals in mind does not make it less useful to us.

Example of a Transformation

Before trying to describe the processes used in STUDENT to translate English statements into algebraic equations, we shall give an illustration, using the word problem mentioned in the introduction. "Translation" here means substantially what it does in translating from one natural language to another. We know, roughly, how to go about translating a statement from English into French: First, the French equivalent of each English word is looked up in a dictionary, and the string of French words substituted for the English string. Then certain rearrangements (and inflectional modifications) are made in the resulting string so that it will satisfy the rules of French syntax rather than English syntax. Of course this is only a rough paraphrase of how the translation would actually be done, but it indicates the essential elements. It is an example of what we shall call a *direct process*.

To simplify the corresponding task of translating from English to algebra, let us pre-edit the text a bit. After we have analyzed the simplified form of the translation, we will return to the original problem.

> If the-number-of-customers-Tom-gets is twice the-square-of two-tenths times the-number-of-adver-isements-he-runs, and the-number-of-advertisements-he-runs is 45, what is the-number-of-customers-Tom-gets?

Now we might find the following in an English-algebra dictionary:

If	:	[not translated]
the-number-of-customers-Tom-gets	:	x_1
is	:	=
twice [= 2 times]	:	2 * [we write * for "times"]

the-square-of : $(...)^2$

two-tenths : .2

times : *

the-number-of-
advertisements-
he-runs : x_2

, and : (end of sentence)

, [question word] : (end of sentence)

what : ?

45 : 45

Replacing the English by the algebraic string, we get something like

$$x_1 = 2 * (.2 * x_2)^2$$

$$x_2 = 45$$

$$? = x_1$$

These equations are the algebraic equivalent of the original word problem, for solving the equations for x_1 gives the answer to that problem. Now, in order to simplify the problem and make it manageable for our crude dictionary-lookup translator, we have "cheated" in several ways. Most obvious and important: no dictionary exists that has "the-number-of-customers-Tom-gets" as an English entry and "x_1" as its algebraic translation. The use of x_1, rather than some other symbol, as the translation for the noun phrase is purely conventional. In the actual program, the translator did not find the equivalence in the dictionary; it simply assigned x_1 as an arbitrary name corresponding to the noun phrase. The only essential condition is that the translator use the *same* name to

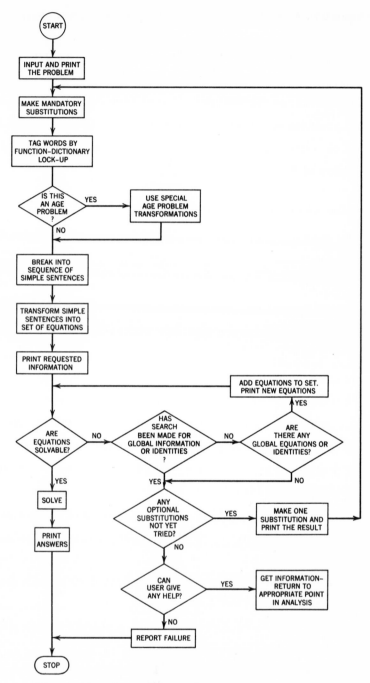

Fig. 1: Flowchart of the Student Program
(From Bobrow 1964a, page 104)

translate a particular noun phrase wherever it occurs in the problem. Thus, in the algebraic equations, x_1 and x_2 each occur twice, as did the noun phrases they stand for in the original problem statement. We have also simplified the translation by introducing the notation "$(...)^2$" to handle the function "square of."

Outline of the STUDENT Program

Having shown very crudely what a translation amounts to, we may now look in more detail at the STUDENT program for accomplishing it.* Figure 1 is a general flowchart of the STUDENT program. The processes in the upper half of the flowchart transform the input text into equations; the processes in the lower half solve the equations. We shall confine our attention to the upper half. Two of the processes represented in the flowchart are concerned only with a special class of word problems—age problems. These are the test labeled "Is this an age problem?" and the process labeled "Use special age problem transformations." We shall omit these also from our present discussion.

What remains is the following sequence of processes (See Fig. 1, top half):

INPUT AND PRINT THE PROBLEM

MAKE MANDATORY SUBSTITUTIONS

TAG WORDS BY FUNCTION—DICTIONARY LOOKUP

---

*The program is described in Bobrow (1964a, 1964b), and a listing provided in Appendix B (Bobrow, 1964a).

BREAK INTO SEQUENCE OF SIMPLE SENTENCES
TRANSFORM SIMPLE SENTENCES
INTO SET OF EQUATIONS

The operation of these processes on the illustrative word problem discussed above is shown in Fig. 2. This figure shows the successive transformations of the problem from the input text to the formal equations.

Mandatory Substitutions

The first step in transformation reduces certain words and phrases that appear in the input text to standard or canonical form, thus reducing the variety of expressions that have to be handled subsequently. As a comparison of the first and second versions of the text in Fig. 2 shows, the mandatory substitutions in this problem are 2 TIMES for TWICE, SQUARE for SQUARE OF, and PERCENT for PER CENT. The mandatory transformations are accomplished with the aid of a simple dictionary of synonyms.

Function Tags

The next main step in the transformation applies tags to some of the words in the text, indicating what grammatical functions these words perform. This transformation is also accomplished by a dictionary lookup. *Functions* are what a grammarian would call *parts of speech,* but STUDENT uses only a very simplified classification of parts of speech, containing three main categories (pp. 53-54, Bobrow, 1964*a*).

> The first category consists of strings of words
> which name objects in the model; I call such strings,
> variables. Variables are identified only by the string of
> words in them, and if two strings differ at all, they define
> distinct variables. . . .

The problem to be solved is:

(If the number of customers Tom gets is twice the square of 20 per cent of the number of advertisements he runs, and the number of advertisements he runs is 45, what is the number of customers Tom gets Q.)

With mandatory substitutions the problem is:

(If the number of customers Tom gets is 2 times the square 20 percent of the number of advertisements he runs, and the number of advertisements he runs is 45, what is the number of customers Tom gets Q.)

With words tagged by function the problem is:

(If the number (of/op) customers Tom (gets/verb) is 2 (times/op 1) the (square/op 1) 20 (percent/op 2) (of/op) the number (of/op) advertisements (he/pro) runs, and the number (of/op) advertisements (he/pro) runs is 45, (what/Q word) is the number (of/op) customers Tom (gets/verb) (Q mark/DLM)

The simple sentences are:

(The number (of/op) customers Tom (gets/verb) is 2 (times/op 1) the (square/op 1) 20 (percent/op 2) (of/op) the number (of/op) advertisements (he/pro) runs (period/DLM)

(The number (of/op) advertisements (he/pro) runs is 45 (period/DLM))

((What/Q word) is the number (of/op) customers Tom (gets/verb) (Q mark/DLM))

The equations to be solved are:

(Equal G02515 (number of customers Tom (gets/verb)))

(Equal (number of advertisements (he/pro) runs) 45)

(Equal (number of customers Tom (gets/verb)) (times 2 (expt (times .2000 (number of advertisements (he/pro) runs)) 2)))

(The number of customers Tom gets is 162)

Fig. 2. Example of direct transformation of algebra word problem (Bobrow 1964a, p. 110).

The second class of words and phrases are what I
call "substitutors." Each substitutor may be replaced by
another string. Some substitutions are mandatory; others
are optional and are only made if the problem cannot be
solved without such substitutions. . . .

Members of the third class of words indicate the
presence of functional linguistic forms which represent
functions in the deductive model. I call members of this
third class "operators." . . . One simple operator is the
word "plus," which indicates that the objects named by the
two variables surrounding it are to be added. An example
of a more complex operator is the phrase "percent less
than," as in "10 percent less than the marked price,"
which indicates that the number immediately preceding
the "percent" is to be subtracted from 100, this result
divided by 100, and then this quotient multiplied by the
variable following the "than." . . .

Some words may act as operators conditionally,
depending on their context. For example, "of" is equivalent to "times" if there is a fraction immediately preceding it; e.g., ".5 of the profit" is equivalent to ".5 times
the profit"; however, "Queen of England" does not imply
a multiplicative relationship between the Queen and her
country.

Only certain words in the text are tagged—those called
operators in the paragraph just quoted. Operators divide, in
turn, into three subclasses: operators (proper), verbs, and de-
limiters. As examination of the transformed example shows,
the operators there are "of," "times," "square," and "percent,"
the verb is "gets," and the delimiter, "?". In addition, the pronoun "he," and the question word "what" are also tagged. Note
that in this case, the dictionary did not list "runs" as a verb,
and the verb "is," which plays a special role, is not tagged.

Simple Sentences

Using the tags, and certain specific syntactical words as clues, the text is now divided into a sequence of simple sentences. For example, if an input sentence has an "if," followed by a string of words, followed by a comma, a question word, and a second string of words, then the first string, between the "if" and the comma, is made into a sentence, and the string following the comma into a second sentence. In the example before us, the text is divided into three sentences.

Algebraic Equations

The final step, the translation into equations, is now quite straightforward. Question words and noun phrases are interpreted as variables and are assigned names. Thus, "what" is given the arbitrary name "G02515," which is equated with "number of customers Tom gets." The other variable is "number of advertisements he runs."

In the particular notation used in STUDENT (so-called "Polish notation"), operators precede their operands. Thus we have "Equal G02515 (Number of customers Tom gets)," that is "Equals (a, b)," instead of the more familiar algebraic notation: "$a = b$." The only remaining subtlety in the transformation program is the set of rules that determines the order in which the various operations are to be performed. Partly this is handled by distinguishing "levels" of operators. Thus, in the example, "percent" is tagged "op 2," and "square" is tagged "op 1," so that the percentage will be taken before the result is squared. The program uses these tags, together with the

sequence in which operators occur in the text, to assign the
right phrase structure.

We have not described in detail the exact grammatical
rules embodied in the syntactical routines of STUDENT because
they are unimportant for our purpose. Much more complex and
complete schemes for parsing English sentences than the
STUDENT scheme have been programmed for computers.
What is chiefly interesting about STUDENT in this respect is
that a rather elementary scheme of syntactical analysis is in
fact sufficient for handling an interesting range of algebra word
problems.

Some STUDENT-like Human Behavior

The remainder of this paper will largely be devoted to a
comparison of the direct translation processes that enable
STUDENT to solve algebra word problems with the processes
that human subjects have been observed using. The raw data
for the comparisons are the thinking-aloud behavior of some
28 subjects who were tape-recorded while setting up equations
for algebra word problems. Ten of the subjects were college
students (except one, a technical school graduate in electronics)
between the ages of 19 and 21. Six of these were male (three
majoring in engineering, two in physics, and one in mathematics), four were female (two majoring in mathematics, one in
history, and one in psychology). Fifteen subjects were high
school students, aged 15 and 16, 11 male and 4 female, en-
rolled in a special summer program of advanced, college pre-
paratory courses for culturally deprived children. These students all had I. Q.'s in the same general range, averaging 118,

and had taken at least a year of high school algebra. They had been selected for the summer program as having high intellectual potential but relatively poor motivation. The remaining three subjects were a male, aged 48, holding a Ph. D. and with extensive mathematics training; a female, aged 27, holding an M.A. degree in psychology; and a male, aged 8, a student in the third grade.

Using this rather diverse group of subjects, and some variations on the basic task (the eight-year-old subject was given arithmetic rather than algebraic problems), we were able to get some impression of the diversity of human behaviors with a number of algebra problems of familiar types. In most parts of this paper we shall be dealing in detail with the behavior of individual subjects. For some purposes, however, we shall use aggregate data from the behavior of thirteen of the high school students, all of whom were given the same tasks.

The subjects in the main series of experiments were instructed as follows:

> We are interested in how people solve problems.
> This experiment is not designed to test your problem-solving ability. It is simply to discover what methods you would use to attack an algebra word problem. There are no time limits on these problems. . . .
> All the problems involve one algebraic equation with a single unknown. You should not attempt solutions using more than one unknown. A problem is completed when you are able to dictate to me an algebraic equation which is equivalent to the verbal statement. . . .
> In order to follow your thoughts we ask that you think aloud, explaining each step as thoroughly as you can. It is a well-known psychological fact that such verbalization is not a handicap to problem solving. The problems will be presented on 5-by-9 cards, and you should begin by

> reading the problem aloud. Try to mention even details
> which you consider trivial, as they may be useful in un-
> derstanding the total thought sequence.
>   To help you remember your place during the solu-
> tion, I will write down on the blackboard parts of the equa-
> tion, formulas, and so on, which you feel are useful in solv-
> ing the problem. You must specify exactly what I am to
> write. . . . You will not be told whether or not the solu-
> tion is correct. . . .

The subjects in the main series of experiments were given the three practice problems followed by the five test problems that are listed in the Appendix of this paper. Some of the early subjects were given a partially different set of problems, but all of the data reported here refer to the problems in the Appendix.

Much of the human behavior, especially on the simpler practice problems, resembles closely the sample given previously of STUDENT's direct translation. A single sample will suffice at this point for illustration. Subject 8 was a woman undergraduate student of mathematics who employed (more than any of the other subjects) careful, direct translation processes. Here is her protocol on Practice Problem 2:

> 'If three more than a certain number is divided by
> 5 the result is the same as twice the number diminished
> by 12. What is the number?'
>   'Three more than a certain number' is x plus . . .
> x plus 3. Write down '$x + 3$.' 'Divided by 5,' so divide the
> whole thing by 5. 'The result is' . . . 'is'—an equals.
> Write '='. 'The same as twice the number,' which would
> be 2 times x. 'Diminished by,' minus—minus 12. That's
> the completed equation.

The single quotation marks have been supplied in the transcription of the tape-recorded protocol to indicate where the subject is obviously reading from the printed problem statement, or dictating something to the experimenter at the blackboard. The wording of the text, taken together with inflectional cues in the tape recording, leave little or no ambiguity in the interpretation.

Clearly, the subject is carrying out a phrase-by-phrase translation, operating in a single pass over the problem statement from beginning to end. In this latter respect, her processing is organized in even a simpler manner than STUDENT's. Implicitly, but not explicitly, she reduces the first sentence to the simpler form, "A certain number divided by five is the same as twice the number diminished by 12." In translating phrase by phrase, she does not notice that the last part of the sentence is ambiguous—could be translated "$2(x - 12)$" instead of "$2x - 12$". At a gross level, the general translational approach of STUDENT gives a pretty good explanation of what the student is doing in solving the problem.

II. SOME DIRECT TRANSLATIONAL PROCESSES IN HUMAN SUBJECTS

In this section, we will examine a number of interesting phenomena that emerge when we compare, in detail, the STUDENT scheme with some examples of human behavior. First, we shall illustrate the range of individual differences, all within a general translational framework, in handling a simple problem. Second, we shall examine some processes for naming quantities that are absent from the STUDENT program, but which are essential if the subjects are to formulate the equations using only one unknown. Third, we shall investigate how ambiguities in naming quantities are handled by STUDENT and by some of the subjects.

In these explorations, we shall use the protocols of three college-level subjects. Subject 8, as already mentioned, is a female undergraduate majoring in mathematics. Subject 5 is a female college graduate in psychology. Subject 6 is a male undergraduate majoring in physics.

An Example of Individual Differences

Figure 3 gives the complete protocols of these three subjects on Practice Problem 1. The protocols show that the subjects proceeded in quite different fashions.

PROBLEM: If a certain number is multiplied by 6 and the product increased by 44 the result is 68. Find the number.

Subject 5	Subject 6	Subject 8
So I would begin by subtracting 44 from 68 and getting 24 and therefore the number is 4.	We'll call the number n. It says that if we multiply it by 6 and add 44 to it, 'the result is 68.' This presents a simple equation of $6n$ plus 44 equals 68.	The unknown is a 'certain number,' which would be x. Multiply x by 6. Write down '$6x$' please. 'Increased by' means add, so you put a plus 44. 'The result is'—indicates equals— write please—'68'.

Fig. 3. Three protocols on Practice Problem 1

The subjects were instructed to set up the equation, using a single variable, not to solve it. Subject 5 disobeyed the instructions. Instead of translating the problem into an equation, she simply finds the answer, working backward from end to beginning, performing arithmetic operations sequentially, and holding the partial answer in memory. If we designate by A the partial answer, we could describe her process thus:

> Set $A = 68$
> Subtract 44 from A [$= 24$]
> Divide A by 6 [$=4$]
> Report: $A = 4$

That this sequence is not simply a hindsight invention is demonstrated by the fact that the subject actually was aware of the partial result $68 - 44 = 24$. We may therefore have some confidence that she went through approximately this sequence in obtaining the answer. In order to do this, she had to replace each operation in the problem statement by its inverse: subtracting for "increased by," dividing for "multiplied by," and she had to interpret the terms "product" and "result."

Subject 8 represents the other extreme—a process corresponding very closely to a direct syntactical translator, as in her handling of Practice Problem 2. The subject treats "the number" as synonymous with "a certain number," and assigns it the name "x." "Is multiplied by 6" is interpreted as transforming "x" to "$6x$." "Increased by 44" is interpreted as transforming "$6x$" to "$6x + 44$." "The result is" is translated "$=$," so that the sentence is translated "$6x + 44 = 68$."

Subject 6 uses a somewhat different process to set up the equation. Like Subject 8, he sets up an algebraic equation, but, like Subject 5, he uses the device of successively modifying a partial result. In the case of Subject 6, however, the partial result is an algebraic expression rather than a number. Again, let us call the partial answer A. The processes of Subject 6 may then be described thus:

> Set $A = n$
> Set $A = 6A$ [$= 6n$]
> Set $A = A + 44$ [$= 6n + 44$]
> Write equation: $A = 68$ [$6n + 44 = 68$]

That the subject is actually proceeding in this way is shown by the fact that he first calls the number n, then multiplies *"it"* by 6, and adds 44 to *"it."* Only on the interpretation we have given above can the "it" refer in both cases to the same object—that is, to the partial answer, A.

To explain how the STUDENT program handles this problem, we shall have to supplement our previous description of it with some new detail. There is involved a new concept here— indicated by the words "produce" and "result." Instead of setting up a new equation for each clause of the sentence, the subjects identify the first clause as designating a new number (the product) that results from performing the operation described by the clause. The clause provides for this new number a *relational name*, "6x," that *relates* it to the name, "x," of the "certain number." Similarly, the second clause, "and the product increased by 44," provides a relational name, "(6x)+44," that relates the "result" to the "product." The main clause now equates this relational name with the number 68, providing the required algebraic equation: [(6x)+44] = 68, where, to emphasize the way in which the equation was developed, we put parentheses around the relational name of "the product" and square brackets around the relational name of "the result."

The STUDENT program in fact contains some processes, not described earlier, that allows it to handle this problem in much the way it is handled by Subjects 6 or 8. For these processes to operate properly, the problem must be slightly reworded, although the present wording could be retained if a few sophistications were added to STUDENT's dictionary and syntactical routines. Figure 4 shows how STUDENT solved the slightly reworded problem:

The problem to be solved is:

(A number is multiplied by 6. The product is increased by 44. The result is 68. Find the number.)

The equations to be solved are:

(Equal G02528 (number))

(Equal (plus (times (number) 6) 44) 68)

The number is 4

Fig. 4   STUDENT solution of (modified) Practice Problem 1.

"A number is multiplied by 6. This product is increased by 44. This result is 68. Find the number." The device STUDENT uses is described as follows:

The sentence "A number is multiplied by 6" only indicates that two objects in the model are related multi-plicatively, and does not indicate explicitly any equality relation. The interpretation of this sentence in the model is the prefix notation product:

(TIMES (NUMBER) 6)

The latter phrase is stored in a temporary location for possible later reference. In this problem, it is refer-enced in the next sentence, with the phrase "THIS PROD-UCT." The important word in this last phrase is "THIS." STUDENT ignores all other words in a variable containing the key word "THIS." The last temporarily stored phrase is substituted for the phrase containing "THIS." Thus, the first three sentences in the problem shown above yield only one equation, after two substitutions for "this" phrases.

In summary, in this problem we find Subject 8 behaving in a manner closely resembling that predicted by STUDENT. Subject 6 also sets up the equation by direct translation, but uses processes a little different from those used by Subject 8.

Conventional and Relational Names

The single simple example of an algebra word problem that we have been considering already discloses some interest-ing ingredients of the process for handling such problems. Of particular interest are the processes for *naming* variables. The names used are of two kinds: *conventional* and *relational*. Since the same distinction can be made among names used in ordinary English prose, we shall first consider it as a general linguistic distinction, then apply it to algebra.

A particular automobile can be identified (that is, named) by its license number, or by naming its owner. Thus, we can speak of "the automobile F34-338," or of "John Smith's automobile." The former method of naming is conventional, the latter is relational, for it identifies the object by a particular relation (ownership) to another object (John Smith). A variety of syntactic devices are used in Engligh to permit relational naming. One of the most common is the noun phrase with "of": "The X of the Y of the Z." "Of" may designate a much more general relation than property ownership: "The prow of the largest ship of the fleet." The definite article, "the," implies that there is one and only one object satisfying the relation— that it defines a function, in the mathematical sense.

In algebra, we use letters of the alphabet to name numbers conventionally. In the problem we have been considering, Subject 6 says, "We'll call the number n," and Subject 8 says, "The unknown is 'a certain number,' which would be x." In both cases, a conventional name in English, "the number," "a certain number," is replaced by a conventional algebraic name: "n" or "x."

The two subjects also use relational naming, however. They translate the phrase, "the result," by the function $(6n + 44)$, or $(6x + 44)$ respectively. Knowing that "the result" is also equal to the number 68, they then state that these two numbers are equal: the number named "$(6n + 44)$" and the number named "68." It is because the former name relates "the result" to "a certain number" that it permits the numerical name for the latter to be found.

The point may be restated in another way. The statement of such an algebra problem asserts that certain relations hold among various numbers, some of them known, some of them unknown. In translating the problem statement into algebra, the information that a particular relation holds can be used in two ways: (1) To state an equation, whose left-hand side is one name for a number, and whose right-hand side is another name for the same number (cf. "John is Fred's uncle"); or (2) to name one number by its relation to another number (cf. "Fred's uncle").

These alternatives may be illustrated if we solve the sample problem we have been examining by setting up three equations in three unknowns, instead of a single equation in one unknown. Call "a certain number" x, "the product" y, and "the result" z. Then we can state immediately the three equations:

$$y = 6x$$
$$z = y + 44$$
$$z = 68$$

We have the same alternatives in English prose. Consider: "His father's car is blue." Let X, Y, and Z be objects (or persons). We can then translate: "X is a person such that Y is the father of X, Z is the car of Y, and Z is blue." Ordinarily, we would have no occasion to make such a translation, but the fact that it is grammatical shows us that there is nothing peculiarly "algebraic" or mathematical about it. There are even certain linguistic devices that allow us to dispense with letters for names of variables: "A certain person is the father of a second person; a certain car belongs to the former; that car is blue."

Returning to the algebra problems, we see that certain tradeoffs are possible between naming variables conventionally or relationally, on the one hand, and setting up more or fewer equations, on the other. In another simple problem (Practice

Problem 3), we see how different subjects make use of these alternatives:

> The difference between two numbers is 12, and 7
> times the smaller number exceeds the greater by 30.
> Find the numbers.

As before, the subjects were instructed to set up the equation using a single unknown, but again, Subject 5 unintentionally disobeyed the instructions. Her protocol begins:

> X minus—would you write—'$x - y = 12$,' and '7 times
> the smaller number' which is gonna be y, so would you
> write '$7y$,' ah, . . .

Here the two numbers are named, conventionally, "x" and "y", whereas "7 times the smaller number" is named relationally, "$7y$." The other two subjects succeed in formulating the problem with a single variable. Subject 6 begins:

> O.K. We'll call one number n —and you may write
> 'n', just jot it down—and the other number $(n - 12)$. Just
> write it down for my reference.

Subject 8 begins in almost the same way, but chooses the smaller, rather than the larger, number to be named conventionally:

> The first number we will let be represented by x.
> Write down 'x' please. The second number is then $(x + 12)$
> since 'the difference is 12.' Write down '$(x + 12)$.'

Since the subjects were instructed to use only a single unknown, they were forced by these instructions to introduce relational names for the remaining variables. (In some cases, as with Subject 5 on Practice Problem 3, they found themselves unable to do so, or forgot the instructions.) In this respect,

STUDENT provides an inadequate description of the human behavior, for it introduces relational names only in the special
case already illustrated by Practice Problem 1, where it is
cued by the occurrence of the word "this." Even had the subjects not been restricted as to the number of unknowns used,
they almost certainly would have used the relational naming
process more freely than STUDENT, and limited themselves
to smaller numbers of simultaneous equations.

We have here an example of how the technique of computer simulation can be used to identify a simple but important
process that enters into the human performance. The difference between using information to create a relational name
and using that same information to create an equation can be
detected readily in the protocols.*

Ambiguity of Names

Frequently, variant phrases are used to name the same
quantity in the statement of a problem. Most often, the second
time a quantity is mentioned, it is denoted by an abridgement
of the phrase that named it on the first mention. Thus: "If
three more than *a certain number* . . . What is *the number*?"
Presumably "the number" of the question is the "certain number" of the first statement. Often, abridgement involves substitution of a pronoun for a noun: "the number of customers
he has" for "the number of customers Tom has." In these

---

*We noted earlier that Miss Garfinkel's program translates all
problems using a single unknown. Hence, it contains more elaborate
processes than STUDENT for relational naming, and in this respect
constitutes a more adequate theory of our subjects' behavior.

cases, the rules for pronoun reference allow the identification
to be made. In other cases, an identifying phrase is omitted:
"the liter" for "one liter of a 90 per cent alcohol-water mixture."

These examples show that a person solving an algebra
word problem must be prepared sometimes to identify with a
single quantity two names that are similar, but distinct. On the
other hand, mere similarity of two phrases does not mean that
the variables they denote are necessarily identical. Consider
this example:

> The number of quarters a man has is seven times
> the number of dimes he has. The value of the dimes ex-
> ceeds the value of the quarters by two dollars and fifty
> cents. How many has he of each coin?

In the first two sentences, there are four noun phrases de-
noting quantities: "the number of quarters a man has," "the number of dimes he has," "the value of the dimes," and "the value of
the quarters." In spite of the fact that the first two phrases
(after replacement of the pronoun by the appropriate noun) differ in only a single word ("quarters" versus "dimes"), as do
also the last two, a native speaker of English would not be likely
to identify the members of either the first pair or the second
pair.

But what about the first and fourth, and the second and
third? Is "number of quarters" the same as, or different from
"value of the quarters"? In this case we would probably decide
they are different, as would any sufficiently careful reader.
This decision, however, certainly does not derive from any inflexible general rule saying that identical quantities must always

have identical names. As a matter of fact, the use of "value" as a synonym for "number" is sometimes idiomatic in English: If the number of dollars a man has is 15, the value of the dollars (in dollars) is also 15.

The STUDENT program provides for matching slightly different phrases referring to the same object, and assigning the same name to them, when the second of the two phrases to appear in the problem statement is contained completely in the first, in the sense that it is a contiguous substring within the first. STUDENT initially undertakes to solve the problem without such identifications, and matches variables if it has been unsuccessful (Bobrow, 1964a, p. 71).

Thus, if necessary in order to solve a problem, STUDENT will assume that "gas consumption" is the same variable as "*gas consumption* of my car," if the second phrase occurs in the problem statement earlier than the first phrase; and under the same conditions will assume that "number of gallons of gas used" is the same as "*number of gallons of gas used* on trip between New York and Boston." It would not, however, identify "number of gallons of gas used" with "number of gallons used between New York and Boston." Thus, although the program illustrates the process—commonly used in interpreting natural language—of identifying "similar" phrases, it is rather inflexible in the way it does this.

Our subjects differed a great deal in the precision with which they handled these kinds of variations in noun phrases. Consider, for example, the protocol of Subject 8 on the coin problem:

> Let's represent—the fir— —x as the dimes. Write down x please. The number of quarters is—is seven times the dimes. Therefore, the number of quarters is repre-

sented by $7x$. Put '$7x$.' 'The value of the dimes exceeds
the value of the quarters by two-fifty'; therefore, x equals—
represented by the value of the dimes—write down 'x' again.

This subject, who was generally quite careful in handling
the problem sentences phrase by phrase, actually writes down
the equation: $x = 250 + 7x$, but then continues:

> Since it really is a money problem we will check
> this and discover that we really should multiply to make
> this—ah—to make it equal in value. Since we have 250
> pennies we have to multiply the dimes by 10. So that
> should be $10x$ and a plus. Since it's quarters it would be
> 7 times 25 times x, on the other side. That's the correct
> solution.

In the initial stages of solving the problem, this subject
equated x with "the dimes," "the number of dimes," and "the
value of the dimes." Perhaps the simplest explanation is to assume that her parsing program identified all noun phrases containing "dimes," and that, operationally speaking, x was defined
as "the variable associated with dimes."

The same subject exhibited similar behavior on another
problem. Here the problem was:

> Mr. Stewart decided to invest 4,000 dollars, some
> at 3 per cent and the rest at 4 per cent. How much should
> he invest at each rate to produce equal incomes?

Here again, four quantities are under consideration: the
amount of money invested at 3 per cent, the amount invested at
4 per cent, the income from the money invested at 3 per cent,
and the income from the money invested at 4 per cent. The subject refers to these quantities in quite ambiguous language: "x
equals 3 per cent invested," "Write down $(4,000 - x)$. This represents the amount invested at 4 per cent, so write down 4 per

cent invested." "We want the number invested at 4 per cent to equal the amount invested at 3 per cent." Although the last sentence sounds like an incorrect statement of the problem, Subject 8 in fact set up the right equation.

The difficulty many subjects have in identifying the variables in the coin problem is vividly illustrated by the protocol of Subject 6 (italics added):

> All right. He has quarters and dimes. I'd like to represent *a dime by x and a quarter by 2.5x,* because a quarter is two and one-half times the dime, so if you'd write down my reference '*x*' for dimes and '2.5*x*' for quarters. O.K. 'The value of the dimes exceeds the value of the quarters by two-fifty' and he 'has 7 times as many quarters as he has dimes' so—put 7 times the denomin— *the notation for quarters* —which is (2.5*x*)—in parentheses. Seven times that exceeds *the value*—oh, let's see, he 'has seven times as many quarters as he has dimes.'The *value of the dimes' which is x* 'exceeds the value of the quarters by two-fifty' so—'a man has seven times as many quarters' —and these are to be solved with one variable only. *X represents the dimes; 7x might represent the quarters.* All right. May I change that? 'A man has seven times as many quarters as he has dimes,' so *call x dimes but call 7x quarters please.* That's a bit of foggy thinking right there. '*The value of the dimes,' which is x* 'exceeds the value of the quarters by two-fifty.' O.K. *The number of quarters is 7x, the value of the quarters is 25 cents times 7x.* Would you write that down please? Just write '25 cents times 7*x*.' O.K. Now 'the value of the dimes exceeds the value of the quarters by two-fifty,' so that 10 cents times *x* minus the 25 cents—no, all right—just put a minus; you already have the 25 cents down, 7*x* equals two-fifty. . . . Ten cents times *x* minus 25 cents times 7*x* equals two-fifty.

III. AUXILIARY REPRESENTATIONS AND CUES

We have used the phrase "direct translation" for the kinds of processes examined thus far, for they amount mostly to a step-by-step substitution of algebraic symbols and expressions for the English words and phrases of the original problem statements. These translation processes involve the meanings, hence the translation, of only those terms in the problem statement that are mathematical in character ("number of," "two times"), or that perform syntactic functions in the sentence ("if," "and"). Other words and phrases are either ignored or replaced by conventional or relational names. Consider again the example:

> If the number of customers Tom gets is twice the
> square of 20 per cent of the number of advertisements he
> runs, and the number of advertisements he runs is 45, what
> is the number of customers Tom gets?

To set up the algebraic equations for this problem requires no knowledge of the meaning of "customers" or "advertisements," or for that matter, who Tom is; as is readily seen from:

> If the number of glubs X biks is twice the square of
> 20 per cent of the number of quonks he dobs, and he dobs
> 45 quonks, how many glubs does he bik?

On the other hand, even small changes in terms like "number of," "twice," "how many" could change entirely the meaning of the problem, or make it meaningless. Certain grammatical cues are also essential: it is important to know that "customers" or "glubs" is a noun, and that "he" is a pronoun that can stand for a person, but not for an inanimate object. Nor can the problem be solved without the knowledge that "is," in this kind of context, stands for "equals numerically."

A distinction is sometimes made between words that carry a substantive meaning and those that are primarily syntactic or grammatical in function. A noun like "customers" is clearly substantive, whereas "if," "the," "and," and "of," for example, are largely syntactic. Taking into consideration words that have special arithmetic meanings ("number," "twice," "times," "square," for example) we can say, as a rough approximation, that translating the word problems into equations requires a knowledge of the meanings of words that play a grammatical role, or an arithmetic one, but not the meanings of those that play a substantive role. The substantive terms, or the phrases constructed of them ("the number of advertisements he runs") are for the most part simply translated into conventional names of variables. All that is required is to be able to decide whether two such phrases name the same variable or different variables.

Let us now return to the coin problem:

> The number of quarters a man has is seven times the number of dimes he has. The value of the dimes exceeds the value of the quarters by two dollars and fifty cents. How many has he of each coin?

The subject cannot solve this problem unless he possesses certain substantive information about dimes, quarters, dollars, and coins. He must know that the value of a quantity of coins equals the number of coins times the value per coin: $V_i = N_i *$ v_i. He must also know that the value per dime (v_d) is ten cents, the value per quarter (v_q) is 25 cents, and the value per dollar (v_D) is 100 cents. The subjects who were successful in setting up the equation for this problem made use of precisely this information.

To a limited extent, the STUDENT program simulates the subjects' use of substantive information. This is accomplished by storing in memory certain definitional equations. For example

"the perimeter of a rectangle sometimes means twice the sum
of the length and width of the rectangle," "distance equals speed
times time," or "distance equals gas consumption times number
of gallons of gas used." If a problem proves unsolvable, STUDENT
searches for relevant relations of this kind in memory, and, if
it finds some, adds the corresponding equations.

We will refer to information of this sort, stored in the
memories of the subjects, as "auxiliary information." We see
that in handling many typical algebra word problems, such information is indispensable as a supplement to the direct translation processes.

Auxiliary Information

In a number of situations, the behavior of the subjects
gives evidence that they are using stored substantive information
that goes beyond the definitional equations we have just considered. The reader may or may not have noticed by now that the
coin problem we have been using is substantively meaningless
since it describes a physical impossibility. The problem states
that there are *more* quarters than dimes (seven times as many,
in fact). The value of a quarter is also more than the value of
the dime; hence, the total value of the quarters must exceed the
total value of the dimes. [$N_q > N_d$ and $v_q > v_d$, therefore
$V_q = N_q * v_q > N_d * v_d = V_d$.] But the problem states: "The
value of the dimes *exceeds* the value of the quarters. ..."

If we translate the problem as given, as our three subjects
did, we obtain the equation: $10x - 7 * 25x = 250$, which has as its
solution, $x = -(50/33)$. Neither Subject 5 nor Subject 8 gave any
evidence of noticing that the solution would be negative. Subject

6, however, immediately on dictating the equation to the experimenter (see the previous quotation of his protocol), continued as follows:

> Now, I've found an incongruity in this problem. When I first saw it—it looked—it looked impossible, I think. I don't know if you want me to say this but if a man has seven times as many quarters as he has dimes and the value of the dimes exceeds the value of the quarters by two-fifty, the quarters must really not be worth too much, because if he has 7 times as many quarters as he has dimes, the number of—the value of the quarters must exceed the dimes by $7 * 2.5 - x$, or what not. The value of the dimes, if they are ordinary dimes, can't exceed the value of the quarters in this case. Therefore, if you solve out you get a negative answer, I believe, which doesn't jibe with—negative quarters—no such thing exists. So, my conclusion is this problem is impossible to solve, in two denominations—quarters, and so forth.

Subject 8 was asked to solve the problem a second time, and immediately set up the equation again—this time without hesitation:

> The number of dimes is x—the number of quarters would be $7x$, and the value of the dimes would be, then, 10 times x, which would equal $250 + 7 * 25 * x$.

The experimenter and subject then continued with the following conversation:

> E: Okay. Now let me show you a diagram—you probably already have this concept in mind, but tell me if looking at that changes the problem in any way. What do you make of that diagram?
>
> S: It just has a—a dime—just has pennies and a dime—and 25 pennies and quarters.
>
> E: Anything else strike you about that diagram?
>
> S: That a quarter is larger than a dime, that's all.
>
> E: Okay. Now look at that problem again.

> S: Now, wait a minute here! If you have more—oh, sure,
> if you have more quarters than you have dimes of
> course the value of the dimes can't be larger than the
> value of the quarters. That one's illogical too.

In both cases, noticing the physical impossibility of the
problem was equivalent to noticing that, under the terms of the
problem, $v_q > V_d$, and hence one could not have "the value of
the dimes exceeds the value of the quarters." Noticing this in-
equality is in no way essential to using direct grammatical cues
to translate the problem statement into an equation—and the
STUDENT program would have performed exactly as Subject 8
did initially.

Spatial and Physical Cues

In the protocols there are numerous instances of subjects,
in handling word problems, applying processes that involve the
spatial or physical relations in the problems. Such cues sometimes lead subjects to discover that a problem represents a
physically impossible situation. They are also used (intentionally or unintentionally) to substitute for the original "impossible"
problem a similar one that involves no physical contradiction.
We have some examples of this for another "impossible" problem (Problem 4):

> A board was sawed into two pieces. One piece was
> two-thirds as long as the whole board and was exceeded in
> length by the second piece by 4 feet. How long was the
> board before it was cut?

Subject 6, who was in general the quickest of the three to
discover contradictions, notices this one immediately:

This is another incongruous one because the first
piece is two-thirds as long as the whole board means the
second piece is one-third as long as the whole board. If
you want to write this down to show the incongruity, put
$(2/3)L$ represents the first piece. The second piece is
represented by $(1/3)L$ . . . Now, $(1/3)L$ exceeds the length
of the first piece by 4, so that we have $(2/3)L + 4 = (1/3)L$.
. . . If we solve this, we have $(1/3)L + 4 = 0$, or $(1/3)L$
$= -4$, or $L = -12$, and this is a negative length and that
doesn't exist either.

Subject 8 did not notice a contradiction, but in fact changed
the problem to make it physically possible. Her equation was:
$(2/3)x = +4 + [x - (2/3)x]$. There is no clear indication in the
protocol of how the transposition took place. The protocol
simply reads:

We want to know the length of the board, therefore,
write down 'x equals length of the board.' 'One piece is
$2/3$ of the whole board,' so $(2/3)x$, write down please, was
'exceeded in length by the second piece by 4 feet' so—we
want an equals plus 4 for the 'exceeded in length.' Now
'the second piece' would be the whole board minus the other
piece, which is $2/3$, so it would be times the quantity—no,
plus the quantity, $[x - (2/3)x]$.

Later Subject 8, now aware that some of the problems
represent physically impossible situations, is asked to do the
problem again. She now notices the impossibility immediately:

Of course, the—the one piece is $2/3$ and the other is
$1/3$. The $1/3$ piece can't be longer than the $2/3$ piece is.
So that is also illogical.

Subject 5 also substituted a physically possible problem
for the given one:

You can just put x equals length for me if you want
to. Ah, $2/3$ of x is . . . 'One piece was $2/3$ as long as the
whole board and was exceeded in length' . . . plus 4 feet—
no, you won't need that—ah, equals x.

Thus, Subject 5 assumes that the 4 feet represent the difference between the first piece and the whole board, not between
the two pieces. Now perhaps we could merely say that Subjects
5 and 8 did not know how to interpret the phrase "was exceeded
. . . by," and hence translated incorrectly. This may well be so,
but it is notable that in both cases the result of the incorrect
translation was to substitute a physically possible problem for
a physically impossible one. One possible explanation would be
to suppose that the subjects were using physical cues as well
as grammatical and arithmetic ones in their processing.

Suppose the problem were reworded as follows:

> A board was sawed into two pieces. One piece was
> two-thirds as long as the whole board, and the difference
> in length between the two pieces was 4 feet. How long was
> the board before it was cut?

Using only grammatical cues, this problem is ambiguous.
If we let x be the length of the board, we know that "one piece"
is $(2/3)x$. But the problem does not state whether the other
piece is $(2/3)x + 4$ or $(2/3)x - 4$. Hence, from grammatical
information alone, we do not know whether to write $x = (2/3)x
+ (2/3)x - 4$ or $x = (2/3)x + (2/3)x + 4$. Of course, if we cal-
culate that the second piece is $x - (2/3)x = (1/3)x$, and that
$2/3 > 1/3$, we will be able to deduce that the "one piece" is
longer than the other, hence that the first equation we have
written is the one intended.

Auxiliary Representations

What processes would lead a subject to calculate that,
since the one piece of the board is 2/3 its length, the other must
be 1/3? This calculation, in the original problem, is not re-

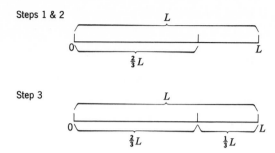

Fig. 5: An auxiliary representation for
Problem 4.

quired in order to set up the equation. Let us hypothesize that
some subjects carry out the following "semantic" processing:

1. Construct a number line. (See Fig. 5)
2. Represent the quantities given in the
   problem on the number line.
3. If certain quantities are named, but
   their numerical values are not given,
   try to compute their numerical values
   or relational names by use of the
   number line.

In the board problem, we construct the number line of
length L (Fig. 5). We mark off the interval from the origin to
$(2/3)L$ as the length of the one piece. The distance from the
end of this to the end of the line is the length of the other piece,
which is not given. By subtraction on the number line, we find
that it is $(1/3)L$, and label it accordingly.

We see clear evidence of this kind of processing in Subject
8's handling of another problem—a mixture problem (Problem 5):

A car radiator contains exactly one liter of a 90 per
cent alcohol-water mixture. What quantity of water will
change the liter to an 80 per cent alcohol mixture?

First, it must be noted that the problem is ambiguous. It is not clear whether the water is to be added, changing the total quantity of mixture; or whether some of the mixture is to be drawn off and replaced by water to make, again, a total of one liter of liquid. Subject 8 took the second interpretation. After reading the problem, she says:

> Ah, the only way I can solve one of these is to draw a picture.

The subject then asks the experimenter to draw a picture, and later another picture that is actually used in solving the problem. The second picture is shown in Fig. 6. The protocol reads:

> So we draw another picture. Then we draw another line across. Now, draw another line below that somewhere —it doesn't matter where. That's x. That's the amount we're going to take out. Let's see—that's one liter when we take out x, and that leaves us 1 minus x liters—quick— put it—write down beside it .9 times—parentheses 1 minus x, and put after that alcohol, please. . . . Okay. Ah—now, I want to get a 90 per cent so I want—I want that, okay, now the amount of alcohol we want to have left is .8 times 1 liter, so I want .9 times the quantity $(1-x)$ to equal .8. That's the equation.

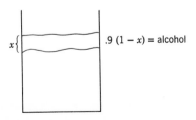

Fig. 6: An auxiliary representation for Problem 5.

How Representations Affect Problem-Solving Performance

The three subjects whose behavior we have been examining in some detail were college students or college graduates, all of whom had studied mathematics through the calculus. Table I gives some data obtained from thirteen of the 10th grade students.

Most of the subjects succeeded in setting up an equation for the board-sawing problem (Problem 4) and for the first two practice problems, but for few or none of the other problems. We may take this as evidence that the problems are really "hard" for high-school students (even those above average in ability) or that these particular students had had poor high-school algebra courses. There is probably considerable truth in both explanations.

After the subjects had undertaken to solve the three practice problems and the five test problems, they were asked by the experimenter to go to the blackboard and make diagrams for the board-sawing, river-boat, and alcohol-water mixture problems. Each diagram was to contain all the information given in the verbal statement. The diagram was to be complete enough to allow the subject to explain the problem to another student who had not read it.

Table I provides some information about how the subjects handled Problem 4, the board-sawing problem, about the diagrams they drew for that problem, and about their performance on the other practice and test problems. The first column of the Table identifies the subjects, the second column shows which of the three practice problems they solved correctly. In Column

TABLE I

Auxiliary Representations Used by High School Subjects

Subject	Practice Problems Solved	Self-Rating	Problems for which:		Problem 4		
			Equations Written	Contra-diction Noticed	Type of Equation	Diagram	Equation
(1)	(2)	(3)	(4)	(5)	(6)	(7)	(8)
Group P1	("Physical" equation, good problem solvers)						
20	1, 2	Good	1, 4	4	(Physical)*	I, i, P	"contradictory"
28	1, 2	Fair to Good	1, 24	4, 5†	Physical	I, i, P	$2/3x - 4 = 1/3x$
Group V1	("Verbal" equation, good problem solvers)						
16	all	Good	2, 3, 4	None	Verbal	I, i, V	$2/3x + 2/3x + 4 = x$
21	all	Fair	1, 4	None	Verbal	U, c, P	$2/3x = 2/3x + 4$
24	all	Good	2, 3, 4	1	Verbal	I, c, V	$2(2/3x) + 4 = x$
25	1, 2	Fair	1, 4	None	Verbal	U, c, V	$2/3x + 2/3x + 4 = x$

Group P2 ("Physical" equation, poor problem solvers)

18	1, 2	Poor	None	(Physical)*	U, c, P	$2/3x + 4 = 0$
22	1, 2	Fair to Poor	4	Physical	I, c, P	$x = 2/3x + 2/3x - 4$
26	1, 2	Fair	4	Physical	U, c, V	

Group V2 ("Verbal" equation, poor problem solvers)

17	1,2	Fair	4	Verbal	U, i, P	$2/3x + (2/3x + 4) = x$
19	1,2	Poor	4	Physical	I, c, V	$2/3x = 1/3x + 4$
				Verbal‡		$2/3x + (2/3x + 4) = x$
23	1,2	Poor	4	Verbal	U, c, V	$2/3x + 2/3x + 4 = x$
27	all	Good	4	Verbal	U, c, V	$4/3x + 4 = x$

*No equation constructed, but evidence of physical interpretation.
†Noticed the ambiguity in Problem 5.
‡First produced P equation; when asked to explain, produced V equation.

(3) is the subject's self-rating of his performance in high-school algebra. Column (4) shows for which of the five test problems the subject was able to construct an equation—whether correct or incorrect. Column (5) identifies the subjects who noticed contradictions in one or more problems. (Problems 1, 3, and 4 were physically impossible; 5 was ambiguous.) Column (6) indicates whether the equation the subject constructed in Problem 4 followed the verbal or a physical translation of the problem. Column (7) shows certain characteristics of the diagram for Problem 4 each subject later drew (See Fig. 7): whether the diagram was integrated (I) (a single figure for the board and its parts) or unintegrated (U)(separate drawings for board and parts); whether the diagram was complete (c)(contained all the information in the problem statement) or incomplete (i); whether the diagram represented the verbal (V) problem or the physical (P) situation. Column (8) of the Table shows the equation each subject actually constructed for Problem 4. In interpreting these data, it should be kept in mind that the subjects constructed the diagrams some time after they derived the equations, with their work on Problem 5 intervening between these two performances.

In Table I, the subjects are arranged in four groups, on the basis of whether they set up the verbal (V) or the physical (P) equation for Problem 4, and whether they were successful (Groups 1) or unsuccessful (Groups 2) in setting up an equation for at least one test problem in addition to 4. Thus, the four groups are labeled P1, V1, P2, and V2 respectively.

Figure 7 provides an example of a diagram drawn by a member of each group. The diagrams in the top half of Fig. 7 are integrated. The one belonging to Subject 20 (P1) is an incomplete (since "4 feet" is nowhere mentioned) diagram of the

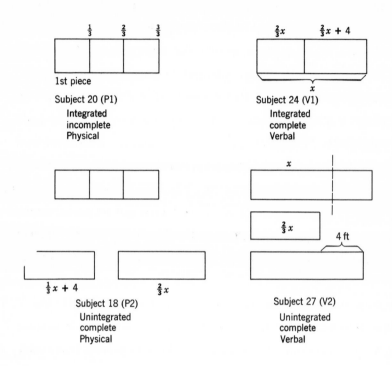

Fig. 7: Types of diagrams for Problem 4.

physical situation. The diagram of Subject 24 (V1) is a complete
diagram of the verbally described situation. The diagrams in
the bottom half of Fig. 7 are unintegrated, consisting of three
parts each. The diagram on the left, belonging to Subject 18 (P2),
is complete but represents the physical situation (the "4 feet"
is added to the one-third piece). The diagram of Subject 27 (V2)
is also complete but represents the verbally described situation.

It will be noticed in the figures that the diagrams that are
integrated belong to subjects in the 1 groups and the unintegrated

diagrams to subjects in the 2 groups. The physical diagrams belong to subjects in the P groups and the verbal diagrams to subjects in the V groups. In the entire set of thirteen subjects these correlations are not perfect, but are visible. Four out of six integrated diagrams,but only two out of seven unintegrated diagrams, were produced by the subjects in the 1 groups.* Four out of six P diagrams, but only one out of seven V diagrams, were produced by the subjects in the P groups.[†] If we call the subjects in the 1 groups the "good" problem solvers, we can summarize these generalizations by saying: good problem solvers tend to construct integrated diagrams, and problem solvers who set up the physical equation tend also to represent the physical situation in their diagrams.

Next, we observe in Table I that the subjects themselves are generally able to predict their own performance. All the subjects who rated themselves as having been "poor" in algebra were unable to construct equations for test problems other than 4, and hence were assigned to a 2 group on the basis of performance. Three of the four subjects who were able to solve Practice Problem 3 were assigned to 1 groups.

Only subjects in the 1 groups noticed contradictions in any of the problems, and both subjects in P1, and only these, noticed the contradiction in Problem 4 as they were attempting to set up the equation. Both of these subjects also drew integrated, incomplete, diagrams on which they represented the physical situation.

---

*The probability of this result, given no relation between integration of diagrams and problem-solving ability, is .13.

[†] The probability of this result, given no association between type of equation and type of diagram, is .05.

With a sample as small as the one before us, we can draw only very tentative conclusions. The data, however, are quite consistent with what our earlier discussion would lead us to expect. In trying to set up the equations for Problem 4, the subjects may use either grammatical or physical clues for translation of the problem statement or some combination of these. The better problem solvers may use either, but if they use primarily the grammatical clues, they will set up the V equation and will not notice the contradiction; whereas if they use the physical clues also (particularly if they notice that $2/3 > 1/3$), they will likely notice the contradiction. If asked to represent the problem in a diagram, the subjects (five of six subjects in 1 groups) will give primacy to representing those types of clues that they responded to in setting up the equations.

About the subjects who are weaker in algebra, similar comments may be made. They may respond to either grammatical or physical clues. Those who respond to physical clues, however, will in this case not notice the contradiction—presumably because they do not also carry out the direct translation in detail. In five out of seven cases, the cues that are given primacy in the diagrams correspond with those that are given primacy in setting up the equations.

From our examination of the behavior of our subjects (at both college and high school level) we obtain considerable evidence that some of these subjects use processes that go well beyond the direct translation processes of STUDENT, even when the latter are supplemented by additional definitional equations. These auxiliary processes used by the subjects involve the construction of some kind of physical representation of the situation

described by the problem statement. When the problem statement defines a physically impossible situation, subjects who
employ auxiliary representations may discover the "contradiction" in the problem, or, if they rely primarily on the auxiliary
representation rather than the grammatical cues in interpreting
the problem, may replace the problem as stated by a similar,
but physically possible one.

Since the problem statements themselves were not literally contradictory (in each case an equation could be written
that accurately translated the statement), the contradictions
the subjects detect must depend on additional premises imported
into the problem through the auxiliary representations. In the
next section, we shall consider specifically how the representations serve as a source of additional assumptions about the
problem situation.

IV. REPRESENTATIONS AS SOURCES OF INFORMATION

In this section we take up three related topics. First, we
analyze in detail the assumptions used by subjects to set up an
equation in the mixture problem (Problem 5). Next, we consider the organization of their reasoning on that same problem.
Finally, we look for evidences of auxiliary representations in
a problem involving rates and distances (Problem 3).

Introduction of Conservation Assumptions

Returning to the three college-level subjects, we examine
in more detail their handling of the alcohol-water mixture problem. We noted previously that the problem is ambiguous. For

definiteness, let us suppose that water is to be *added* to the mixture, changing the total quantity.

There are at least nine distinct quantities of substances that are involved in the physical situation described in this problem, and to some or all of which the subject might attend in solving it:

Initial Situation	Changes	Final Situation
T_1 —total quantity of original mixture	ΔT—quantity of liquid added	T_2—total quantity of final mixture
A_1—quantity of alcohol in original mixture	ΔA—quantity of alcohol added	A_2—quantity of alcohol in final mixture
W_1—quantity of water in original mixture	ΔW—quantity of water added	W_2—quantity of water in final mixture

The statement of the problem mentioned explicitly that: (1) The total quantity of the original mixture is 1 liter; (2) 90 per cent of the original mixture is alcohol; (3) water is added to the original mixture; and (4) 80 per cent of the final mixture is alcohol. That is:

$$T_1 = 1 \text{ liter}$$
$$A_1 = .9 \ T_1$$
$$\Delta W \neq 0$$
$$A_2 = .8 \ T_2$$

This information is not sufficient to solve the problem (try it). In addition, the derivation of the solution must also make use of one or more of the following premises:

$$T_2 = T_1 + \Delta T; \quad A_2 = A_1 + \Delta A; \quad W_2 = W_1 + \Delta W;$$
$$\Delta A = 0; \ T_1 = A_1 + \ W_1; \ T_2 = A_2 + W_2; \ \Delta T = \Delta A + \Delta W.$$

These sets of relations are postulates about the physical situation. They are not logically necessary, although they may seem "obvious" to some persons given the problem. To see that they are actually physical assumptions, consider what would happen if water were a compound containing alcohol as a component. Then when water was added to the original mixture, some of the new water might dissociate in reaching the new equilibrium, and we could not assume that $\Delta A = 0$, even though no alcohol were added. In the same way, $T_2 = T_1 + \Delta T$ is a physical assumption, whose truth can be known only by adding one substance to another and determining whether the volume relation is in fact additive (when the one substance dissolves in the other, it isn't additive).

The physical postulates are precisely the sorts of *conservation laws* that Piaget has emphasized in his analysis of the cognitive development of children. $\Delta A = 0$ and $A_2 = A_1 + \Delta A$, for example, might be translated: "If you add no alcohol to a mixture, then the amount of alcohol in the final mixture is exactly the same as the amount in the original mixture." The subjects who succeed in solving the mixture problem supply these additional premises (usually without comment) from their own previous store of knowledge. Before turning to their protocols, let us examine a rigorous derivation of the solution, to see exactly how the physical premises enter in.

(1) $T_1 = 1$ (given)

(2) $A_1 = .9T_1$ (given)

(3) $A_2 = .8T_2$ (given)

(4) $A_2 = A_1 + \Delta A$ (conservation assumption)

(5) $\Delta A = 0$ (conservation assumption)

(6) $A_2 = A_1$ $[(4) + (5)]$

(7) $A_1 = .9$ $[(1) + (2)]$

(8) $A_2/T_2 = .8$ $[(3)]$

(9) $A_2 = .9$ $[(7) + (6)]$

(10) $T_2 = A_2 + W_2$ (conservation assumption)

(11) $W_2 = W_1 + \Delta W$ (conservation assumption)

(12) $T_1 = A_1 + W_1$ (conservation assumption)

(13) $W_1 = .1$ $[(7) + (12)]$

(14) $W_2 = .1 + \Delta W$ $[(11) + (13)]$

(15) $T_2 = .9 + .1 + \Delta W$ $[(10) + (9) + (14)]$

(16) $.9/(.9 + .1 + \Delta W) = .8$ $[(8) + (15) + (9)]$

At five points in this derivation, conservation assumptions, not explicitly included in the problem statement, are required. Of course, different derivations are possible, but they would not differ essentially in this respect—all would use the conservation assumptions.

Now let us compare this derivation with the transcript of Subject 6. In the left-hand column, we will indicate the numbers of the equations, in the above derivations, that correspond with the subject's statements.

ΔW	The quantity of water which we will add we will call q.
T_1	The car radiator already contains 90 per cent alcohol-water mixture. O.K. Which means it contains 90 per
(2)	cent—ah—alcohol, which means it contains 10 per cent
(13)	of—of—water. O.K. What quantity will change the liter
(3)	to an 80 per cent alcohol mixture? The alcohol content
(6)	will remain the same. Ah—90 per cent of the original mix. This is another one that can't be done exactly for this reason: we can only give a percentage of water— It says 'what quantity of water will change' . . . O.K.

(1)   The car contains one liter. Good. We can do it, I'm
         sorry. Ah—the total volume of alcohol is .9 of one
(7),(9) liter—would you write that down as .9L please, for me,
         and I'll remember, I think, that it's alcohol. All right,
         the total water in this final mixture will be .1L (just
(14)   write that down to the right of it) + q. O.K. Now the
         total mixture is comprised of .9L of alcohol plus
(15)   (.1L + q) water, so we'll take the .9L and divide it
         by—just put .9L divided by .1L plus q plus the alcohol
         —plus .9L—just add plus .9L in the denominator—
         those L's are irrelevant and you can erase them if
         you want because we know that that's a liter and the
         answer will be in liters. Upon solving that, .9 over
         1 equals—I guess we'll have to add about .9 liters—
         .09 liters, I'm sorry. O.K.

         Experimenter: Is this your final analysis?

(16)   Subject: That would be my final—ah—what will—what
         will I equate that to? Let's see—equals .80.

The first thing we note about this transcript is that it
follows closely the second derivation we gave above. The
crucial steps are (6), "The alcohol content will remain the
same," and (8), which the subject does not mention explicitly,
but which guides his whole derivation from "Now the total
mixture is comprised of . . ." to the end.

The second thing we note is that the subject in his derivation mentions premises, like (1) and (2), that are explicit
in the problem statement, and that he mentions all steps in
the derivation *except* (8) and *except* for those steps [(4), (5),
(10), (11), and (12)] that are simply statements of conservation assumptions.

The third point of interest in the transcript is the way
in which the subject identifies and names the various quantities that are represented in the physical situation. The prob-

lem statement itself mentions explicitly only T_1, "one liter of a
90 per cent alcohol-water mixture"; ΔW, "what quantity of water
will change the liter ?"; and T_2, "80 per cent pure alcohol." The
derivation (omitting the unmentioned conservation assumptions)
refers also to A_1, A_2, W_1, and W_2. These quantities (with a qualification mentioned below) are also named specifically by the
subject. The subject refers to ΔW as "the quantity of water
which we will add," and as "q." He refers to A_1 as: "90 per
cent alcohol," "the alcohol content," "90 per cent of the original mix," "the total volume of alcohol," ".9L of alcohol," "the
alcohol," and ".9L." Since he early notes that $A_1 = A_2$, he does
not adopt distinct names for these two quantities. W_1 is alluded
to by "it contains 10 per cent of water." The quantity W_2 is
identified as "the total water in this final mixture," which he
subsequently denotes as "$(.1L + q)$."

Especially interesting are the subject's references to the
total mixture. For T_1, the subject uses the phrases, "90 per cent
alcohol-water mixture," "the original mix," while for T_2, he
uses "80 per cent alcohol mixture," "this final mixture," "the
total mixture." Note that in all of these examples, a quantity
is usually first called by a name that is close to the language
of the problem statement. Names used later are often clearly
relational, for example, "90 per cent of the original mix."
When the same object is referred to by different names, the
name used in a given instance is usually determined by the
particular relation in view at that moment. So, we have "the
total water in this *final* mixture," when $W_2 = W_1 + \Delta W$ is in
consideration; but "the *total* mixture," when the subject is
using $T_2 = A_2 + W_2$. That is to say, terms like "original" and

"final" are used when a relation is being considered between the mixture before and after the water is added, while "total" is used when the composition of the mixture at a given point in time is in question.

The evidence from the protocol, then, including the subject's choices of words and phrases, suggests strongly that he followed something like the second derivation. If so, where did he obtain the appropriate conservation assumptions which are not contained in the problem statement? Let us propose a hypothesis. We suppose (Fig. 8) that the subject constructs an internal representation of the problem situation from the problem statement. We do not insist that this representation be "visual" in any literal sense, but we do require that it contain in implicit form the same relations (for example, among T_1, A_1, and W_1) that are implicit in the diagram.

We note that the four crucial conservation assumptions can be read directly off the figure: (6) $A_2 = A_1$; (10) $T_2 + W_2$; (11) $W_2 = W_1 + \Delta W$; and (12) $T_1 = A_1 + W_1$. Two of these [(10)

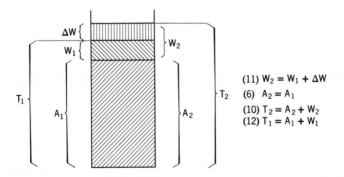

(11) $W_2 = W_1 + \Delta W$
(6) $A_2 = A_1$
(10) $T_2 = A_2 + W_2$
(12) $T_1 = A_1 + W_1$

Fig. 8: A hypothetical representation for the mixture problem.

and (12)] are obtained by adding lengths vertically; the other two [(6) and (11)], referring to the "before" and "after," are obtained by comparing lengths on the left and right sides of the diagram. Again, the details are not important; many variants on the basic diagram would permit the same deductions, or equivalent ones, to be made.

For what it is worth, this interpretation of the derivation of the conservation assumptions is confirmed by the subject's later introspections. First, after he solved the problem, the subject was asked to explain his equation. He says,

> Now .9 is the percentage, if you want to call it percentage, the percentage of one—ah—liters of alcohol. This doesn't change when you add water. O.K. Now the denominator —the .1L refers to the water that's already in there. There's a tenth of a liter of water already in there. To this we add q, the—the quantity of water which is to be added. That's the total quantity of water—ah—however, since this is a percentage of alcohol in the entire mix, we have to add .9L at the bottom too, so that the numerator represents the alcohol in there to start out with and to finish with and—and the denominator represents the whole final mixture, so that what we have is .8 is a—is a percentage—it represents the amount of alcohol divided by the total mixture.

Later, the experimenter asked the subject what imagery he had used. The subject stated that he had had a "picture" of the container with blue alcohol and red water. The experimenter then produced a diagram, much like Fig. 8, but colored, asking: "Like this?" The subject exhibited considerable amazement since, he said, that except for the fact that the colors of water and alcohol were reversed, the diagram was identical with his mental image.

The important issue here is not whether the subject em-

ployed imagery—some subjects may not. It is whether he employed some kind of, conscious or unconscious, representation,
functionally equivalent to a diagram like Fig. 8, that enabled
him to "read off" the conservation assumptions directly. The
evidence seems rather overwhelming that Subject 6 proceeded
in this way.

Conservation Assumptions and Representation

In a previous section, we have already commented briefly
on the behavior of Subject 8, who explicitly had the experimenter
draw a diagram for her. Let us now consider Subject 5, who
failed to solve the mixture problem.

Subject 5 also interprets the problem as one of changing
an initial situation into a new situation. Unlike Subject 6, she
does not immediately identify the specific quantities involved
in each situation and their relations. (She also suffers from
some confusion as to whether the unit of measurement was an
"unknown" or not, but we will leave this difficulty aside.) She
refers to T_1 as "the liter" and T_2 as "80 per cent pure alcohol,"
echoing literally the problem statement.

Subject 5's crude model seems to be something like this:

(initial mixture) + (water added) = (final mixture),

or

> we've got 90 per cent of a liter that is now alcohol
> and you want to add some water to it. So you really want
> $.90L + x$—you don't have to write this—$.90L + x = .80$—
> $.90 + x = .80$. That's just too simple. Don't write it be-
> cause I don't think it's right.

This translation involves a kind of vague metaphor, a
metaphor that represents the physical situation inadequately.

"Initial mixture" is translated as "90 per cent of a liter that is now alcohol," which becomes, in turn, ".90L." Similarly, "final mixture" is identified with "80 per cent pure alcohol," which is translated ".80." By simple substitution, then,

(initial mixture) + (water added) = (final mixture)

becomes:

$$.90 + x = .80$$

With further thought, the subject begins to disentangle the several quantities involved. A little later, she says

> Ninety per cent of a liter is alcohol now, and you want 80 per cent of the liter plus x to be alcohol.

Here she appears to be on the point of solving the problem but fails to set up the equation. The protocol is unclear as to the nature of the remaining difficulty, but probably it is her failure to note the crucial conservation assumption—that the amount of "alcohol now" equals the amount of "to be alcohol."

Much later, after being shown a diagram, the subject solves the problem. Summarizing her solution, she says,

> One liter plus x is the new—the new quantity, x being the amount of water. Eighty per cent of that has got to be the alcohol in it, so that's got to be equal to 90 per cent of—because you didn't add any alcohol—90 per cent of the liter.

In this final statement, the subject has unambiguous names for most of the important quantities: T_2 is "the new quantity," ΔW, "the amount of water," A_2, "the alcohol in [the new quantity]." She has also used the information in the problem statement to deduce $A_1 = .9T_1$ and $A_2 = .8T_2$. Finally, she expresses two crucial conservation laws, $T_2 = T_1 + x$ and $A_1 = A_2$. With these, she is able to solve the problem.

Solving the mixture problem, then, depends on identifying and naming the principal quantities involved, and using the important conservation assumptions that relate them to each other. But these conservation assumptions do not derive from direct transformations of the problem statement. They are physical assumptions supplied by the problem solver, and the principal means he has for supplying them is to construct some kind of physical or spatial representation in which they lie implicit, and from which he can extract them by processing the representation.

The protocols of the high school students on the alcohol-water mixture problem provide further evidence for some parts of our analysis, and cast further light on the differences between the subjects who tend to handle problems verbally (that is, by direct translation), and those who handle them physically (that is, who use auxiliary representations of the physical situation).

None of the high school students solved the mixture problem, although eight of the thirteen set up some kind of equation. Seven of the eight equations were essentially the same as the original incorrect equation set up by Subject 5 (90 per cent $+ x$ = 80 per cent). Four of the five subjects who, on the basis of their protocols from the board-sawing problem, we classified as "physical" set up this equation, but only three of the seven subjects we classified as "verbal" did so.*

As mentioned previously, each of the subjects was asked, at the end of the experimental session, to draw a diagram that would explain the problem. The diagrams can be classified in three groups (Fig. 9): (1) diagrams (*W*) that show the "water added" as a separate quantity, or as being poured into the original mixture, (2) "before-and-after" diagrams (*B − A*), showing the original mixture and the final mixture separately, and (3) diagrams (*C*) in which all the percentages are marked on a single container of liquid. Of the seven subjects who produced the incorrect "additive" equation, five drew the *W* diagram, and two the *B − A* diagram. Of the six subjects who did not produce this equation, three drew the *B − A* diagram, and three drew *C* diagrams; none drew the *W* diagram.[†]

Thus, our earlier interpretation of Subject 5's behavior on this problem is confirmed. Underlying the translation is a representation that identifies the physical process of "adding" water with the arithmetic process of adding *x* to the original mixture. But, through inability to deal with percentages, or for some other reason, the subjects are unable to sort out the various quantities contained in the mixtures, hence to determine

*As a matter of fact, two of the three V subjects who set up the faulty equation in Problem 5 also behaved anomolously (in comparison with other V subjects) in some other respects. Subject 24 was the only one among the V subjects who noted a contradiction in any problem (Problem 1). Subject 19 first produced the P equation on Problem 4, and then the V equation. See Table I.

[†]The probability of this result, on the null hypothesis of no connection between drawing the W diagram and producing the erroneous equation, is less than .01.

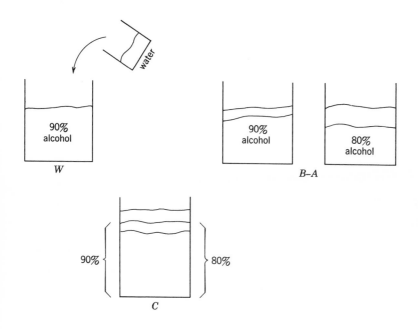

Fig. 9: Examples of (W), $(B - A)$ and (C) diagrams for the alcohol-water mixture problem.

exactly to what "initial mixture" the water is to be added to obtain the "final mixture." They use the conservation assumption, $T_2 = T_1 + \Delta W$, but are unable, because of the inadequacies of their representations or of their understanding of percentage, to find the other conservation assumptions—in particular, the crucial assumption $A_1 = A_2$.

Organizing the Solution Process

We have left unexplained one important part of the procedure used by someone like Subject 6 to solve an algebra problem as complicated as the mixture problem. The derivation of the solution, in all its detail, contains a substantial number of steps. How is the problem solver able to take these steps in approximately the right order? What prevents him from wandering aimlessly, rather than moving relatively directly to the solution?

From other research on problem solving, particularly the General Problem Solver, we would hypothesize that the subject compares the "givens" of the problem with the desired result (Newell and Simon, 1963; Simon and Newell, 1964). Finding one or more differences between them, he tries to transform one or the other to reduce, and finally eliminate, these differences. There is one important difference between the algebra problems and problems of proving theorems, which were the original task environment tests of the GPS theory. In theorem proving, the subject knows the desired result in detail —the theorem to be proved; whereas in setting up equations, he only has a general description of the desired result—an algebraic equation in which the "unknown" appears together with one or more of the known given quantities, but in which no other unknown quantities appear.

One way in which a subject can proceed to this goal, under the conditions of algebra word problems, is to set up some equation, from the problem statement, containing one or more unknown quantities, and then, by substituting relational definitions for the unknown quantities, to arrive at an equation with the necessary properties. Let us examine the sequence from Equation (8), above, to Equation (16) from this viewpoint. The initial equation the subject sets up (8) makes use of the fact that the percentage of alcohol in the final mixture is 80. Since "percentage of alcohol in total" is translatable "A_2/T_2", a rather direct translation process will yield $A_2/T_2 = .8$. Neither A_2 nor T_2 are known quantities, and the unknown, ΔW, does not appear in the equation; hence it must be transformed.

Taking A_2 under consideration, the only other known relation in which it appears is (6) $A_2 = A_1$. Taking A_1 under consideration, it is also unknown, but appears in the relation (2) $A_1 = .9T_1$. Considering T_1 next, by (1) $T_1 = 1$, hence is a known quantity. Hence, the first equation, (8), can be transformed into $1/T_2 = .8$. This equation is still unsatisfactory, since it has the unknown T_2, and does not contain the unknown ΔW. But T_2 occurs in the conservation assumption (10) $T_2 = A_2 + W_2$. Repeating the same process, we replace the A_2 in this relation by .9; and using another conservation assumption, we express W_2 as $W_2 = W_1 + \Delta W$. Again, from $W_1 = T_1 - A_1 = 1 - .9 = .1$, we get, eventually, $T_2 = .9 + .1 + \Delta W$, which is exactly what the subject substitutes in the denominator of (8) to obtain (16).

Thus, it appears that the mechanisms that provide direction in GPS are also appropriate to explain the sequence of expressions that Subject 6 considers in solving the mixture problem. He starts by setting up an equation—any equation, and then proceeds to try to modify any part of that equation which contains an unknown other than ΔW. This process leads him fairly directly to the solution.*

*Miss Garfinkel's program (See Part II, 1960), which also requires that a single equation in one unknown be set up, uses a somewhat different process, more syntactic in spirit, to remove the superfluous unknowns. *Op. cit.*, Part II. The program also makes provision for introducing certain conservation assumptions.

When the process is organized in this way, it tends to keep the cognitive strain—the load on the subject's immediate memory —within reasonable bounds. He starts out with a single relation (in this case, $A_2/T_2 = .8$), and by application of relations explicit in the written problem statement, or derived from conservation assumptions stored in permanent memory, modifies this relation step-by-step, by substituting new quantities for the unknowns. At any given moment in this process, there is only a single statement (the most recent modification of the initial relation) that he has to retain in immediate memory.

Further Comments on Conservation Assumptions

Problem 3, involving a launch traveling up and down stream, provides another situation where the introduction of conservation assumptions, and their physical nature, is particularly clear. The problem states the rate of flow of the stream, and the speed at which a launch can go in still water. To set up the equations, the subjects had to determine the speed of the launch downstream and upstream. All three of the college subjects, and most of the high school subjects, *added* the two rates to obtain the downstream speed, and *subtracted* them to obtain the upstream speed.

Subject 8 makes the assumptions with a single comment about their physical character: "Now the distance [misspoken for "rate"] downstream is going to be 8 miles per hour plus two. Write down 8 plus 2, so that the stream helps." And later: "rate of the launch which is 8, minus the rate of the stream, which is 2."

For Subject 6, the relation of the rates is also "natural":

> Going downstream the launch will travel at the
> velocity of 8 miles an hour plus 2 miles an hour because
> it—the stream will carry it along, naturally, so that the
> rate of the launch will be 10 miles an hour downstream.

Subject 5 is explicitly aware that the physical assumption
may be incorrect:

> The launch can go at the rate of 8 miles per hour in
> still water, so it's going downstream at the rate of 10 miles
> per hour . . . it goes 10 miles per hour, and coming back
> upstream, ah, I assume—I don't know much about motors—
> it goes 6 miles per hour . . . so I think those two values are
> correct, because I assumed that all this is additive, al-
> though I'm not really certain, but I assume that if you can
> go 8 miles per hour and the stream is flowing 2 miles per
> hour, it's 10.

From these protocols, we conclude that addition of veloc-
ities is an assumption the subjects, particularly Subject 5, do
not make quite automatically. They are still aware of the physical origin of the assumption to an extent they are not in the
case of the conservation of quantities and additivity of quantities
in the mixture problem. What holds only "naturally" in the
former case, holds "obviously" and without comment in the
latter.

Characterizing the conservation assumptions as "physical"
does not imply, of course, that direct translation processes could
not be incorporated in an algebra-word-problem processor to
handle them. For example, if we assume that some means
(radar, for example) exists for measuring speed directly, then
"distance equals rate times time" is a physical assumption.
STUDENT incorporates this assumption directly in its direct
translation scheme, permitting the term "distance," when it

appears in a problem statement, to be replaced by "rate times time."

All three of the college-level subjects use the relation among distance, rate, and time in trying to solve the launch problem. Subject 5 uses the relation as though it were physically derived, and never mentions the formula. Subjects 6 and 8, however, behave like STUDENT, as though they had the formula stored in memory, and employ it for direct translation. Subject 6 says: "There's a little equation that says that in these cases distance equals velocity times time." And Subject 8 says: "Distance equals rate times time—so that you want to divide x by that. . . . Dividing the distance by the rate equals . . ."

SUMMARY

We have examined the behavior of human subjects setting up equations for algebra word problems, using as our base of reference the direct translation schemes proposed by Garfinkel and Bobrow. Our particular interest has been in detecting the extent to which the human subjects make use of direct processes like those incorporated in the STUDENT program, and the extent to which they employ auxiliary cues and internal representations of the physical situation.

We have seen that the human subjects differ a great deal in the extent to which they rely on direct and auxiliary processes respectively. Among our college-level subjects, Subject 8 (a mathematics major) is an example of a good problem solver who usually relies chiefly on direct translation—in close parallelism with the STUDENT program. Subject 6 (a physics major) is an example of a good problem solver who makes extensive use of auxiliary cues and physical representations.

A set of "contradictory" problems that represent physically impossible situations has proved to be a useful tool for detecting the relative uses of direct and auxiliary cues by the subjects. In the face of a contradictory problem, the subject can respond in three main ways: (1) He can set up an equation for the problem as it is stated literally; (2) he can set up an equation for a related, physically possible, situation; or (3) he can recognize the physical impossibility of the situation. If he is using primarily direct cues, he will make the first response; if primarily physical cues, the second; if he is attending to both, the problem description will be redundant, and he may detect the contradiction.

We were able to classify a group of high school students into those who were primarily "physical" in their responses, and those who were primarily "verbal." The differences between the two groups showed up quite consistently in (1) the extent to which they detected the contradictions—the "verbal" solvers didn't, the "physical" sometimes did; (2) whether the equations set up represented a physical situation, or were literal translations of the words; and (3) whether the diagrams they drew contained the physical relations that were implicit in the problems. The data from these high school students were consistent with the hypotheses derived from more detailed examination of the protocols of the college-level subjects.

In addition, we identified some of the important processes

that a person must acquire in order to do algebra word problems successfully. A number of these had already been incorporated in Bobrow's STUDENT program. Several of the others, present but not emphasized in that program, have to do with identifying the quantities that have to be handled in setting up the equations, and devising relational names for these quantities that incorporate part of the information in the problem statement. The processes for constructing auxiliary representations of the problem situation are not currently part of the STUDENT program, and will have to be added to that program if it is to provide a satisfactory theory of the human behavior observed in handling these problems.

APPENDIX

ALGEBRA WORD PROBLEMS USED IN EXPERIMENTS

Practice Problems:

1. If a certain number is multiplied by 6 and the product increased by 44, the result is 68. Find the number.

2. If 3 more than a certain number is divided by 5, the result is the same as twice the number diminished by 12. What is the number?

3. The difference between two numbers is 12, and 7 times the smaller number exceeds the greater by 30. Find the numbers.

Test Problems:

1. A man has 7 times as many quarters as he has dimes. The value of the dimes exceeds the value of the quarters by $2.50. How many has he of each coin?

2. Mr. Stewart decided to invest $4,000, some at 3 per cent and the rest at 4 per cent. How much should he invest at each rate to produce equal income?

3. A stream flows at the rate of two miles per hour. A launch can go at the rate of 8 miles per hour in still water. How far down the stream does the launch go and return if the up-stream trip takes half as much time as the downstream trip?

4. A board was sawed into two pieces. One piece was two-thirds as long as the whole board and was exceeded in length by the second piece by 4 feet. How long was the board before it was cut?

5. A car radiator contains exactly one liter of a 90 per cent alcohol-water mixture. What quantity of water will change the liter to an 80 per cent alcohol mixture?

4

DONALD W. TAYLOR
Yale University

Discussion of Papers by Adrian de Groot and by Jeffery M. Paige and Herbert A. Simon

Five years ago I wrote (Taylor, 1960, p. 112): "I am inclined to believe that one recent development in the psychology of thinking offers exceptional promise for increasing our understanding of the processes of thinking. This is the approach initiated by Allen Newell, J. C. Shaw, and Herbert Simon which involves treating the thinker as an information processing system (Newell, *et al.*, 1958)." It will not be surprising, therefore, that my response to the two papers just presented is, in general, quite favorable. The second paper, as the most recent in a series by Professor Simon and his colleagues, seems to me to continue to provide clear support for my earlier optimism. The first paper continues the excellent work on chess first reported by Professor de Groot nearly twenty years ago (de Groot, 1946). That earlier work anticipated important aspects of the information processing analysis of problem solving. His present paper makes clear the similarities between the approaches of the two speakers.

Because I find very little to disagree with in the second

paper and have only limited questions concerning the first, these comments will be brief. Let me first highlight certain aspects of each of the two papers, beginning with the second one.

In the study of decision making, the distinction between a *normative* model and a *descriptive* model is a familiar one (see, for example: Taylor, 1965). The former is intended to tell the decision maker how he should make that class of decisions for which the model is appropriate; the latter is intended to represent as accurately as possible the behavior of the decision maker. The terms *artificial intelligence* and *simulation* have been used, but unfortunately not consistently, to make an analogous distinction with respect to intent in the construction of computer programs which solve problems. The objective of the former is to construct a program which will solve problems well, never mind how people solve them; the objective of the latter is to represent as accurately as possible the behavior of the human problem solver.

Although that is not its primary purpose, the construction of a normative model of decision making may nevertheless aid in the understanding of how people do make decisions. Thus, for example, the concepts of game theory, a widely known normative model, have made important contributions in the analysis of actual behavior.

The fact deserves emphasis, I believe, that the intent of the STUDENT program constructed by Bobrow was that of artificial intelligence. The author did not intend to simulate human problem solving. By comparing in detail, however, the behavior of human problem solvers with that of the STUDENT program, Paige and Simon have made significant additions to our understanding of the processes which human beings employ in solving algebra word problems. Thus the use of what may be regarded as a normative model has again been found to aid in the understanding of actual behavior. In passing, it may be noted that the reverse also occurs. Thus, for example, the objective of both Tonge (1961) and Gere (1962) was essentially that of artificial intelligence, but both found this objective best served by the analysis of how people in fact solve the kinds of problems under investigation.

There are two other points in the second paper to which I would call special attention. The first is the use that was made of problems impossible of solution in the illumination of the processes involved in problem-solving behavior. The employment of such problems seems to me to have been particularly fruitful in the present instance. This technique may well deserve more widespread use than it has had in the past.

Finally, I would call attention to the analysis of individual differences in the processes employed in solving algebra word problems. One of the strengths of the information processing approach is that it encourages such analysis. The distinction in the present study between those who respond primarily to grammatical and those who respond primarily to physical cues carries the understanding of process well beyond that which would have been achieved had attention not been given to such individual differences.

In his earlier analysis of thinking in chess (de Groot, 1946), the author of the first paper made clear the role of heuristic processes. In the present paper, he has made vivid the importance of individual differences in perception and memory in playing chess and the difficulty of understanding the processes involved. I, at least, shall look forward to the results of the future work aimed at increasing understanding of the coding processes and memory organization of the chessmaster.

In organizing his paper, Professor de Groot employed a series of eight statements. Attention here will be limited to the first six. With some qualification, I would endorse each of the first five, but I have some questions about the sixth.

That it is worthwhile to attempt "analysis of high level, complex, cognitive processes . . . in a real-life-like setting" is, I believe, clear. I would emphasize only, as I think Professor de Groot would agree, that it is also worthwhile to study simple rather than complex tasks and to investigate behavior in laboratory settings in solving problems especially devised for use in research. As an example of the latter, I would cite the use in a number of studies of problems in symbolic logic originally devised by O. K. Moore (1954). (No one would question that chess is a complex task, but I cannot help wondering whether there would be general agreement that it is "real-life-like.")

The use of "thinking aloud" has repeatedly proved fruitful in the analysis of process. That this is true in the investigation of algebra word problems has just been demonstrated for us by the second paper. As another example, I would cite the construction of the General Problem Solver (Newell, *et al.*, 1959) on the basis of protocols obtained from subjects engaged in solving the Moore type of problem. Insofar as introspection is concerned, many investigators would, I believe, agree that examination of one's own experience and that of others in solving problems is a fruitful source of hypotheses—hypotheses which should then be subjected to rigorous tests by other means.

The clearest evidence that problem solving "can be conceived as a linear sequence of operations" is provided by the extensive work on simulation of cognitive processes here and elsewhere. This same work also provides clear evidence of the importance of hierarchical relations not only in problem solving but in other kinds of behavior. One may note, for example, the analysis of a variety of behaviors by Miller, Galanter, and Pribram (1960). Evidence of the acceptance of the importance of hierarchical relations is also found in the widespread use of the concept of the decision tree. In the introduction to the second edition of his well-known book *Administrative Behavior*, Simon (1957, p. xxix) has called attention to the ubiquitous nature in modern theories of behavior of the concept of the tree of possible future behaviors. He suggests: "The fact that this concept has been seized upon independently in such a variety of contexts to provide a framework for a theory of behavior suggests that it represents the real core of the new behavioral *Zeitgeist.* "

A more adequate analysis and classification of the variety of processes employed in thinking is prerequisite to the development of a more adequate theory of problem solving, or of thinking more generally. At this stage, it may well be most fruitful to focus upon the development of limited theories of problem solving (for example, a theory of chess playing or of the solving of algebra word problems). One would hope, however, that in the identification of processes in these limited areas, one might proceed to the construction of more general theories (that is, theories which include the processes involved in solving several classes of problems as, for example, is true to some extent in the General Problem Solver). One might hope eventually for a quite general theory which would cover a broad range of problems. But whether "it must be possible to develop an ordered classification . . . to cover every method, trick, heuristic, transformation that may be instrumental in productive thinking" is a question that I doubt will receive empirical answer within the lifetime of those here present.

Professor de Groot's sixth statement raises questions for me. The first question may indeed show that my interpretation of one or more of the first five statements differs somewhat from that which the author intended. The sixth statement in part indicates that the ordered classification referred to in the fifth statement is to be "derived from, largely introspective, experimentation." My own expectation is that the more adequate understanding of the processes employed in thinking will instead result from the use of the information processing approach. As I have already said, I do believe that the use of "thinking aloud" has repeatedly proved fruitful and that the introspective analysis of experience may provide a fruitful source of hypotheses concerning process. But I also believe that it is essential that such hypotheses be subject to rigorous tests. One method of rigorous testing is through simulation— through the expression of one's hypotheses in the form of a computer program and the comparison of the behavior of the program with that of human subjects. Another is the use of the familiar methods of experimental psychology.

The sixth statement also indicates that it must be possible to systematically relate the classification of processes referred to in the fifth statement "to the outcome of statistical analyses of cognitive achievements." At some very general level, I could not disagree. But I must confess to considerable skepticism concerning the more specific suggestion that it will be possible "to predict the factor composition of any kind of complex cognitive process" on the basis of the analysis of the kinds of operations derived from either an introspective or an information processing approach to problem solving. A full statement of the reasons for my skepticism is beyond the scope of this discussion, but at least two may be suggested here.

One reason involves the kind of tasks which at least thus far have been employed in factor analytic investigations (see also: Taylor, 1963). A single such investigation ordinarily involves the administration of a fairly large number of tests to each of a large number of subjects. As a consequence, the time which can be allotted for each test is small. To be reliable, the test must often be composed of a number of items. The time available per item hence is even smaller. The result is that the problems included in such tests are typically very short. This leads me to believe that processes employed in solving longer and more complex kinds of problems may escape discovery by the factor analytic investigator. For example, it seems doubtful that this approach will lead to the identification of processes of the kind exemplified by the "means-end" or the "make-a-plan" heuristics of the General Problem Solver or the heuristics involved in playing chess. I doubt, therefore, that analysis of such complex problems in terms of such operations would permit one to predict the correlations between a large number of tests, such as those employed by Guilford (1960), and either performance on tasks for which the General Problem Solver is appropriate or achievement in playing chess.

My second reason for skepticism stems from the nature of the factor analytic model (Harman, 1960). This model assumes that the performance which is to be accounted for in terms of factors can be represented as a simple linear additive combination of the factors upon which the problem is loaded. That the kinds of processes which are identified by an introspective or an information processing approach may be expected to be linearly related to performance and to combine additively seems to be doubtful. The existence of nonlinear and even nonmonotonic relations seems probable. The existence of multiplicative relations must in some instances, I think, be expected; that is, the contribution of one process to performance must be dependent upon (multiplied by) a second. If these conjectures have merit, then the effort to predict the loadings of complex problems on orthogonal factors from an analysis of operations based on an introspective or an information processing approach will indeed be unlikely to succeed. Accurate predictions in the reverse direction may be expected to be similarly unlikely.

In closing, I would at least raise the question as to whether there may not be a fundamental inconsistency between the assumptions of the factor analytic model and any model which emphasizes a hierarchy of processes.

5 | ROBERT M. GAGNÉ
American Institutes for Research

Human Problem Solving: Internal and External Events

The experimental study of human problem-solving behavior has continued in a somewhat sporadic fashion over a good many years. No one seems particularly happy about the findings as yet, although an obvious increase in the number of investigations devoted to this area in recent years is generally agreed to be a hopeful sign of better things to come. It is admittedly not an easy kind of behavior to study. On the one hand, it can readily evade the grasp of the experimenter with a "naturalistic" bent who may find himself cherishing a problem that practically none of his subjects can solve. On the other hand, a problem can just as easily slip away in the other direction, by becoming the kind of activity that subjects can do perfectly well, but which no one will agree should properly be called a "problem." The difficulties are such that psychologists, who are supposed to study such phenomena, sometimes give up and turn to other things.

Since sooner or later I shall have to say what I mean by problem solving, perhaps this task can be approached first of all by mentioning several things to which I am not going to turn. One of these is creativity. I assume that studying the conditions and the correlates of creativity is a legitimate enterprise. Naming this kind of human activity, however, obviously does not begin to solve the problem of defining it, nor of distinguishing it from other forms of intellectual behavior, as even a cursory examination of the literature in this field will show (Guilford, 1958; Taylor, 1958; Getzels and Jackson, 1962; Gruber, Terrell, and Wertheimer, 1962; and Taylor, 1964). Most writers on this subject, I take it, consider creativity much too exalted a kind of activity to be thought of in relation to problem solving. Although I do not believe this is a self-evident matter, I should prefer to agree with the majority for the moment, and thus choose a convenient way of limiting the scope of this paper so that it does not even try to deal with creativity.

A more recently stated distinction, and a rather convincing one, has been made by Mackworth (1965), between problem solving and problem finding. The former is a matter, he says, of "choosing correctly between existing programs," whereas the latter requires "choosing correctly between existing and expected future programs." It seems reasonable to suppose that there is a perfectly valid distinction here, although it is much more difficult to decide how important the distinction is; that is, how far apart these two kinds of human activity really are. There is also some danger of the risk referred to previously—by defining problem solving as choosing among existing sets of mental rules, it may seem to be too "routine," and thus not considered to be legitimate problem solving at all.

Whatever the answer to this question turns out to be, it

should be quite clear that the making of this distinction does not add much to our understanding of problem solving. Problem finding may turn out to be something else, but problem solving remains a type of complex human behavior which is not yet well understood. It seems that the solving of a problem is an event which needs to be classified, so far as the individual's behavior is concerned, as an act of learning. One of the fundamental criteria of problem solving is that a kind of performance which could not be exhibited before the "problem" was solved *can* be exhibited after the "problem" is solved. In other words, the observed events in problem solving comprise a change in human performance, and this in turn leads us to infer a change in human capability. Before one begins to examine the process of problem solving, he needs to have firmly in mind what the product is, as Duncan (1959) points out. The notion that one can consider problem solving as having the outcome of a change in human capability appears to be a clarifying first step in this direction.

What sort of change in capability occurs in problem solving? What is it that has happened for the first time in a subject who has "solved" Maier's (1930) pendulum problem, or Katona's (1940) card-trick problem, or seen that a point of inflection in a mathematical function represents a minimal rate of change?

The most important characteristic of this newly acquired capability is its lack of specificity, or to say it another way, its inherent generalizability. The investigator is simply not convinced that problem solving has occurred unless he performs what is in effect a transfer experiment. Katona's (1940) work, for example, is based upon this principle. The performance of a given matchstick problem which could not be done previously does not permit the conclusion that problem solving has occurred. The solution may have been memorized in one way or another. But the performance of a *class* of matchstick problems (or representative members of the class) which could not previously be solved does make possible the inference of a newly acquired "problem-solving" capability (See Ref., Gagné, 1964).

The kind of human capability that is acquired in problem solving seems to be a capability of *applying a rule* to any number of specific instances. This does not imply that the individual can state the rule—far from it. Many of Katona's subjects showed transfer to card-trick and matchstick problems without being able to state the rule they were following. Maier's subjects were not asked to state the complex rules they were following, but merely to demonstrate the solution of the problem. Brown and Fraser (1963) discuss the rules of syntax that young children learn. They are quite complex rules, and were quite successfully followed by young children, yet there was no question that they could not be stated by these children. In fact, modern linguistic scholars have continued to devote much effort to the precise statement of syntactic and grammatical rules that are followed by literate adults. On the whole, it is quite difficult to state these rules, yet no one doubts that oral speech does follow them.

The rule or principle that is acquired in problem solving must be a novel one, so far as the individual learner is concerned. Before one can infer that problem solving has occurred, one must demonstrate that the rule cannot have been otherwise acquired. There are a number of alternate ways it could have been acquired, of course. The principle might have been simply recalled from somewhat remote past experience. Or it might have been retained from more recent experience as a verbal statement, such as, "zero divided by any number is zero." Another possibility is that the performance may depend simply on stimulus generalization, as would perhaps be the case in using toothpicks for matchstick problems. All of these simpler possibilities need to be ruled out, if one sets out to demonstrate problem solving. It follows that the *second* performance of the same class of problems cannot be assumed to be problem solving at all. One uses a second, third, or fourth problem of a class to demonstrate that the new generalizable capability is truly inferrable. But the change that brought it about (that is, the problem solving) must have occurred on the first occasion only.

The definition suggested by this discussion is this: Problem solving is an inferred change in human capability that results in the acquisition of a generalizable rule which is novel to the individual, which cannot have been established by direct recall, and which can manifest itself in applicability to the solution of a class of problems.

EXTERNAL CONDITIONS OF PROBLEM SOLVING

Having defined the outcome of a problem-solving event, it should now be possible to examine the conditions of what is called the "problem situation." These are the conditions external to the learner which have been investigated for their potential effects in bringing about the problem-solving behavior. These conditions have been critically discussed in previous review articles (Gagné, 1959; Duncan, 1959). It is possible, however, that a more rigorous classification of these variables will be suggested by the definition just given.

Stimuli

Various sorts of physical stimuli may be employed as a part of the external situation for problem solving, and it is quite impossible to classify them in any meaningful way. Obviously, the physical stimuli in a card-trick problem are the playing cards; in a matchstick problem the patterns of matches; in a hat-rack problem a set of sticks and clamps; and in an anagram, an arrangement of printed letters on a page. As I have argued elsewhere (Gagné, 1964), it seems to make no sense to suppose that the individual is reacting to any of these as physical stimuli per se. A mediation process, a coding of the stimuli, must be assumed. The individual engaged in solving the problem is not reacting to the playing cards but to the numbers represented by their spots. He is not responding to matches but to patterns of squares; not to sticks but to constructions of sticks; not to printed marks on a page but to letter sequences. In other words, the individual in the problem-solving situation is dealing with concepts of which the physical objects present in the situation are simply representatives of a class.

In contrast, then, to simpler forms of learning, the stimulus situation for problem solving needs to be described in terms of the concepts (classes of objects or events) of which it is composed. This may be the reason why it is possible to think of problem solving as a task of "information processing." If one can assume that the physical stimuli are first conceptualized (and thus that they convey information), it is reasonable to suppose that the next step is one of processing this information. It needs to be pointed out, however, that assuming the stimuli for problem solving to be concepts does not at all help to explain how they got that way. There still remains the very difficult job of accounting for the transformation of card spots into numbers, or matchsticks into squares, or printed marks into letters and words. In other words, a process of "stimulus processing" underlies the formation of concepts, which in turn become the stimuli to be considered in problem solving.

Perhaps there are other aspects of the physical situation of importance to problem solving. Such environmental stimuli as noise, extremes of temperature, oxygen pressure, and other surrounding conditions may well be supposed to affect the solving of problems. There is not a great deal of evidence about the effects of these variables, and the major reason may arise from the difficulties encountered in attempting to measure problem solving in some reliable and at the same time uncontaminated fashion.

Verbal Directions

Another part of the external situation that needs to be mentioned is a set of verbal directions which are used for the purpose of confronting the individual with the problem. They may, for example, direct his attention, by saying "Look at the

spots on this card," or "Notice the numerator of the fraction,"
or whatever. They may direct a sequence of behavior, as in
saying "First look at the card on the left, then at the one on the
right," and delivering other similar commands. The existence
of verbal directions is noted here primarily to distinguish them
from instructions, which are to be discussed next. Presumably,
directions are of some importance in bringing about the problem solving. But they do not in themselves convey or represent
the content of the problem, as do instructions.

Instructions

Instructions, as opposed to verbal directions, have the
function of eliciting the mediating processes for problem solving. In brief, they may stimulate recall of the concepts represented by the stimulus objects, or the recall of principles relating these concepts to each other, or certain sets or strategies which appear to play a part in the finding of a solution to
the problem.

Instructions, whether given all at once or at various
times during the course of problem solving, can be seen to
perform different functions for the learner. Some of these are
fairly easy to appreciate, and some of them are less obvious.
I shall summarize here what seem to me to be the major ways
in which they operate (Gagné, 1964):

(1) Informing the problem solver as to the nature of the
    solution required. Presumably, this must be done, if
    the problem solver is to recognize when his own per-
    formance matches some standard, so that his behavior

may be brought to a close. An example: The solver of an anagram is told at the outset that he is looking for a common word.

(2) Distinguishing relevant aspects of the stimulus situation. If the problem solver is to seek a rule involving the color of a card as well as the number of its spots, instructions may be used to point out both color and number of spots. Unless relevant features are pointed out, the problem may be failed for what would be considered a trivial reason.

(3) Stimulating recall of appropriate concepts or rules. This is one of the most evident functions of instructions, and can be seen clearly in most problem-solving studies. An example: In his pendulum problem, Maier (1930) gave instructions which recalled to the subject "part" rules that could reasonably be supposed to be involved in the total solution. One of these, for instance, was how to make a long pole out of two short ones, using a clamp.

(4) Guiding the thinking process in certain directions. The most obvious way in which this can be done is by urging the subject to ignore certain hypotheses about solution, thus narrowing the process of search for possible courses of action. Other forms of guidance are presumably possible, though. There is considerable evidence that "guided discovery" is an effective technique in bringing about problem solving (Gagné and Brown, 1961; Wittrock, 1965).

It may be realized, then, that the external part of the situation for problem solving comprises the three major elements of physical stimulus objects, verbal directions, and instructions. Ordinarily, all three are present. That stimulus objects are not responded to as such is attested by the fact that they may be eliminated, and the problem stated verbally. Verbal directions may also be virtually eliminated under such circumstances, so long as the problem solver understands that he is expected to answer the question put to him. But instructions (which of course are also verbal in form) appear to be quite essential for problem solving. If the experimenter is not there to give them, it is not unreasonable to suppose that the problem solver will supply them to himself. If one were determined to investigate the effect of instructions on problem solving, presumably he would want to manipulate them in terms of the different functions they may be performing, four of which have been described.

INTERNAL CONDITIONS

Having described the external conditions for problem solving, it is now possible for me to turn my attention to the internal conditions. Many people would perhaps claim that these are the only really interesting aspects of problem solving performance. I agree that they are the most interesting. But it seems quite important to recognize that there is an intimate set of relationships between the external and internal events in problem solving. In all probability, we cannot fully understand the processes of problem solving until we can account for the linkages of these events.

The Process of Problem Solving

Most writers on problem solving agree that the process takes a certain appreciable amount of time and proceeds through certain stages. These latter have been variously described, but perhaps they can be summarized as follows: (1) statement of the problem; (2) defining the problem, by distinguishing essential features; (3) searching for and formulating hypotheses; (4) verifying the solution. Some writers emphasize a stage of "preparation," occurring between (1) and (2), and in certain practical instances, such a stage of activity does in fact occur. For present purposes, however, it may be assumed that "preparation" has already been done; the significance of this statement will become apparent in the discussion which follows.

Of the four stages mentioned, it is apparent that (1) refers to external events considered previously. The remaining stages may be considered as inferences about the internal process of problem solving, concerning which there is considerable agreement. Accordingly, I shall not question these stages in this discussion, but will adopt them for the purpose of describing the interrelations between external and internal events.

The central column of Fig. 1 illustrates the internal processes that may be inferred as necessary to problem solving, beginning with the recall of subordinate capabilities and ending with the acquisition of the solution rule which solves the problem. At the left of the figure are shown the external instructions that function to stimulate and guide these processes. At the right are indicated the kinds of individual differences in processes which may be expected to influence problem solving,

FACTORS IN PROBLEM SOLVING

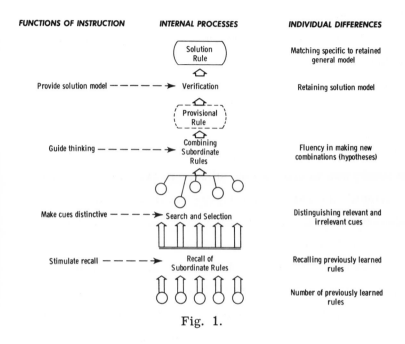

Fig. 1.

that is, to have the effect of making one individual better at it than another.

The diagram states that problem solving depends upon the presence of certain previously learned rules (or in simpler cases, concepts). In other words, if the problem is one of finding a new relationship between the sides of a right triangle, the individual must already know what the right angle is, the principles relating adjacent sides to hypotenuse, the principles relating sine and cosine to size of adjacent angle, and so on. If the problem is one of solving an anagram, the individual must already know the word that constitutes the solution, and a number of additional principles regarding the probable letter combinations in English. These previously acquired capabilities are essential.

The previously learned rules and concepts must be recalled, as a first step. At this point, as has been pointed out, instructions may enter the picture to stimulate recall. They may say something like: "You remember how to find the hypotenuse when the two other sides of a right triangle are known." Or, as in Maier's (1930) experiment, they may say, "You remember how to make a long stick from two short ones, using a clamp." However it is done, the externally applied instructions presumably function to increase the vividness (or "availability") of some previously learned entity.

At the next stage, the individual searches for and selects the recalled rules that are specifically relevant to the stimulus situation, and rejects those which are not. Here he may be aided by external instructions which emphasize the relevant features of the objects he is attending to, thereby making them more distinctive. There is bound to be a good deal of "noise" at this stage of the game, and the process is one of distinguishing the noise from the relevant signals. For example, if the problem solver is searching for a new trigonometric relationship, the size of the triangle may be quite irrelevant. If he is searching for a new pattern of matches, the direction of the match-head in the pattern may be irrelevant. Conceptualizations of these features of the stimulus situation may have been recalled; but they now must be distinguished from other concepts and discarded.

Combining subordinate rules is the next stage of problem solving, often referred to as "formulating hypotheses."

There are many ways in which recalled rules and concepts may be combined; the object is to find the correct one. It seems likely that the process may be guided by some strategies of the sort emphasized in Bruner's (1956, 1961) writings. It surely can be strongly affected, though, by external instructions having the specific function of guiding thinking. This variety of instructions was used by Maier (1930) to give "direction" to thinking. The demonstrations used by Katona (1940) in his experiments may be said to have had the same purpose. In both cases, such instructions were found to lead to problem solution more frequently than when they were not used. In research on "guided discovery," several investigators have found that the use of guiding instructions speed up or otherwise improve problem solving (Craig, 1953; Gagné and Brown, 1961). Presumably, such instructions operate to narrow the search for likely combinations, and thus reduce the time of search (Gagné, 1965b).

At the next stage, the problem solver arrives at a provisional rule which he believes may solve the problem. This rule is then subjected to verification by carrying out the operations it suggests with reference to the stimulus objects. But before verification is carried out, the provisional rule must itself be "matched" (See Refs., Miller, Galanter, and Pribram, 1960) to an internal model, which may be called the "solution model." This internal model is the general form of the answer, rather than being the answer itself. It is a process by which the problem solver reminds himself that he is looking for "open patterns" rather than "closed patterns" of matches; or that he is looking for a "food word" in an anagram; or that he is seeking a linear distance in finding the unknown part of a right triangle. The solution model is often conveyed to the learner by external instructions, and often these are given at the very beginning of the problem. Accordingly, the solution model must usually be "carried in mind" throughout the other stages of problem solving; that is, it is subject to recall at any moment.

A final stage of problem solving is verification. Here, the provisional model is checked by application to a specific example (usually an external one). Should verification not work, the problem solver returns to the task of trying new combinations of rules. When verification does work, it may be said that a solution rule has been acquired. This may be further checked by requiring the problem solver to make additional applications of the general rule to specific instances of the problem class.

In summary, then, it can be seen that the internal events of problem solving may be influenced by instructions that constitute a part of the external situation. The recall of previously learned concepts and rules may be stimulated by instructions to "remember" or "recall." The process of distinguishing between relevant and irrelevant cues in the stimulus situation may be affected by instructions which increase the distinctiveness of these cues. The combining of rules, that is, the making of hypotheses, may be externally guided by instructions which have the effect of narrowing the search for rule combinations. And finally, the "solution model" or general characterization of the solution, usually carried in mind throughout the problem-solving activity, is typically conveyed by instructions at the very beginning of the problem.

Individual Differences

The events of problem solving described in Fig. 1 suggest some interesting possibilities of individual differences that may affect the process. These are shown in the right-hand column of the figure. Although it is not supposed that this is an exhaustive list, those differences that are indicated might be expected to have the strongest relationships with problem solving.

Amount of information stored. Beginning at the bottom of the figure with the earliest stage, it is reasonable to suppose that people will differ with respect to the size of the store of previously learned concepts and rules they possess. It would be difficult to overemphasize the importance of this very obvious kind of individual difference. One person is better at solving a problem than another because he *knows more*—because he *has more information* of the sort that ultimately turns out to be relevant to the problem or to the process of solving it. Among all the possible reasons why the score on an intelligence test may be significantly related to problem solving (McNemar, 1965), this possibility should not be neglected. People who score high on intelligence tests have a lot of verbal and quantitative rules stored in their memories, and this is surely one important reason why they are able to solve problems successfully.

Ease of recall. The rules and concepts which have previously been learned must be recalled. There is a possibility that some people can recall more of them, without getting them confused with each other, than can other people. Recall, as is well known, is subject to interference (Underwood, 1964), a

process which may well vary in amount or intensity with the
individual. It is not at all evident that this particular kind of
ability has ever been systematically measured. Presumably,
it would have to be done by teaching a group of individuals the
same set of "facts" or "principles" to the same criterion, and
then testing them at a later time for recall of these principles.
Although this is not necessarily an easy job of testing to under-
take, short cuts do not appear advisable. For example, there
is no particular reason to suppose that the retention of a sequence of nonsense syllables ten minutes following learning
would reflect the same ability as is suggested in the figure.

Concept distinction. Still another ability difference is
suggested at the next stage of problem solving. Here the individual must distinguish relevant from irrelevant aspects of the
stimulus situation. Presumably, this is not simply a matter of
"discrimination ability" in a narrow sense. Instead, the problem solver sorts out the conceptualized features of stimuli;
perhaps he must deal with the color and shape of the stimuli,
but not with their number or arrangement or size. Yet these
latter features may be continually present in the situation, and
may therefore tend to interfere with the process of selection
for purposes of the problem. People may differ from each
other in this ability to select and maintain conceptual distinctions in the face of potentially conflicting cues. Beyond this
statement, I do not feel confident in describing the kind of
measurement that might be employed to reveal this individual
difference. Some exploratory attempts will undoubtedly be required for the purpose of increasing the precision of meaning
of this ability.

Fluency of hypotheses. An important difference in individuals can almost certainly be identified at the next stage. This is a difference in the facility with which people combine rules into new hypotheses. Presumably, this is related to, if not the same as, some of the intellectual fluency factors identified by investigators of creativity, such as Guilford (1958), Taylor (1958), Getzels and Jackson (1962), and others. Of course, it needs to be recognized that some part of "fluency" may be determined by how large a store of recalled rules the individual has at his command. However, it is reasonable to suppose in addition that some individuals are much more "ingenious" and "flexible" about forming hypotheses than are others.

Retaining the solution model. The general form of solution required by the problem, the "solution model," may be transmitted to the problem solver by instructions given as an early step in the establishment of the problem situation. When this is done, it must be retained in the face of many potential interferences, in order that the problem solver will be able to match a provisional solution with the model. This kind of retention appears to bear some resemblance to the "running memory span" studied by Yntema and Mueser (1960, 1962), among others. The typical situation is one in which a series of messages is presented about the states of several variables. Changes are announced in subsequent messages. These are interrupted at random intervals, and the individual is required to answer a question about the current state of one of the variables. With this procedure, it may be said that what is being measured is the ability of the subject to retain several "models" which are subject to mutual interference. It seems likely that retention of this sort is at least highly related to the demands of retaining a solution model in problem solving.

Matching instances to a general class. The stage of verification in problem solving appears to demand that the individual be able to assign specific instances to the class represented by the solution model, and reject those instances which are not representative. This is the operation that must be performed in order for the problem solver to "check" his solution, or to "know he is right," and thus bring the problem activity to an end. Presumably, people differ in such an ability to a degree that may be quite important for problem solving. One person may see immediately that a particular construction constitutes a pendulum, or a hat rack, whereas another may have to go through a more elaborate procedure, and therefore take more time to satisfy himself that a "match" has been achieved.

MODELS OF PROBLEM SOLVING

There is considerable interest nowadays in constructing models of human problem-solving behavior. A number of investigators are interested in mathematical models (Luce, Bush, and Galanter, 1963). Several others are intrigued by computer models (Simon and Newell, 1964). It will be apparent from the discussion so far that I am very fond of mechanical, or perhaps it is electromechanical, models. The kinds of characteristics such models have can be illustrated by reference to my model of problem solving. They may be described as follows:

1. Sequential action. First there is one set of events, and the completion of this action causes another set of events to occur. The model does not intend to predict an unvarying sequence for any act of problem solving. What it does state, however, is that successful completion of any stage depends upon the existence of a capability in the preceding stage.

2. Threshold phenomena. Sometimes, certain states must reach a given point of "strength" before anything happens to produce the next stage of the process. The most obvious instance of a threshold phenomenon in the model of Fig. 1 is the recall threshold.

3. Non-graded responses. Another characteristic of such a model is that action resulting from some preceding event is positive and non-graded. It either takes place or it does not. A cue is either discriminated or not; a hypothesis is either formed or not; it cannot be partially formed. Of course if there are collections of cues, or collections of hypotheses, one can presumably expect a kind of "graded" response. Its basis, however, is clearly a sampling of elements.

4. Multiple connections. Any event can contribute to one or a number of subsequent events, or conversely, any number of events can be required to produce just one subsequent event. In the model represented in Fig. 1, for example, many different hypotheses are possible; some may require a combination of one rule with another; others of one rule with several others; and so on.

The events depicted in Fig. 1 suggest two different kinds
of experimental studies that could be carried out to test the
model. First, a number of studies are suggested regarding the
effects of *instructional variables* on problem solving. Different
methods of stimulating recall, for example, could be devised to
bring about the recall of subordinate rules. The effects of such
treatments on recall, and subsequently on problem-solving
success, could then be measured. Similarly, experimental
studies could be designed to explore the effects of making cues
distinctive, of guiding thinking, and of providing a solution
model. In each case, the procedure in such studies would be to
vary the functions of instructions as independent variables, to
observe their effects on internal processes by means of measures specifically designed for this purpose, and then to test
the action of these events on problem-solving performance.

Second, the possibility is suggested of investigating the
relations between *individual differences variables* and problem
solving. Obviously, for any given class of problem, the number of previously learned rules (and concepts) that are relevant to that class may be measured independently as individual
differences and related to problem-solving success. As another example, differences in individuals in distinguishing the
relevant and irrelevant cues of the stimulus situation may be
measured and then related to performance in problem solving.
Other kinds of individual differences described in the figure
can in a similar manner be systematically investigated to determine their relationships with problem-solving behavior.
On the whole, it appears to me that this model suggests an extensive program of research which could reveal a great deal
about how human beings solve problems.

6 JOHN R. HAYES *
Harvard University

Memory, Goals, and
Problem Solving [†]

This paper is intended to provide a brief review of the
program of research I have been carrying out for the last two
years on the solution of certain types of problems. Some problems are solved suddenly and in a single step, as Maier (1931)
puts it, ". . . like the perceiving of a hidden figure in a puzzle-
picture." Others are solved in a sequence of well-defined steps
like the tracing of a path through a complex maze. All of the
studies I will describe concern problems of the second kind—
problems solved by a sequence of discrete steps. Our purpose
in these investigations was to explore the functioning of human
information processing in the solution of such problems. We
paid particular attention to the function of subgoals in guiding

*The author is now at Carnegie Institute of Technology.
†The research reported in this paper was in part performed at
the Decision Sciences Laboratory as part of project 7682, "Man-com-
puter information processing" and further reproduction is authorized
to satisfy the needs of the U. S. government. The research was also
supported in part by a contract from the National Sciences Foundation
#GS-192 to Harvard University, Center for Cognitive Studies.

the solution process, and to the effects of coding, or information format, on retrieval. The nature of the research can probably best be conveyed by proceeding directly to a description of the experimental task and method.

The experimental task was to solve "spy" problems. In the spy problems, the S was asked to imagine that he was running a spy ring, and that for security reasons not all of his spies could talk to each other. Before each problem, the E gave the S a list, called the "connection list," of the spies who could talk to each other. A typical list is shown in Fig. 1. The first pair, for example, indicated that the spies "shower" and "clerk" can talk to each other.

SHOWER ⟶ CLERK

DROUGHT ⟶ HILL

LARYNX ⟶ BETH

ADJECTIVE ⟶ SHOWER

HILL ⟶ HORSE

BEEF ⟶ LARYNX

ADJECTIVE ⟶ PARCHESI

DROUGHT ⟶ KEVIN

SHOWER ⟶ BEEF

LARYNX ⟶ DROUGHT

BEEF ⟶ TAFT

Fig. 1: A typical connection list.

The S was required to learn the connection list to a criterion of three successive error-free trials. Any change in word order was counted as an error. When the learning criterion had been met, the E stated the problem for S both in spoken and in written form. The E might say, for example, "Get a message from 'adjective' to 'hill'," and simultaneously hand the S a card on which was printed "adjective-hill." The S was then required to solve the problem aloud but without the aid of pencil and paper. He was instructed to tell the E everything that he was thinking in the course of the solution. When they are chained together, the pairs given in the connection lists form a structure such as is shown in Fig. 2.

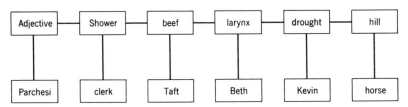

Fig. 2: The structure of the connections in Fig. 1.

The spy problems were chosen as the experimental task because they have three properties which promote the analysis of the solution process and which are not usually present in arbitrarily chosen puzzles. These properties are homogeneity, information control, and modularity. (a) The spy problems are homogeneous in that the various steps are all of the same kind and approximately the same difficulty. (b) The information necessary for the solution of a spy problem is contained in the connection list which is under the E's control. In most puzzles, on the other hand, the S is expected to supply information beyond that contained in the puzzle statement. (c) The spy problems are modular in that one can construct a spy problem of any length and any number of blind alleys. Many problems would be spoiled if we attempted to make them a step longer or a step shorter.

The first experiment* was concerned primarily with the relation of problem topology or structure to solution time. Twelve college students solved five problems of each of the

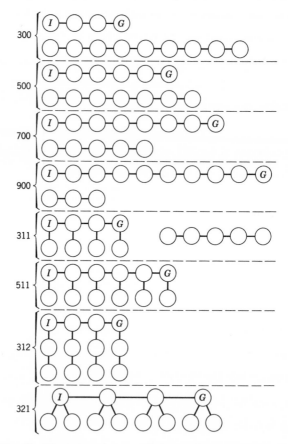

Fig. 3: The structures of the eight problem types in Experiment I.

*The first three experiments discussed below are described in more detail by Hayes (1965).

eight structures shown in Fig. 3. The various problem types differ from one another in length, that is, in the number of steps required for solution; in the number of blind alleys attached to the solution chain; and in the length of the blind alleys. A three-digit code will be used to designate the problem structure. The first digit will indicate the problem length; the second, the number of blind alleys attached at each point on the solution chain; and the third, the length of the blind alleys. Thus, "500" represents an unbranched problem of length five, and "312," a length three problem with one double-length blind alley at each point on the solution chain.

In order to avoid confounding effects of the length of the connection list with the effects of problem structure, all of the connection lists contained exactly eleven pairs. For some problem types, "300" and "500" for example, it was necessary to add "filler" pairs to bring the number up to eleven.

It would be misleading to proceed directly to a formal account of the results without first trying to make clearer what it is that the S's do in solving problems. When the S tells us what he is thinking in the course of solving a spy problem, what he says consists almost entirely of pairs from the connection list. The S does not announce the pairs randomly. Rather, he arranges them in chains; for example, shower to beef, beef to larynx, larynx to tree, etc., which form connected paths through the problem structure.

The S may work either in the forward or in the backward direction by starting the path either at the beginning of the problem or at the goal. In Experiment I, 25% of all paths were backward. Many authors have noted the use of backward solution

process. Duncker (1945); Johnson (1955); Newell, Shaw, and
Simon (1958); and Polya (1957) are examples. In our experiments, the backward strategy seems to be a secondary one, in
the sense that it is most often used when the forward strategy
has already failed. Classifying paths by the order in which they
occurred within problem solutions, only 12% of first paths were
backward, whereas between 35% and 40% of all later paths were
in the backward direction.

What the S says while he is solving a problem reflects in
many ways what he must remember and how he remembers it.
For example, when the S is constructing a path, most usually
he simply announces the pairs in sequence without any intervening comment. On occasion, however, rather than simply an-
nouncing a required pair, the S either will recite the connection
list by rote until he comes to the pair or will state that he is
reciting it subvocally. (The S's were instructed to report such
recitations.) This process, which we call list searching, occurs
relatively infrequently—55 times in the 3200 steps of Experiment I. The retrieval times provide evidence that list searching
really is a process distinct from the more usual retrieval
method (to be called "direct accessing"). List searching takes
about ten times as long as does direct accessing. Later, we
will discuss data which bear on the nature of the direct accessing process.

In the early stages of this research, I expected that the
length of problem that the S could solve would be limited by the
length of solution chain which the S could retain in his immediate memory. I was disabused of this notion by two brushes with
reality. First, I found that S's could solve spy problems as

much as 20 steps in length. Second, I looked more carefully at what it was that the S's were doing. They were not storing up the whole solution chain in their memories. Rather, they seemed to store only enough information to allow them to generate the chain a very few links at a time. This information appeared to include: (*a*) their present position in the problem (an S might say "Joe can talk to Bill, so the message is at Bill. Bill can talk to Sam, so the message is at Sam" etc.) and (*b*) the direction from which they had come. Direction must have been recorded in some form since the S almost never retraced his path. Having gone from Joe to Bill, the S rarely returns to Joe.

A final aspect of the behavior which seems to bear on memory is the strong tendency, mentioned above, of the S's to describe the paths with pairs. That is, the S's say, "Joe to Bill, Bill to Sam, Sam to Ed." They do not say, "Joe to Bill to Sam to Ed." When questioned about it, S's give as explanations such statements as, "Well, that first Bill is part of one thought, and second Bill is part of another thought." Perhaps we can interpret such statements as reflecting a difference between the word "Bill" when it is a content retrieved by the question, "Who can Joe talk to?", and the word "Bill" when it is in turn used as a cue to memory.

As one would expect, the solution time of the problems in Experiment I increased with increases in the problem length, in the number of blind alleys attached to the solution chain and in the length of the blind alleys. Increases in length, whether of the problem or of the blind alleys, however, caused more than proportional increases in solution time. The length nine problem (900), for example, took six times rather than three times as long to solve as the length three problem.

In the branched problems, the proportion of blind alley entrances decreased markedly as the S approached solution. This improvement in performance over the course of the solution suggested that the more-than-proportional increases in solution time might be a kind of "end effect." The second experiment was conducted to explore this possibility.

In Experiment II, the S's solved exactly the same problems that were solved in Experiment I. The data were treated differently, however, in that the sequence of steps by which the S progressed to the solution was tape recorded. The S was counted as making a "step of progress" whenever he

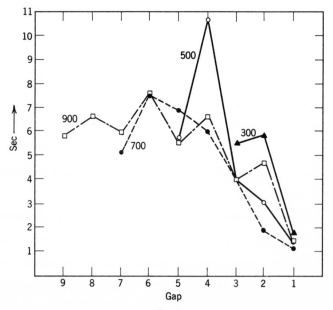

Fig. 4: Progress times for the unbranched problems in Experiment II.

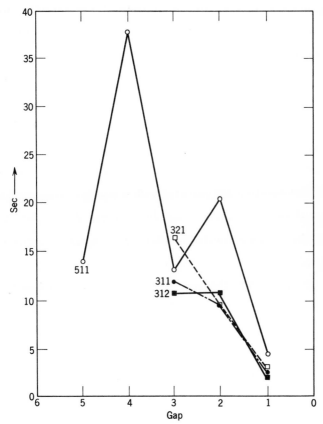

Fig. 5: Progress times for the branches problems
in Experiment II.

executed a step on the solution chain either in the forward or
the backward direction which he had not executed before. The
results of this analysis are shown in Fig. 4 for the unbranched
problems and in Fig. 5 for the branched problems. These curves
show the median time required to take a step plotted as a function of the number of steps which the S still needs to execute in
order to reach solution. It is clear that the rate of progress increases over the last three or four steps as the S approaches

solution. The acceleration is statistically reliable in this experiment and as we shall see it appears repeatedly in later experiments.

It is tempting to compare the solution acceleration with the goal accelerations observed in animal maze learning studies. Such a comparison would be misleading however. The goal acceleration phenomenon observed in maze-learning studies appears gradually with repeated traversals of the goal path. The solution acceleration, on the other hand, appears on the S's first traversal of the solution path. Maier (1940) has effectively argued that fundamentally different processes are involved in the two types of experiments.

People have often suggested a theory to me which relates the solution acceleration to the number of pairs available in the connection list. Briefly, the theory holds that the solution process "uses up" pairs and that as solution proceeds, the S accelerated because he has fewer pairs to choose among. This theory cannot be correct. In all of the problems the S's learned the same number of pairs (eleven). Thus, after taking three steps, the S should be making progress at the same rate whether he is solving a "300" problem or a "900" problem. As Fig. 4 shows, this is not the case. The S's rate of progress seems to depend not on how many steps S has completed in the problem but rather on how many steps he has yet to complete.

Another theory which is consistent with the data is that the solution acceleration results from a process of "planning" or "foresight." By these terms I mean some process by which the S stores up information for later use in the solution. At least two kinds of processes suggest themselves as possibilities.

We have called these "local planning" and "remote planning."
Probably the easiest way to discuss these processes is by way
of illustration. Suppose that an S is proceeding to work through
the chain A-B-C-D-E-F from A toward F. The S is planning
remotely if in the course of searching for the A-B connection,
for example, he notices that E connects to F. Thus, while looking for one set of connections, the S notes the presence in the
list of others which can be used in the last few steps of the
problem. Having been thus preorganized, the last few steps can
be executed more rapidly than could the earlier steps.

The S is using local planning if before taking the step A-B,
he covertly explores a few steps ahead of his present position to
determine what the outcome of such a move might be. With local
planning we would also expect the last few steps of the problem
to be executed rapidly. The reason is that when the S comes
close enough to solution, his plan will include the goal. When it
does, the S will recognize that his plan solves the problem, and
he will execute it rapidly.

In order to differentiate among these mechanisms, an experiment was performed which included some problems in which
the S could not plan remotely. Without discussing Experiment III
in detail the result indicated that the solution accelerations observed in Experiments I and II resulted both from remote and
from local planning.

When these results had been obtained, H. R. Rubenstein*
suggested that the same sort of acceleration should be obtainable
with subgoals. In an attempt to obtain the result, we executed
Experiment IV.

*Personal communication.

Basically, the method consisted in comparing the temporal course of the *S*'s progress in solving the problems with subgoals and without them. The subgoal problems were just like the standard problems in everything but the statement of the problem. In a standard problem, *S* might be told, "Get a message from Joe to cat." In the subgoal form, the same problem might become, "Get a message from Joe through ape and waterfall to cat." The subgoals were always inserted fairly. That is, in order to get from Joe to cat, the *S* had to go through ape and waterfall (in that order) in any case. The subgoals, then, might be considered as aids or hints. They were in no sense misleading.

Figure 6 shows the problem structures used in Experiment IV. The X's indicate the positions in which the subgoals were placed when the structure was used for a subgoal problem.

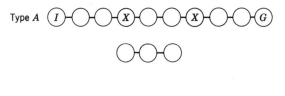

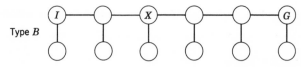

Fig. 6: Problem structures used in Experiment IV.

The *S*'s were twelve college students. Each *S* solved twenty problems: five problems with subgoals and five without in each of the problem structures.

Figure 7 shows the results for problem type A and Fig. 8 for problem type B. In each case, the solid curves, which contain the results for the standard problems, show clear evidence of the solution acceleration found in the previous studies. The broken curves show the results for the subgoal problems. In both Figures there is evidence of acceleration as S approaches the subgoals. The results are statistically reliable for the two subgoals in problem type A. These results were much as expected. We did not expect to see what happened immediately after the subgoals, however. In all cases, the S appears to progress more slowly than one would expect on the steps which follow subgoals. Comparing the steps following a subgoal with the corresponding steps in a standard problem, we find that the

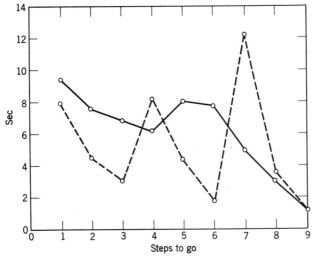

Fig. 7: Progress times in problem type A with subgoals (broken curve) and without subgoals (solid curve).

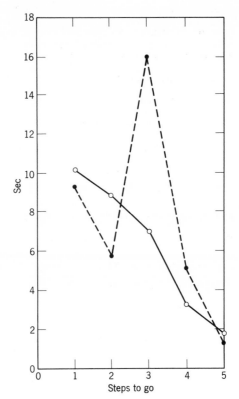

Fig. 8: Progress times in problem
type B with subgoals (broken curve)
and without subgoals (solid curve).

aftereffect is significant in problem type B, and for the second
subgoal in problem type A.

Problems of type A are solved significantly more quickly
with subgoals than without them, in spite of the subgoal aftereffect. In problem type B, however, the subgoal aftereffect is so
marked that the subgoal problems were actually solved significantly more slowly than the standard problems. Before making
these observations I had always believed that at worst, a

subgoal could be useless. Here, clearly, is an instance in which a fair subgoal actually impedes problem solving performance.

What is it that causes the subgoal aftereffect? A possibility which early suggested itself was that after accomplishing one subtask, the S relaxed to some extent before going on to a new task. This simple explanation doesn't cover all of the facts.

To obtain further information on the nature of the subgoal aftereffects, the problem-solving protocols were examined for evidence of memory difficulty. The occurrences of three types of events were noted.

1. List searches—these were defined above.
2. Errors—incorrect assertions that a pair is in the connection list.
3. Reversals—these are changes in direction. For example, after progressing from x to y, the S moved back to x.

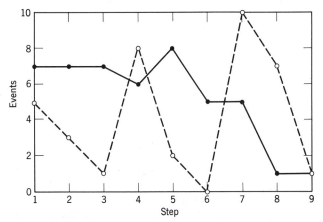

Fig. 9: Frequency of events in problem type *A* with subgoals (broken curve) and without subgoals (solid curve).

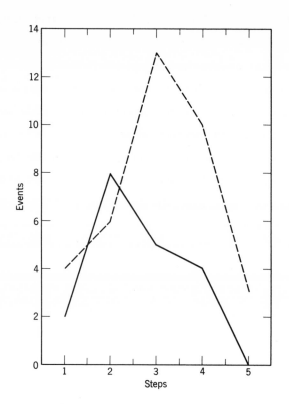

Fig. 10: Frequency of events in problem
type *B* with subgoals (broken curve) and
without subgoals (solid curve).

These three types of events are taken as evidence of
memory disturbance.

Figures 9 and 10 show that these events become less frequent before subgoals and more frequent after them. This result
is reminiscent of the Zeigarnic effect (Zeigarnic, 1927)—the tendency of *S*'s to remember better tasks which they had been prevented from completing than tasks which they had been allowed
to complete. Perhaps the result is a kind of running Zeigarnic
effect.

Rate of progress, memory difficulties, and, as our most recent data show, blind alley entrances, are all influenced in much the same way by goals and subgoals. Research is currently under way in an attempt to relate these phenomena in a manner similar to Miller, Galanter and Pribram's (1960) analysis of planning and the Zeigarnic effect.

The evidence of planning or foresight in problem solving should be placed in the context of a theory which is concerned not only with the chaining together of discrete problem-solving steps, but the theory should also take account of the various levels of activity which the S may bring into play in solving a problem and the various costs and levels of commitment involved in each.

To illustrate what I mean more concretely, consider that we have set an S a construction task, perhaps Maier's (1930) pendulum problem. In working on the problem, the S may explore the steps available to him by actually taking them—that is, by exploratory construction, by talking about them, or by thinking about them. Usually exploratory construction is the most expensive procedure, the steps being costly to execute and errors relatively difficult to undo. Thus to make a given exploratory construction requires more of a commitment by the S than would talking about the same sequence of steps. Talking about the steps, in turn, would require more commitment than thinking about them. The sensible thing for the S to do, if circumstance allowed, would be to explore at a low level of commitment and let sequences of inexpensive acts serve as plans for sequences of expensive acts.

If the planning activity in itself cost nothing, then the

advice to "think before you act" or "look before you leap" would always be appropriate. But the planning activity is not free. Not only is there a cost associated with the formation of a plan, there is also a cost of retaining it. The result of taking these costs into account is that the amount of foresight which the S exhibits may be expected to depend on the particular response that is being observed. If we look only at what the S builds, his behavior may appear thoroughly planned and insightful. If we ask him to talk through the solution, however, we may find as we do in the present studies that the S plans some but not all of the way to the goal. If we were to eavesdrop on the S's thoughts, perhaps we would find no foresight at all. Thus, we do not want to assume that the amount of foresight that the S shows is a fixed parameter of the cognitive system—e.g., three or four steps as suggested in our studies. Rather, we assume that the amount of foresight that a subject exhibits will be a function of the costs and commitments involved in the particular problem.

In all of the studies discussed above, the factor of interest was the underlying problem structure. The form of the connection list was kept simple and constant. In the two studies to be discussed below, the problem structure was kept constant while

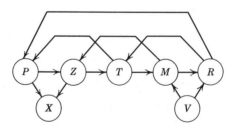

Fig. 11: The problem structure
used in Experiments V and VI.

the form of the connection list was varied.

Figure 11 shows the problem used. All the connections are one-directional—that is, P can talk to Z, but Z can't talk to P. Each of the spies on the solution chain can talk to two spies and be talked to by two (different) spies. There were 25 of these problems, five in each of the five formats shown in Fig. 12. In the A format, each connection was represented by a separate pair. The pairs were arranged randomly with the restriction that successive pairs should share neither the same first nor the same second spy. In the B and C formats, each statement in the connection list embodied two pairs. In the B format, the S connection list consisted of statements of the form "Joe can talk to Bill and Sam," and in the C format, statements of the form, "Al and Ed can talk to Joe." In the expanded formats, such statements were replaced by the separate pairs of which they were composed, as shown in Figure 12.

In Experiment V, ten S's learned the 25 connection lists and solved the 25 problems. The A format took longer to learn than did the other four formats, which were learned with about equal speed. On solution, however, the B format took significantly less time and the C format significantly more time than the A format. (See the solid curve in Fig. 13.)

The advantage of the B format over the C format depended on the direction in which the S solved the problems. The one S who solved the C format problems backward, solved them at the same rate as the B format problems which he solved forward.

In Experiment VI, another ten S's learned the 25 connection lists, but rather than solving the problems, they were given an information retrieval task. For each spy on the solution chain,

	A	B	BX	C	CX
1.	Z → T	T → M,P	T → M	M,V → R	M → R
2.	V → R		T → P		V → R
3.	P → X	V → M,R	V → M	P,M → Z	P → Z
4.	M → Z		V → R		M → Z
5.	T → P	P → Z,X	P → Z	R,T → P	R → P
6.	Z → X		P → X		T → P
7.	R → P	R → T,P	R → T	V,T → M	V → M
8.	T → M		R → P		T → M
9.	P → Z	Z → X,T	Z → X	P,Z → X	P → X
10.	R → T		Z → T		Z - - T
11.	M → R	M → Z,R	M → Z	Z,M → T	Z → T
12.	V → M		M → R		- M → T

Fig. 12. Connection list formats used in Experiments V and VI.

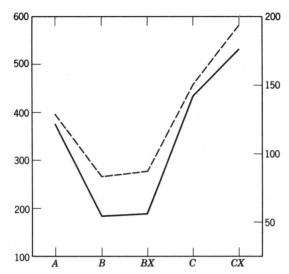

Fig. 13: Median solution times obtained in
Experiment V (solid curve) and median retrieval times obtained in Experiment VI
(broken curve).

they were asked who that spy could talk to. The retrieval time
was the time which the S required to produce both connections.
Figure 13 shows the retrieval times of Experiment VI (broken
curves) plotted together with the solution times of Experiment V
(solid curve), for each of the five formats. The units of measurement have been adjusted so that the two curves lie close
enough together for convenient comparison. It is clear that the
differences in retrieval time could account very well for the
differences in solution time.

     One further result of Experiment VI bears on the nature
of the direct accessing process. When the S's were required to
retrieve both of the connections of a given spy, they tended to

retrieve them in the order in which they were arranged in the connection list. In format A, same-order retrievals outnumbered inverted-order retrievals by two to one. This result suggests that the direct access process may involve some list searching; the list searched might be the left column of the connection list.

The experiments I have described summarize the program to date. Future research will be concerned with

1. the relation of planning processes to costs and values and to memory,

2. the influence of notation and format in the retrieval processes involved in solution, and

3. the attempt to generalize present results and procedures to more complex solution processes.

7 | ALLEN NEWELL
Carnegie Institute of Technology

Discussion of Papers by Dr. Gagne and Dr. Hayes*

Let me first discuss the Gagné paper. I am perhaps somewhat more sanguine than Bob Gagné about the current health of research in problem solving—even while agreeing that it is always appropriate to bow in the direction of our ignorance. But it seems to me that the amount and quality of recent work in concept formation; in empirical studies of language, especially in characterizing children's grammars; and in analyzing the systems of rules that lead to complex problem solving, all are indicative of both progress and health.

That problem solving is an act of learning seems quite acceptable to me. Indeed, by any reasonable definition of learning, any problem solver learns the solution. However, Dr. Gagné uses this as an entry point to an effort at defining problem solving. Now, in general I am not keen on definitions of

*The work for this discussion was supported by the Public Health Service Research Grant—MH 07722 from the National Institutes of Health.

large umbrella terms like "learning" and "problem solving."
It seems to me that their exact formulation is one of the last
things that happens in a science, since they continue to stand
for domains of empirical phenomena, independently of what
theories exist. It seems to me better to leave them to their
ostensive ways, and to leave matters of precision to the claims
of formalized theories.

But the definition posited by Dr. Gagné makes me uncom-
fortable in other ways. Upon reflection, I think my discomfort
stems from his concern about how to infer that problem solving
has occurred, as opposed to other simpler behaviors. So he
evokes transfer, generalizability, and so on—desiderata that are
meant to ease the inference of problem solving rather than to
characterize the phenomenon itself. Working as I do with rather
complex instances of problem solving, few concerns of Dr.
Gagné become mine. More important from a definitional point
of view, many of my examples do not fit his mold. Let me give
just one. Recently in my class in complex information processing we have been asking how to build a program that would discover a solution to the following problem, called the Firing
Squad Problem (Moore, 1964) originally formulated by J. Myhill.
I give it in two forms: one vivid, one precise.

   1. A long line of soldiers in a dense fog is to fire simul-
      taneously upon command of the General, who stands at
      the end of the line. However, each soldier is only aware
      of the men immediately to the right and left of him.
      The General gives the command "Fire when ready."
      (Note that only the man next to the General is aware

initially that this command is given.) What system of communication is to be used by the soldiers so that they can all fire at the same time? It is also assumed (and this is what makes the problem hard) that not only is the length of the line unknown, but that neither the soldiers nor the General can count above some number, say 1,000, whereas the line can be many times as long, say 1,000,000.

2. Consider a finite sequence of N identical finite state machines (the soldiers). A finite state machine is a device which can be in one of K configurations, S_1, S_2, ..., S_k at each instant of time, but which makes a transition to a new state at each instant, $t = 1, 2, \ldots$. Each machine is connected to the machines adjacent to it in the sequence, so that the new state that it assumes is a function of its own current state and the current states of the two adjacent machines. That is, for machine i, $S_i(t + 1) = T[S_{i-1}(t), S_i(t), S_{i+1}(t)]$, where T is called the transition function. Initially, all the machines are in state Q ("quiescent"). At time 0 the first machine (the General) is put into state R ("fire when ready"). At some time t_F all the machines (including the initial one) are to be in state F ("fire") and at no time prior to t_F is any machine to be in the state F. The number of states is to be a fixed integer K, independent of the number of machines in the sequences, N. The problem is to specify the states and the transition function (T) of the machines, such that the above happens.

This is a reasonably hard problem. It was originally thought to have no solution, but has since been solved. (If you wish to try, the time to fire for the usual solutions is proportional to either $3N$ or N^2; no solution can take less than $2N - 1$ steps, the time it takes for a signal to go from one end of the line to the other and back, and minimal solutions exist.)

There is little doubt that it is a problem. Yet it does not fit Gagné's definition in any natural way. One shows he has solved the problem by giving the solution; there is no need to generalize, nor to show transfer to some other task. We are not concerned with whether the subject has memorized the answer or knows it by rote. These are possibilities (as in all other tasks), but are to be dealt with administratively rather than by experimental design—we would characterize a subject as dishonest who did not admit to knowing the solution beforehand. Further, there is no simple sense in which this problem is solved by applying a rule. Rule applications exist in abundance, but the solution itself is slowly constructed out of pieces, like a house.

Finally, solving the Firing Squad Problem appears to involve finding other ways to represent the problem than that immediately available in the problem statement. Many people seem to carry out their thinking in a "problem space" that contains such phenomena as "waves," "reflection," "velocity," "interference," etc. These terms, however familiar to humans with human experience, are not part of the formal definition of the problem. One of my students used, instead of a wave-like metaphor, the process of syntactic analysis in computer programming as an analog—considering various possible states of soldiers to be analogous to matching parentheses. Thus, several problem spaces may be involved in solving a problem, the problem solver working back and forth between them. Concern with representation has already shown up strongly in Dr. Simon's paper, and I will return to it again. The point is that this aspect of problem solving appears nowhere in Dr. Gagné's definition.

Let me comment briefly on one other aspect of the Gagné paper: the stages in problem solving. This notion has a long history. It seems to be a response to at least two ideas: that different things must be done in solving a problem—different functions must be performed; and some of these functions must have logical priority over others—the latter not being possible until the former has been done. In a "stage" model these two ideas are welded together with the yet stronger assumption that problem solving occurs as a long, linear sequence of processes. Often some statement is included, as there is in the Gagné presentation, that the sequence is iterated or sometimes only occurs partially, but it is clear that if such caveats are taken too seriously, little empirical content is left in the model.

My point is not just to note that the "stage" models are rather primitive, but to observe a parallel to them in the construction of problem-solving computer programs. Problem-solving programs are often built according to a "fixed stages" scheme. Bobrow's program, STUDENT, discussed extensively by Dr. Simon, provides an excellent example. Go back to Fig. 1 of his paper. Notice that the program first makes mandatory substitutions in the sentences, then tags words by functions, then extracts the kernel sentences, then converts each sentence

to an equation, and finally solves the equation. Now this is certainly a reasonable way to proceed, and STUDENT demonstrates
that it is sometimes effective, since STUDENT solves problems.
However, when one tries to identify the deficiencies in STUDENT,
viewed either as a theory of human problem solving or as a
problem solver, one of them (rigidity) stems directly from the
fixed structure of its behavior. Whereas a human (or a more
flexible program, hopefully) can do all the things shown in the
flow diagram (make substitutions, write an equation corresponding to a kernel sentence, etc.), they are for him tools freely
available to be used as the problem demands, rather than fixed
points in a sequence. Often, especially when the problem is
simple, the tools are used in a sequence like that in the flow
diagram, but also, especially when the problem is hard or ambiguous, the "normal" sequence does not occur.

Why was STUDENT built with fixed stages? Chiefly, I
would hypothesize, because this is the simplest first approximation, and more flexible organizations are not easy to come
by. Thus the scheme represents not so much an insight into the
true nature of problem-solving behavior as a concession to the
frailty of the investigator. Incidentally, there do exist programs
for some task areas that go at least part way toward providing
more flexible organizations (Newell and Simon, 1963).

Let me now turn to the paper of Dr. Hayes. My first reaction when reading this paper was "Fun!" Somehow, when a
new task shows up having a structure both clean and provocative, the temptation is to drop everything and play with it. The
usual vagaries of symposium communication prevented me from
receiving Dr. Hayes' paper until a few days ago, but I immediately

put together some cards and gave myself the task. I verified promptly that memorizing the list of component associations gives no insight into the structure of the total graph, and further that it is possible to follow the correct path through the maze with only the most tenuous grasp on the components (as it happened, I was somewhat rushed when doing the task and did not fully memorize some of the lists). But let me resist further impulses to play, and ask instead what questions of importance to psychology might be served by serious work with Dr. Hayes' task. I can think of four possibilities.

1. It could provide an existence demonstration. Such demonstrations have played an important role in psychological experimentation. One seeks to demonstrate that there is an effect of motivation on perception, or that there are Gestalt principles of perception not reducible to more atomistic explanations. In Dr. Hayes' work the aim would be to demonstrate the existence of complex internal processes—or rule governed behavior, covert search, strategic organization. However, this no longer needs to be done, it seems to me, in view of the very large amount of work on both language and problem solving accomplished in the last decade.

2. It could be used to discover and explicate a particular system of rules and strategies. Now, we already know that to a large extent such strategies are conventional —that is, learned. And we know that variation in the task will lead to variation in the strategies. Since there are lots of different tasks, literally an unbounded

number of them, we have to ask (sometime) what is the purpose of discovering and cataloguing the strategies and heuristics of a particular task. One motivation is to show that such cataloguing can be done rather completely—an existence demonstration again. Since we have provided almost no such demonstrations of completeness, I believe this is worth doing. Another is to discover new methods of processing—new ideas about strategies and heuristics to add to our total stock. But Dr. Hayes' task is of such a simple nature that it appears an unlikely candidate for such discovery.

3. It could be used as a jumping off place to explain more complex behavior. This is the principle of gradually working up from the simple and familiar (which for psychology has usually been thought to be conditioning and learning of nonmeaningful material), effecting a kind of reduction as one goes. The trouble with this path for Dr. Hayes is that considerable work has already been done on tasks several orders of magnitude more complex than his. Examples of this work were given by Dr. de Groot and Dr. Simon earlier in the conference. Their work is already adequately reductionistic, working back as it does to specific programs of elementary information processes. Thus Dr. Hayes will find that the high ground he was aiming for has already been occupied by friendly troops. This does not seem a likely possibility.

4. Finally, the experimental arrangement of Dr. Hayes seems well adapted to exploring the question of internal

representation. Can we discover the detailed structure
of information about the tree that is held internally,
and discover how it is processed? I have already indicated that I think questions of representation are extremely important. I think Dr. Hayes has a chance of
making a significant contribution to this question with
his task, and I would commend the issue to him. Let
me develop it in more detail.

We are incapable at the moment of thinking of information
processing without conceiving of some kind of structure (the
representation) that encodes information, and some processes
that are capable of extracting information from this structure
and encoding additional information into it. In some sense the
structure only exists ("makes operational sense" might be a
preferred phrase) because of the processes that encode and
decode it. Still, we find it convenient to summarize the properties of a collection of encoding and decoding processes by describing the structure. I can conceive of at least three kinds of
representations of Dr. Hayes' task. There may well be others;
it would be worthwhile to invent or discover them.

One representation holds the information about the tree
as a list of associated pairs, essentially as it is provided to the
subject by the experimenter. The list may be searched sequentially, accessing successive pairs in the order in which they
were memorized. A second representation would associate with
each word the set of its successors. That is, the subject holds
a direct representation of the tree, but is only able to perform
local operations on it. Having obtained several successors to a

given word he has no further information about them—that is, about what lies beyond. Both of these representations are easily defined explicitly. It is easy to build computer versions of them and to calculate the effects of different strategies of processing.

About the third representation I must be somewhat vague, since we understand less about spatial perception than about associational structures. Suppose I were to draw the graph of one of Dr. Hayes' tasks, as in his Fig. 1, and ask someone to solve the task while looking at this representation. The task is trivial. Why? The subject has available not only the successors to each word, but can "see" the direction to be taken to get to the solution word. This additional information is encoded by the (implicit) convention that the solution path runs generally from left to right across the figure. If the points were placed at random on the page, with connecting lines that looped and crossed, then all directional encoding could be destroyed, and the spatial graph reduced to the second representation where only local operations of finding successors are possible. However, the interesting question is not whether global processes can be made ineffective; it is whether the human has available any representations that are richer than the first two. Does he have some way in which he can "see" where he is going, and if so, can we discover the nature and laws of this representation?

Already in Dr. Hayes' report there is considerable information about these representational issues. Apparently the first representation mentioned (sequential list search for pairs) remains available to the subject but is used infrequently and can often be identified, when used, by the time it takes. If this is so, it implies, of course, that some other representation is also

available to him. It is clear that subjects do not have available
so neat a representation as that of Dr. Hayes' Fig. 1, or his
task would be no problem for them.

Most provocative, of course, are Dr. Hayes' findings that
the number of branchings taken by the subject are less than the
number that would be taken by chance, and that there is an acceleration of the solving process as they get toward the end of
the tree. Setting aside the possibility of experimental artifact,
which does not seem to me likely, there are at least two possible
explanations for these phenomena. One revolves around the
distinction between overt and covert processes. The effects
noted may exist not in his search behavior but in his reporting
behavior. The planning schemes discussed by Dr. Hayes rest
primarily on this idea. The other explanation revolves around
a representation that does permit the subject to obtain some
global information—some information about direction.

It seems to me of great importance to discover which explanation is correct. In particular, most of our ideas about information processing in either men or machines make use of
representations that admit only local operations. We have a
chance here of determining experimentally what sort of representation is used by a human subject. The answer will be fascinating and significant whichever way it turns out. I assume, of
course, that one would not be content simply to demonstrate
that some nonlocal information was being used, but would press
on to determine the nature of this representation and the information processes that encode and decode it.

Such a concern leads in the direction not of more complex
tasks but of more ingenious experimental arrangements to settle

the issue. Can one "mark" the next to the last word in the solution, so that it can be detected even when the subject processes
it covertly? Then one might detect when he is working back-
wards. What is known about the global structure of the graph
after memorization of the list but before the task is given (or
within seconds afterwards)? What sort of answers do we get
to the question "Is K between X and Q?" asked immediately
upon giving the task? Such a concern also leads in the direction
of trying to invent additional representations and to the study
of their properties under various strategies of processing.

In summary, I hope that my lengthy discussion of Dr.
Hayes' task communicates my feeling that it is not only fun but
fruitful, and that my obvious inclination to try to affect the
course of his further work with it indicates that I think it provocative.

8

ISRAEL GOLDIAMOND*
Institute for Behavioral Research[†]

Perception, Language, and Conceptualization Rules[‡]

The type of problem solving we shall consider is that in which the task is to find the commonality in a group of disparate situations, or the rule for classifying a particular situation as a member of a specified set of situations. For example, a set of pictures is presented serially, and the viewer is asked to indicate what they have in common. If words are not to be used, either according to the design or because S is nonverbal, he

*Written under Research Career Development Award, National Institute of Mental Health, 1963-1968, K3-MH19430-03 at IBR. Also on appointment as professor of psychology, Arizona State University, Tempe.

[†]Mailing address: 2426 Linden Lane, Silver Spring, Maryland, 20910.

[‡]The animal research reported is being performed under grant NsG-450, National Aeronautical and Space Administration. The research in pigeon ratio perception was performed under contract DA-49-193-MD-2288 with the Office of the Surgeon General.

The research in human concept formation is being performed under the Office of the Surgeon General contracts DA-49-193-MD-2448 with the Washington School of Psychiatry, and DA-49-193-MD-2638 with the Institute for Behavioral Research.

may have to choose from among grouped presentations, which
one follows (or does not follow) the rule—a complex discrimination task. Intelligence tests abound in such items. These
tasks are often called abstraction or conceptualization.

Analogy tests may be considered extensions of the same
basic problem. Here, there are two pairs of items, governed
by the same rule of relation. One pair and an element from the
second pair are presented. The subject's correct choice of the
missing element indicates operation according to the rule. The
items may be verbal, pictorial, or mathematical. The completion of verbal, pictorial, or mathematical progressions is yet
another extension.

These tasks have interest not only in their own right but
because of their traditional relation to perception, learning, and
language. It is upon this relation that we shall focus.

Abstraction and concept formation have been regarded as
extremely important in behavioral analysis and training, but
their importance has not in general been matched by the rigor
of the procedures used to study them. Perception and learning, however, have developed sophisticated methods of analysis
and control. A bridge between these two methodologically
sophisticated areas, on the one hand, and concept formation, on
the other, may make available a body of recently developed procedures which can be extended to the analysis and controlled
alteration of conceptual behaviors. A purpose of this discussion
is to consider some recent developments in learning and perception which may provide such methodological links.

The notion of a methodological link between learning-
perception and conceptualization is not new, of course. In

Gestalt psychology, for example, a schema for the analysis of perception was extended to the study of abstraction, cognition, and problem solving (Koffka, 1935). Verbal concepts and perceptual configurations were considered as imposing organization and structure upon perception and learning. In this regard, we have been bequeathed with such terms as *Einstellung* and *set*. In current perceptual research of a more mathematical nature, procedures that restrict response alternatives, and procedures that involve set theory, play similar roles in the analysis of perception and signal detection processes. In operant research, abstraction is being studied within the context of discriminative behavior, and procedures for controlled establishment and alteration of abstractions are being developed. In other systematic and eclectic branches of perceptual research, verbal instructions and other procedures for limiting response alternatives find constant use.

Although there is considerable historical support for such methodological linkage, there is also historical support for separation of research in perception and conceptualization, on the one hand, and discrimination and abstraction on the other. A critical difference seems to be the use of verbal behavior in human research and nonverbal behavior in animal research. This difference characterizes both the behavior of the E as well as the behavior of O. With regard to E's behavior, he gives verbal instructions to humans, but not to animals. Instructions telescope a long history of training which the training procedures used with animals often make explicit. Never having been allowed the luxury of simply verbalizing to the animal what he is to do, investigators in this area have devel-

oped procedures for control and analysis of behavior of great
power and promise. With regard to the behavior of O, verbal
responses are made by humans, whereas other behaviors are
the dependent variables when animals are used. The range of
alternative buttons, levers, and similar manipulanda is more
greatly restricted than the alternatives available when words
are used, and the nonverbal situation accordingly does not seem
as complex, rich, or multivariate as the verbal case. Further,
button responses or red stimulus lights seem to be more capable of classification in physical and quantifiable terms than
words are when used either as responses or as stimuli. This
seems to be especially so when we are concerned with meaning
of words. Concepts seem to require verbal behavior, and the
animal literature has accordingly been overlooked or treated
as irrelevant, overly simplified, or overly dependent on inap-
plicable physical description.

We shall attempt to indicate during this discussion that
the control and analytical procedures developed for animals
precisely because we cannot verbally instruct them are quite
useful for the study of human concepts. They are useful not
simply as a method for control but as a method of studying
words themselves, with attention not merely to their rate or
form but to their meanings. Stated otherwise we can, using
these methods, readily treat meaning as a dimension. We can
control it, shape it, teach it, and study it. At the same time, in
a kind of reverse lend-lease, we can ask of the animal experiment, which does not use instructions, just where the instructions are. The answers may be of interest.

LOGICAL AND METHODOLOGICAL COMMONALITIES

We shall open our discussion with a consideration of perception, called discrimination when animals are O's. We shall
attempt to develop what can be considered a trivial (in the logical sense) relation between perceptual research and conceptual
research of the abstracting type.

Perception is often defined by a matching operation. In
the adjusting procedures, we ask O to adjust one stimulus so
that it matches another. Or we may ask O to match a color by
picking a color chip from a collection of chips stored in an Ost-
wald book. Such selection from a literal storage of chips is
analogized to retrieval processes by information theorists when
a word is used as a match in a descriptive naming of the color.
The matching notion is so embedded in perceptual theory that
even in the absolute methods, where the stimulus to be matched
is not presented, it is often assumed that a match is being made
with a criterion. The criterion may be located inside O's head,
or may simply be part of a theoretical model, as in signal detection research (Swets, Tanner, and Birdsall, 1961). It can be
argued that oddity problems (analogous to forced-choice procedures in detection research), or the extended oddity problems
of color blindness tests, also involve categorization on the basis
of matching and nonmatching.

An animal implementation of the matching definition of
perception is, of course, the method appropriately named "matching to sample" (Skinner, 1950). Here, there may be a linear array
of three keys. The outer two are unilluminated as indicated in
Line 1 of Fig. 1 in the upper set. This is called the sample. In

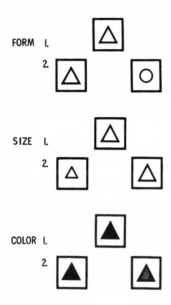

Fig. 1: End states of a match to sample procedure, where selection of the appropriate match defines different types of perception or discrimination.

more conventional perceptual language, it is the standard. The pigeon pecks the key, or the child touches it or a button corresponding to it, and the light may go out, simultaneously illuminating the two outer keys, as in Line 2. These are the matching stimuli or the comparison stimuli of classical psychophysics.

Our present discussion will be limited to end states, that is, the product of considerable training. The training procedures themselves will be discussed separately.

If O comes to respond constantly to the triangle, no matter what its position, size, color, and so on, we say that he has matched the sample, or that he is engaging in form discrimination. Similarly, we may talk of size discrimination for the middle set in the figure, or color discrimination for the lower set, and so on.

The sample or standard may be presented concurrently with the matches or comparison stimuli, or we can impose a time delay between the termination of the standard and the onset of the comparison stimuli (Blough, 1959; Berryman, Cumming, and Nevin, 1963), and may thereby study memory qua memory, or relate it to perceptual variables. We need not restrict ourselves to two comparison stimuli. We can use only two keys, and have the standard switch position. In research we are currently undertaking, there are twelve comparison stimuli in a row, ranging in a spectrum from violet to red, giving the pigeon a rather large vocabulary of color responses. The standard is an afterimage and the appropriate match will tell us about pigeon Purkinje perception, or that of other animals once we develop the procedures. An adjusting procedure may also be used, in which the pigeon in the Pelican continually alters the comparison stimulus to match a standard (Skinner, 1960). In a recent experiment (Pliskoff and Goldiamond, 1965), pecking a red key turned it off, simultaneously illuminating two white keys. If the red key went off after five pecks, the left white key produced food; but if it went off after 95 pecks, the right white key produced food. The ratios were then altered in stages to 25:75, 35:65, 40:60, 42:58, and 50:50. The pigeon was discriminating his own ratio, a form of self-perception. As this experiment suggests, the matching-to-sample procedure readily lends itself to research in the theory of signal detection, since O can make two types of errors (pecking L when R correct, or R when L correct) and be correct in two ways (L when L and R when R). This is formally similar to responding Yes or No when signal-plus-noise or noise alone is

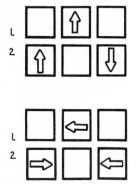

Fig. 2: A more complex match to sample. The *O* must match (Row 2) the sample (Row 1).

presented, a classical psychophysical situation, represented by instructions such as: Say Yes if you heard the tone, etc. By attaching different consequences or payoffs to the four possibilities entered into a 2 × 2 decision matrix (LR, LL/RR, RL), detection rate can be affected in accord with signal detection theory (Goldiamond, 1965*b*). In all events, the matching procedure can be extended considerably beyond its original literal match.

A more complex perception task than those of the preceding figures is presented in Fig. 2. Here, again, we are discussing only the terminal state, and perception of the arrow which is pointing upright will be indicated by a match, perception of the arrow which is pointing left by another, and so on, as we alter the direction of the arrow in each sample.

Quite a different situation is presented in Fig. 3, in which there is no literal match. In the first series, the correct response is the arrow on the right. In the second series, the correct response is the arrow on the left. If we presented more of these, you would get the rule, namely, select the one which is rotated −90°. This experiment would not be considered a perception ex-

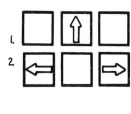

Fig. 3: Match to sample used to analyze concept formation.

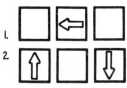

periment, but falls more closely into the range of concept experiments. If O finally performs accurately, we would probably
not discuss perception, but would state that O had learned the
rule, or had formed the appropriate concept. The rule can be
expressed in words, but I think that an animal might be taught
to perform according to the rule by procedures which we will
discuss later.

This situation seems to differ from the perceptual match
to sample, in that a rule *mediates* between the standard and the
comparison stimulus, and conceptualization might be concerned
with such mediating rules. Does perceptual matching lack such
rules? In concept research of the kind discussed, we might
have mediating transformations of 90°, or 45°, or of an infinite
variety. The perceptual case might be characterized as the
case where the transformation is zero. Accordingly we might
define the perceptual match as a limiting case of a conceptual
experiment, where the rule for selection is one of zero trans-

form from the standard.* Rather than stating that concepts develop out of percepts, we might with equanimity state that perceptual matches are limiting cases of concepts.

If we wish to teach a child the appropriate behavior in the
concept case just cited, we might tell him the rule immediately.
We might thereby bring his behavior under the immediate control of the rule as we do when we tell the driver to make necessary adjustments when the indicator moves into a certain range.
Or we may simplify the task considerably, and tell the driver to
get gasoline when the fuel light registers red. With regard to an
animal, we would have to develop special procedures to establish control of his behavior by such a rule. As a matter of fact,
by virtue of the fact that we do not know his language, we must
use special procedures even in the limiting case where the rule

---

*The zero transformation noted is only along the dimension of
the rule, to be discussed later, since the standard and comparison
stimuli are two different stimuli.

The zero transformation which defines a match along some dimension, specified by a rule or abstraction, need not be in physical
terms. In many perceptual oddity problems it is, as when a group of
stimuli which match each other is presented, along with one which does
not share the abstraction. An example is 0 0 o 0. Selection of the
nonmatch implies a match among the others, or abstraction, or zero
transformation, according to a rule of size. However, in the oddity
presentation 5 7 6 X, the abstraction is Arabic numerals, and in Mary,
Bill, Jane, Edna, it is sex name. Such extension is discussed later in
this paper, but these oddity problems may be classified as sharing with
certain types of perception a zero transformation along a dimension.
In some *analogies*, the task is to match *rules*, a higher order match, or
zero transformation, so to speak. For example, P:p::Q(p,q,r,Q) involves
abstracting, of all the possible relations between P:p the capital-lower
case one, since this is the only rule matching a rule relating Q with any
of the choices. In the case of P:R::C(B,G,S,R), homophonic relation between Cyrillic and Latin alphabets is involved (S is correct), and for
P:r::C(R,S,s,r), the further relation of capital-lower case is added. A
metric for analysis is presented later in the discussion.

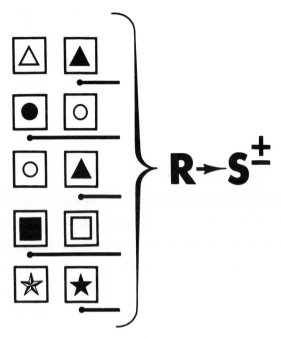

Fig. 4: An example of abstraction. The red figure is always chosen because it was differentially reinforced.

is of zero transformation, that is, in perceptual matching research, or where abstraction is involved.

A hypothetical end state in which pairs of stimuli are presented to an animal, who always responds to red, is presented in Fig. 4. The terminal behaviors were produced by a program of presentations, each involving differential reinforcement of red and nonred. The O was reinforced when he responded to the red presentation, regardless of its shape, position, and so on, and was not reinforced when he responded to a presentation of a different color. If the type of discrimination represented continues through all possible variations, we would state that the animal had *abstracted* the rule, namely, Respond to red (Holland and Skinner, 1961). We might even say he remembered red, or was matching the stimuli to an implicit standard. An explicit match would, of course, involve the match-to-sample procedure. Here, the rule of zero transform would be, Select the one with zero color transform, and if the color of the sample to be matched always changed, we might make statements beyond the abstraction of red; we could assess the color vision of the animal. In the human case, where we wish to assess color vision, we may tell O simply to respond to color. Or we may instruct him to move his finger or his eyes along the circles or a similar color, and to name the form or figure so described.

In the human case, we have given the human the instruction; when we state that the animal has abstracted, we are stating that the animal has learned or has induced the instruction. In this simple case, the instruction or rule for operation is distinguished from the abstraction or concept by whether it is taught before the training session, or emerges after, and as a result of, the training session. Otherwise, they seem to be identical. The difference seems to be in the training procedure whereby we put the organism under the control of this rule. Where human O's are used, and we wish to establish initial control by the rule, we can, of course, use words, although we need not do so. If we wish O to "find out for himself," or wish to have the concept "emerge," we may use the animal training procedures.

The rule can be an exceedingly complex one that cannot be defined in terms of simple stimulus dimensions. For example, Herrnstein and Loveland (1964) have recently demonstrated that a pigeon may be taught to abstract in terms of the rule, Human versus nonhuman, responding differentially to slides containing and not containing people. The people on the slides differed in size, race, number, state of dress, and so on. Among the mistakes the pigeons made was to classify a house with an active chimney as people, but not when there was no smoke emerging. The rapidity with which the pigeons picked up the discrimination suggested to the authors that they had taught them the specifics of the experimental situation, namely, how to respond to the apparatus, when to respond, and so on, rather than teaching the pigeons the concept. They felt the pigeons already had the concept of people when they started the experiment. In terms of the present discussion, we would state that what the pigeons had learned was the rule which they were to apply to the task of selecting correctly from among the slides (or getting food for their selections), rather than being taught that people were significant parts of their environment.

A more formal statement is presented in Fig. 5, which can be considered the operant or instrumental paradigm. The terms are given operant designations, but the elements are familiar to students of instrumental behavior. Reading across the main line, we have S^D/S^Δ, the discriminative stimuli in whose presence behavior is reinforced (S^D) or not reinforced (S^Δ), as exemplified by red and nonred presentations in the example cited in Fig. 4. The response is designated by R. The designation $S^\pm$ refers to the consequences which maintain or attenuate behavior by being contingent upon it, such as reinforcing stimuli, aversive stimuli, and extinction. The maintaining or attenuative properties of these stimuli can be manipulated by certain variables designated DV,

or deprivation variables; food deprivation may make food an effective reinforcer.* The experimental constraints, which when
altered produce the disruption of the behavior pattern hitherto
established and attributed to stimulus change or novel stimuli,
are represented as the constant stimuli, designated SS^c. In instrumental experiments, the major variables are referred to as

---

*The paradigm can be used both to provide functional definitions
and to suggest procedures. Stimuli which are topographically similar
can have different effects upon behavior, depending on their relation to
the paradigm (Azrin, 1958). A book, for example, can be an S^D, when it
occasions studying to which consequences are attached. It can be an
S^R when it is given as a prize, contingent on behavior, or when understanding it becomes contingent on studying. It can be a DV, that is, can
make some consequence effective in its maintenance of behavior.

A term such as motivation can refer to any of the entries in the
paradigm. This is exemplified by the following four statements, each
describing the behavior of a child "motivated by hunger":

(1) Definition by variables which make a consequence effective:
    He has been deprived of food (or with water, has been so de-
    prived, or kept in the sun, etc.). Hence the mother who says
    to her child: "You haven't eaten all day; you must be hungry."
(2) Definition by behavior: Those behaviors which have in the
    past produced food are now at a high level. Hence, the moth-
    er's statement to her child: "How come you keep taking
    apples? You just ate."
(3) Definition by a consequence itself: Food will serve to rein-
    force behaviors hitherto unrelated to it. Hence, the mother's
    statement: "You're hungry? Go make your bed first, then I'll
    give you food."
(4) Definition by discriminative stimuli: Stimuli in whose presence
    behavior has produced food are now quite potent in occasioning
    that behavior. The refrigerator and the cookie jar seem to
    control behavior; the child can't let them alone.

Such translation of motivation into observable relation may not
only allow us to deal with the classical phenomena of motivation and
meaning (where the meaning of a behavior is defined by its consequences)
but to focus on explicitly stated and manipulable variables (Goldiamond,
Dyrud, and Miller, 1965).

THE OPERANT-INSTRUMENTAL PARADIGM: SIMPLE

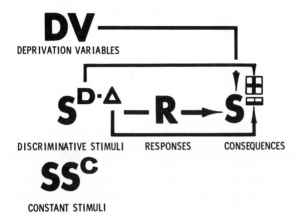

Fig. 5: The major variables governing
simple operant or instrumental behavior.

cue, response, reinforcement, and drive (Dollard and Miller,
1950). Figure 6 represents a simplification of this paradigm, in
which we are dealing only with the main line, namely, the discriminative stimuli, the behavior, and two differential consequences.

THE OPERANT-INSTRUMENTAL PARADIGM: SIMPLIFIED

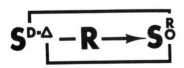

Fig. 6: An oversimplification of the
operant-instrumental paradigm. The
discriminative stimulus is defined by
reinforcement of behavior in its presence. The other variables have been
omitted.

THE OPERANT-INSTRUMENTAL PARADIGM: SIMPLIFIED PERCEPTUAL

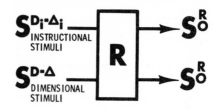

Fig. 7: An oversimplified paradigm for
perceptual, discriminative, or concept research. Note the two classes of discriminative stimuli. In some research, the two
consequences may be combined into a single
one. The other variables have been omitted.

We have complicated this paradigm by presenting the
paradigm for perceptual or conceptual research in Fig. 7.
Here, it will be observed that two different sets of discriminative stimuli are controlling the behavior. One class of discriminative stimuli is the instructional stimuli. These serve
to restrict the response alternatives to the dimension along
which the experimenter presents his other discriminative
stimuli, which we shall call the dimensional stimuli. For example, in an airplane recognition test, slides are projected
containing different planes. The O may respond to them by referring to their size, or color, or seating capacity. The experimenter is concerned with their military identification. Accordingly, he may say, Name the airplane I am about to present.
The airplane is then presented and the subject says, Mig, rather
than, How big. In color experiments, the instructional stimuli
may be, Name the color I shall flash. The O then reports the

color presented. Both sets of stimuli are discriminative stimuli. Stated otherwise, they owe their control over behavior to the fact that differential consequences are systematically attached to differences between them. Such control by instructional stimuli is exemplified by the military adage, "Never give an order you are not prepared to back up." In an experiment by Ayllon and Azrin (1964), mental hospital patients were differentially reinforced with ice cream for picking up utensils on a cafeteria line. The behavior was not appreciably altered thereby. They were then given instructions, but without consequences attached. There was a sharp rise in the desired behavior on the first day, which was then followed by a drop to the status quo ante. However, when differential consequences were attached to following or not following the instructions, the instructions exerted good control over the behavior.

The paradigm just given is similar to that used in animal discrimination research, or human concept research, formally presented in Fig. 8. Here, a complex set of procedures is utilized, in which only the discriminative stimuli are varied, along with systematically related differential reinforcement. After a while, the animal may come to respond to the stimuli only in terms of certain of their properties, as evidenced by his choice of stimuli containing elements in the appropriate set, over those which do not. Stated otherwise, his responses now come under the control of instructional stimuli which the experimenter never built in explicitly (to the animal), but intertwined into his program. When we state that the animal has developed an abstraction, we are stating that he is behaving as if he has imposed upon himself a set of instructional stimuli, which

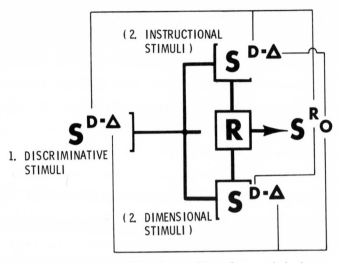

Fig. 8: An oversimplified paradigm for certain types
of human concept and animal discrimination research.
Here, discriminative stimuli differing simultaneously
along many dimensions (1), for example, color, form,
brightness, position, are initially presented, with responses reinforced only to certain of them. After a
while, discrimination along only a specific dimension
may occur, as evidenced by choice of the stimulus
containing an element along that dimension. Responding along the dimension may be considered abstraction, conceptualization, or instructional control (2),
and control by the stimulus adhering to the rule in
each presentation as dimensional control (2).

now govern the dimensions along which he will respond with regard to the dimensional stimuli. He has, so to speak, given himself an *Einstellung*. In the animal perception or human concept
formation paradigm, we also have a single consequence contingent upon behavior in the presence of both S^D's, rather than
to have each S^D control behavior through a separate reinforcement.

Explicit separation of instructional from dimensional stim-

uli in animal research occurs in research in conditional discrimination.

Conceptualization has been related to verbal vehavior, and
the relationship would appear to be reiterated by Skinner's (1957)
analysis of verbal behavior. In these terms, the instructional
stimulus is a *mand,* and when O comes under its control by responding differentially to the dimensional discriminative stimuli,
he is *tacting.* The analysis suggests an interesting relationship
between verbal behavior and perception, as well.

An example of the emergence of appropriate instructional
control and its relation to differential reinforcement is provided
by an experiment by the author. Human O's were run through a
psychophysical, two-choice, forced-choice task. A triangle was
presented in either a left or right window, at varying intensities,
ranging from fully invisible to fully visible, with O required to
respond L or R. A constant method was used, with intensities
randomized. Classical psychophysical curves relating intensity
and accuracy were obtained. After a rest, O was given a ques-
tionnaire soliciting his views on extra-sensory perception. He
was then instructed that when the two windows lit up, E was
thinking of a triangle L or R, and O was to stare into the windows, then press L or R, depending upon his contact with E's
thoughts, guessing if necessary. If his extra-sensory perception was accurate, the illumination in the windows would immediately go out. If it was inaccurate, nothing would happen,
and he was to correct himself. A triangle was always projected
into window L or R, that being the correct window. An ascending Method of Limits was used, with the initial signal-noise

ratio (triangle to window illumination) zero, followed by a descending method.

In the ascending procedure, many of the O's displayed
typical "insight" curves. There was an initial and prolonged
period of chance responding, followed by a sharp inflection to
almost perfect, then perfect accuracy. In the ascending procedure, as the triangle became increasingly brighter, it became more visible, but did not systematically control accuracy.
However, as it became more visible, the relationship between
its position and reinforcement (accuracy, in this case) also became clearer. Eventually, the relationship would become controlling. This would occur at a high intensity presentation,
which would also control a high rate of detection, hence the
sharp inflection in the curve. Stated otherwise, detection was
contingent upon two separate properties of stimulus intensity.
One involved detection rate as a function of signal-noise ratio, and
the other involved substitution of instructional control to respond
to the triangle, systematically related to differential reinforcement, for instructional control by E.S.P. instructions which
were not so related. Detection rate was contingent upon prior
establishment of appropriate (to reinforcement) instructional
control, which developed through the establishment of a relationship between differential reinforcement and increasing
signal presentations.

On the descending curve, the psychophysical curves obtained during the session preceding the E.S.P. session were re-
obtained, since there was control by the same instructional
stimuli. In the E.S.P. experiment, such control emerged during
the experiment, but in the previous psychophysical experiment,
it was established through instructions given prior to the pres-

entations. The difference between the ascending and descending E.S.P. curves reflected differences in detection which were functionally related to differences in instructional control. That "insight" curves were obtained, with an occasional "Ahah," suggests that the Ahah phenomenon in perceptual research may be considered in terms of instructional rather than (or as well as) discriminative insights. Curves with such inflections are often obtained mathematically when two separate functions are involved, and the insight literature might be considered in these terms.

One O, incidentally, became steadily worse as the signal-noise ratio increased, scoring perfect zero detection (rather than the 50 per cent of chance) at the highest intensities. He reached the nadir of perfection, and on the descending curve gradually returned to chance. He gave no explanation of his behavior. There was no evidence of E.S.P. One O with an anomalous record informed me afterwards that the Orient had far more wisdom in occult matters than the Occident, and when he had heard that the experiment was on E.S.P., "I leaned back in my chair, put my fingers on the keys, and closed my eyes." He told me that he had performed extraordinarily well. The anomaly in his record which occasioned this conversation was that he had scored pure chance.

Most animal discrimination experiments are typified by intermingling of instructional and dimensional stimuli. That they are not separated in such research has suggested to some human investigators that rigorous (i.e., animal-like) research with humans requires dispensing with instructions, and that instructions should not be used to shape human be-

havior. Rather, the intermingled stimuli should be applied directly. This point of view has been justly criticized by Bandura
(1962). Indeed, the Ayllon and Azrin study mentioned indicated
not only that instructions were discriminative stimuli, that is,
they required differential reinforcement for their control, but
that the simple use of differential reinforcement alone was not
effective in the time period studied. In other words, words can
save a lot of time and effort. The methodological kinship between perception, learning, concept formation, and verbal behavior suggests that procedures developed for rigorous analysis
in one area can be extended to the other.

If instructional and dimensional stimuli are intertwined
in animal research, they are often confused in human research.
In hypnotic research, for example, telling O that he is to see
red roses when yellow ones are presented has resulted in
systematic changes with regard to other colors reported (Goldiamond and Malpass, 1958). For example, yellow was not only
responded to as red, but orange as a deeper red, and so on.
There *was* a systematic relation between dimensional stimuli
and behavior, which we describe as stimulus control. The behaviors are seldom random. Rather than suggesting that a perceptual shift has occurred because of hypnotic instructions, the
data are more readily explainable in terms of a shift in the instructional stimuli, hence the stimulus control (the dimensional
stimuli are still punctiliously controlling behavior), and hence
its anomalous nature (the instructional stimuli have shifted from
their usual control). The development of size constancy may be
another case in point. I recall disputing a statement made by a
child psychologist that three-year-old children do not have size

constancy. As evidence, he cited his daughter, who referred to a distant chimney as being two fingers high, whereas I gave it 24-30 inches. When he next brought his daughter around, I asked: "If Santa Claus was carrying so much that he couldn't climb into that chimney when he landed on the roof, what would you put there so that he could just step into the chimney?" She pointed to a table of the appropriate height. This is not intended to settle the nativist-empirist controversy in this area, but rather to suggest that much of our perceptual developmental data may not necessarily involve development of perception with age, but rather, the control of instructional S^D's in an increasingly adult direction, since exposure to the differential reinforcements dispensed by the adult world increases with age. Data to this effect appear to exist with regard to persistence of global statements and perceptions by mentally retarded children, who are behaviorally segregated from their environment, and may thereby be removed from this shaping process (Goldiamond, 1959). Both size constancy and its absence could probably be demonstrated for animals under conditional discrimination procedures, where a red light might serve as the instructional S^D for matches which are size constant (they are reinforced when the red light is on), and a green light might serve as the instructional S^D for matches which are not size constant, that is, are made to the retinal image. Other perceptual anomalies discovered in the clinic, especially in aphasia, may stand scrutiny in terms of the present discussion; as might the literature on response bias and perception (Goldiamond, 1958, 1962, 1964*a*).

PROCEDURES FOR TRAINING AND ANALYSIS

As was suggested earlier, the response in a perceptual-conceptual experiment is under the joint control of both instructional and dimensional discriminative stimuli. A major difference between human perception experiments and human concept experiments is that in the perception experiments, control by the instructional discriminative stimuli is established first in order to obtain control by the dimensional discriminative stimuli, but in the concept experiment, control by the instructional discriminative stimuli emerges during the experiment. It may be made manifest by the dimensional control appropriate to it. Since many animal discrimination experiments are of this type, it would appear that such experiments are more closely related in procedure to human concept experiments than they are to human perception experiments. This relationship is possibly occluded by the fact that many human concept experiments end with the verbal naming of the concept found. If, instead, other operation by O is required to demonstrate the acquisition of the concept (that is, acquisition of control by the instructional stimuli), as in the transposition tasks, the human concept experiment is procedurally identical to many animal discrimination experiments. Be this as it may, a consequence that emerges from this analysis is that some promising procedures recently developed in the animal discrimination laboratory may be profitably extended to human concept research and training.* These

---

*Two other consequences which merit mention are, of course, the extension of animal laboratory procedures to human perceptual research, and the reverse, possibly strengthening a field legitimately

animal discrimination procedures, incidentally, are to a large
extent derived from human programmed instruction (which is
certainly not divorced from verbal concept training). This in
turn is related to basic animal research involving the Method
of Successive Approximations. Such an interplay between basic
and applied research has, of course, characterized disciplines
other than psychology (See Ref. Goldiamond, Dyrud, and Miller, 1965).

In the Method of Successive Approximations, or *shaping*,
an animal's behavior is gradually changed from some initial
behavior to a specified terminal behavior. The *E* starts with
the behaviors that exist, and when some cluster of behaviors
contains an element in the direction toward the criterion, he
reinforces. As the name of the method suggests, the cluster
may now contain behavior closer to the criterion, and there is
further reinforcement. Within a few minutes, every pigeon, who
normally pecks on the ground, is converted into a woodpecker,
standing erect and pecking at a high disk (in which case the pro-

---

called animal perception, as opposed to animal discrimination.

The field of experimental animal perception cannot presently be
considered in detail, but its nature can be suggested. Suppose in a conditional discrimination experiment, size is the dimensional S^D. When
the light is red, the appropriate size match is retinal, but when the
light is green, the appropriate size match is of size constancy. In a
second experiment, colors are the dimensional S^D. When the light is
red, the appropriate color match is "retinal" (purple snow is matched
by purple), but when it is green, the appropriate match is the constancy
(purple snow is matched by white). In a third experiment, forms are
the dimensional S^D. When the light is red, the appropriate form match
is "retinal" (a rectangle in perspective is matched by a trapezoid), but
when it is green the constancy match is made (the rectangle is matched
by a rectangle). If red then generalizes to control "retinal" matches
and green to constancy matches in other areas, we are discussing one
form of animal perception research.

gram can now be automatically controlled through a relay rack). In programmed instruction, a similar logic is followed. The program starts with stimuli, the correct behavior to which is in the organism's repertoire. The E introduces new elements into the stimulus cluster which, with each frame, alter the set controlling O's correct behavior. The behavior is presumably maintained by the reinforcement of behavior the preceding set occasions, and by the similarity of the new set to the preceding one. Eventually, a totally new set of stimuli, the terminal set, may control correct behavior. The procedure whereby control of behavior is transferred from one set to another is called *fading*, presumably since elements in the old set are faded out as elements in the new set are faded in.*   In both shaping and fading, the learner sets the response pace (procedures exist to alter rate), but since in fading it is E who directly sets up the stimulus packet, whereas in shaping it is O who sets up the response packet, fading seems capable of greater experiment control.[†]

Recently, Terrace (1963*a*, *b*) has developed procedures which extend fading to basic research in animal discrimination. It is normally very difficult to get pigeons to discriminate be-

---

*Both shaping and fading may be described in terms of set theory, where the behaviors, stimuli, or functional relations between the two are conceptualized as a set of vectors in n-space. If one of the vector elements is in the direction and on the dimension desired, the entire set is reinforced, and otherwise not. This may alter the elements or their distribution in the set, and further differential reinforcements continue the shift.

†The precaution is necessary since in a functional definition of stimuli, their relation to behavior defines them, rather than their topographic definition. In common language, O's interpretation of the stimulus may define it, and an interpretation is behavior.

tween fat horizontal bars and fat vertical ones, and may take thousands of trials. Control by color difference is easier to establish, and the forms are embedded in different colors. The colors are gradually faded out, and control is transferred to the forms alone, in a relatively short time, and almost without error. What seemed to have been an almost impossible task has been made simple. These procedures have been extended to training preschool children in form discrimination (Moore and Goldiamond, 1964), to getting psychotics to speak with progressively more words (Sherman, 1965), to having stutterers speak in a new pattern of speech as the originally maintaining stimuli are withdrawn (Goldiamond, 1965c), among others. They are being systematically investigated and extended to control of animal and human discrimination by Sidman (1965)*.

*Although all fading procedures have in common the errorless transfer of control of behavior from one dimension to another, the dimensions faded out may differ widely, some examples being hue (Terrace), circularity (Sidman), brightness (Moore and Goldiamond) words (Sherman), verbal response-auditory feedback delay (Goldiamond). Similarly, the dimensions faded in differ. Procedurally, these all have the commonality stated, and a functional relation (law) can be made between the procedure and the results. It would, however, be interesting to note what else they have in common. Some interesting suggestions for research are supplied by other areas in which fading occurs. In learning to read, for example, the child's verbal response, controlled by printed material, may affect him the way that stimulus would when someone else produced it. Stated otherwise, hearing himself say the word may affect him the way hearing someone else say it does, and this dual feedback may be involved in reading with meaning (Goldiamond and Pliskoff, 1965a; cf. Staats and Staats, 1963; Skinner, 1957). There is, however, a progressive fading out of reading aloud, for those children who start this way. The voice is lowered, unvoiced lip movements occur, lip movements diminish, and, as Edfeldt (1960) indicates, appropriate muscle potentials are found for larynx and lips during silent reading, apparently being lower for more fluent than less fluent readers. This suggests a

Apparently, animal and human discrimination are being brought under the same precise operant control, using fading procedures, that has hitherto characterized such control of behavior, using shaping procedures. One occasionally hears the statement that operant investigators are merely technicians interested in demonstrating how they can control performance, and are not interested in basic learning processes. This statement raises two issues. One involves the fact that control can be used to validate a theory, as well as prediction. Since control also produces prediction, but prediction does not necessarily imply control, control is the more powerful way to validate one's theory (See Ref. Sidman, 1960). The second issue raised is that of the metric used. Many studies use as their dependent variable the number of trials to acquisition. This is related to other variables to assess their influence upon acquisition. Such research shares three properties with fading-shaping research. They both start out with some initial discrimination (or behavior, or both). They both wind up with a different terminal

continuation of fading out from such muscular feedback control, and transfer to textual control. To what extent eye movements, photochemistry, nerve, or brain are involved in such transfer would seem to be an interesting area for research here, as well as for the more general problem of fading.

Another example of fading may be in thinking and dreams. When S is asked to think of picking up an object, potential change has been reported along some of the muscles which would be involved if he actually picked it up. The potential is not as great, but neither is the image. Analogous data on REM periods in sleep have occasioned speculation on these points, which will not be materially extended here. Indeed, there is a considerable literature linking thoughts and *petites perceptions*, going as far back as Leibnitz (1765), at least. The fading method, however, does seem to provide a *procedure* for accomplishing the transfers, associations, and substitutions such speculations sought to *account for*.

discrimination (or b or b). They both differentially reinforce correct and incorrect responses. The difference between the trials-to-acquisition research and the fading-shaping research lies in what constitutes correctness, or what is differentially reinforced. In the trials-to-acquisition research only the terminally desired discrimination (or b or b) is reinforced. It is sink or swim at each trial. In shaping-fading procedures, there is a program of discriminations (bb), each differing from the preceding, and each likely to be reinforced, that is, to be correct. In both cases, the acquisition of control of behavior by instructional stimuli emerges during the experiment, but in one case the acquisition emerges without errors on the part of O, and in the other case with numerous errors; indeed, making errors has been considered integral to the learning process. Acquisition is involved in both cases. Both study the learning process, but the trials-to-acquisition research seems to confound learning with extinction processes. Generalizing from trials-to-acquisition data, Spence (1936) considers extinction necessary to certain types of learning. Indeed, in Krech's term, one hypothesis (instructional stimulus) after another is rejected (Krechevsky, 1938). Behavioral patterns may vary from one O to the next as different superstitious behaviors are inadvertently established or extinguished. There may be differing runs of extinction. Averaging becomes necessary. In all events, the fact that there exist two different types of programs, the sink-or-swim and approximation program, which mediate between initial and terminal behavior, suggests that the mediating program is an independent variable, and that much of the learning and discrimination theory which has

been extended to learning in general is based upon research in
which the program variable is set at a limiting value. No doubt
both programs represent learning situations encountered outside the laboratory. Their generality may be related to such
similarity. We suspect that the extended program occurs in
more cases than the other. Further implications are being considered elsewhere (Goldiamond and Pliskoff, 1965).

If the program mediating between initial and terminal behavior is to be treated as an independent variable, is there a
metric as readily available as trials-to-acquisition? Research
of this type is not well advanced enough to supply a definitive
answer, but two possibilities suggest themselves. One is the
minimal number of errorless steps required to bring about the
new control, which Terrace refers to as transfer across continua. This might be labeled the *difficulty* of the transfer, using
one fading procedure. The other might be the minimal number
of mediating programs required, which might be labeled the
complexity of the transfer, or the concept.

It will be recalled that in Fig. 3, the concept mediating between the sample and the match was, Rotate the arrow −90°. A
possible procedure for errorless establishment of such control
is offered in Fig. 9. The upright arrow is in sample position in

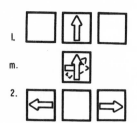

Fig. 9: Match to sample
used for concept research,
with the explicit mediating
variable either visual or
motor rotation (right).

Row 1. The child touches the sample, and it is entered in the mediating row. It then rotates −90°, and is also entered in Row 2, the matching row. The child then makes the match. Other sample arrows in different positions are then presented, with similar mediation. The mediating row may then be faded out, and conceivably the match will be made in its absence. Is stimulus mediation or response mediation involved? We have added a knob for the child to turn. Each movement of the knob produces a rotated mediating figure. Whether it is stimulus or response mediation or both should be ascertainable by these procedures, for which we have constructed equipment at our laboratory, and hope to experiment with it.

If difficulty is defined by the number of fading steps required, complexity may be defined by the number of different mediations. In Fig. 10, the wedge on the left is the correct match to the sample. This may require a mediating step of rotation, as before, and then an additional mediating step in which the arrow turns into a wedge. Finally, there is the perceptual match. This

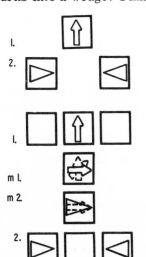

Fig. 10: A more complex concept, involving two explicit mediating steps, one of rotation, and the second of form transformation.

Fig. 11: Topographically different stimuli classified in the same functional class ("meaning"), since in the presence of any, the same behavior will be reinforced.

is a more complex concept than the preceding.

These illustrations are not intended to exemplify actual procedures, since these can at the present be developed only empirically. Rather, they are intended to suggest a framework in which complex concepts might be handled, and in which mediation and mediating rules might be made explicit. Nor is the match to sample the only procedure. Sidman (1965), working with mental retardates, has used an oddity procedure with twelve disks arranged in a circle and one of the figures differing from the others. Several rules were required to switch from one discrimination to another, and one type of fading produced different results from another, for the same concept.

Can these procedures be utilized for meaning of words? Words such as girl, jill, dame, broad may be in the same stimulus class, since the same behavior of looking when called may result in the same consequence. But this is not confined to words alone. Visual images serve the same function, as indicated in Fig. 11. Here, the images are in the same stimulus class. The concept, or the rule for inclusion in this class, is that the behavior of stopping is reinforced. The figure also serves to illustrate the difference between a functional and topographic analysis of stimuli. Topographically, it is difficult to classify these stimuli as similar. Their functional relation to behavior, as S^D's controlling the same behavior, puts them into the same functional operant class. Conversely, Azrin (1958) has indicated that topographically similar noises can have totally different effects upon behavior if they are S^D's related to different consequences, or constant stimuli, or consequences themselves. The abstraction depicted in this illustration is analogous to the pigeon situation described earlier, where people differing in size, shape, number, and race were responded to identically.

Establishment of a rule that has no nonhuman analogy but follows from the animal laboratory is indicated in Fig. 12. This experiment has been run by me with an N of over 2,000, individually, in small groups, and in large lecture halls (Goldiamond, 1964b). The O's are told to imagine that they are pigeons, and are to circle the A or B on their paper. A show of hands is called for, and B is announced as correct. The procedure is

I. A	B	10. DAISY MAE	LI'L ABNER
2. B	D	II. ROBERT	MAY
		12. ANNETTE	BOB
3. B	Q	13. BOY	GIRL
4. 0	B	14. SONNY BOY	BETTY ANN
5. JB	AQ	15. BRUCE	BETSY
6. URB	VOX	16. EDNA	WILLIAM
7. BULL	COW	17. LOUISE	GEORGE
8. SOW	BOAR	18. EDWARD	RACHEL
9. BUSTER	NANCY	19. JOHN	ROBERTA

Fig. 12: Sequence used to demonstrate fading to control of behavior by a dimension of meaning. The subject is instructed to read the words from pair 7 on.

then followed for the other pairs. It will be noted that in Presentations 7-13, the B is also embedded in a male animal or
name. At 14 and 15, the discriminative property of the B is
faded out, and control is faded to the male name alone. At
19, the B is rejected. Operant control has been established in
which *meaning* is the rule, and defines the operant class, with
generalization occurring along it. It would seem that this
paradigm may be quite useful in the study of verbal behavior.
The errors of O as control of his behavior is transferred from
one meaning to another might be a dependent variable relatable
to other variables. Ozier and I are currently studying rhyming
by aphasics in this manner. Our population of two have both
broken down at the same rhyme, and the program, the independent variable, is being altered to keep O correct. For a
normal O, or an aphasic at a better state of recovery, these
extra steps would not be necessary. The number of steps

necessary for maintenance of errorless behavior may thus be a meaningful variable.

In all events, these procedures demonstrate that word meaning can be treated as a dimension, and programmed errorlessly, using the perceptual procedures developed with stimuli classifiable in physical terms. We have considered perception in terms of matching rules, and the analysis suggests that the rules involved in analogies may be similarly programmed. In analogy tests two constructs are related by some rule whose identification through a match is O's task. That analogies may also be pictorial reiterates the relationship between perception, language, and conceptualization we have been discussing. The advantage of this relationship is that it allows us to use procedures developed in one area to investigate and program the others, including meaningful and logical rules.

OTHER LANGUAGES

Up to the present century, our primary method of storing information, and therefore of imparting it, was through the written word. An extreme example of the equation of knowledge with words is the statement: If you can't put it into words, you don't know what you're talking about. On the other hand, the radiologist examining X-Ray plates is often hard put to define the basis of his diagnosis. Verhave (1959) trained pigeons in quality control of good and bad pills for a drug house. The women at the end of the assembly line could not verbally define their bases for selection, but could select reliably. The pills they accepted were S^D to the pigeon, and the pills they rejected were S^Δ.

Stated otherwise, differential consequences were attached to
pecking at a disk when a pill previously classified as good by
the women appeared, as opposed to such behavior when a pill
classified bad appeared. The pigeons rapidly learned the
women's classificatory system. Incidentally, the procedure was
turned down by the Board of Directors, presumably because of
the effects on public relations of a box marked: Inspected by
Pigeon 205.

In our current research with psychiatrists, in which we
are concerned with a behavioral analysis of psychotherapeutic
transactions, we have noted the interplay between verbal and
nonverbal communications.* Words can be multiple S^D's as
well as maintaining (or aversive) stimuli, constant stimuli,
other variables, and multiply-determined responses. They can
be entered anywhere in the operant paradigm. They can be
used to shape discriminative behavior. They can be faded to
produce the emergence of implicit instructional control by concepts the patient may not verbalize. Simultaneously, gestures
and nuances in tone and expression enter, as well as the ther-
apist's own reactions. It has been argued that all this must be
put into words, but as the experience of the radiologist suggests, and as Verhave's more mundane pigeons indicate, it is

*Psychotherapy research being performed under contracts DA-
49-193-MD-2628, "Behavioral procedures in psychiatric practice," Jarl
Dyrud, M.D., principal investigator, Israel Goldiamond, Ph.D., and
Miles D. Miller, M.D., co-investigators; and DA-49-193-MD-2448,
"Study of interviews (therapeutic and interrogative) by operant condi-
tioning methods," Israel Goldiamond, Ph.D., principal investigator, Jarl
Dyrud, M.D., and Miles D. Miller, M.D., co-investigators. See acknow-
ledgement in Footnote ‡, p. 183.

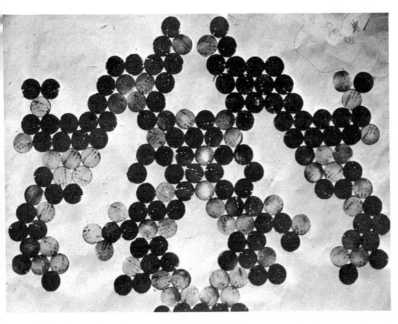

Fig. 13: Use of corks to establish mathematical abstractions. (Courtesy of H. L. Cohen.)

not necessary to be able to classify in words in order to com-municate and train in similar abstractions and rules.

An example of shaping along complex academic concepts which are not readily stated in words, is provided by Cohen, et al. (1964), who report a special program for college freshmen in the lowest third of their graduating high-school class. They would normally not have been admitted in the university system of their state. Among their exercises was to apply a bottle cork to a stamp pad, and then stamp out corks tangent to each other in various patterns. An example of one student's work is indicated in Fig. 13. Exercises were made of abstracting the evident con-

Fig. 14: Use of ping-pong balls to establish physical
abstractions. (Courtesy of H. L. Cohen.)

figurations and mathematical relations. The students were then
given ping-pong balls to glue together in related patterns. An example is presented in Fig. 14. Again, regularities are evident,
and further exercises were given. The students were then given
sticks and asked to imagine the ping-pong structures they had
made before and to connect the centers as indicated in Fig. 15.
When the course of study moved to vector analysis and physics,
many of the students had little trouble with the abstractions necessary for these.

R. Buckminster Fuller (1965) reports that a Nobel laureate

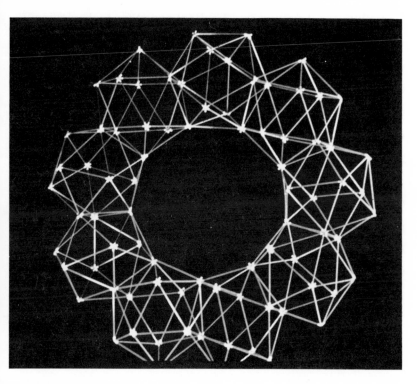

Fig. 15: Abstraction of vectors from ping-pong abstraction in preceding figure. (Courtesy of H. L. Cohen.)

in chemistry remarked of one of Fuller's structures, similar to those displayed, "Why that's the structure of the molecule I've been working with." Quite obviously, that is not the structure, but it is a useful model for it, that is to say, it is a reinforced rule or instructional S^D to set up dimensions for observations of chemical reactions. The chemist had come to this structure by having to tear down the verbal language which he had been taught. It has been noted that psychiatrists also have developed a special language, which may serve to set up dimensions not readily established by conventional language.

With the development of optical and other technologies, it is now possible to store information eidetically and in other ways, and to train people, utilizing these nonverbal methods of communication and information. A critical consideration for education and research is the explicit use of this current technology. Included in such control is the physical space itself, which may set up rules for behavior (Cohen, 1964). Our technology of communication and information storage may be used to develop abstractions and dimensions in new languages which may be more appropriate to the subject matter than verbal language. The verbal language may be useful in one area, the visual language in another, the spatial language in another, and interpersonal language in yet others. The very modest research reported from the laboratory suggests that an experimental analysis of behavior is not restricted to any of these but is generalizable to all. Verbal behavior can contribute to, and can be analyzed and controlled by, procedures developed in nonverbal designs. A general discipline of communication may produce procedures relevant to verbal, visual, and other forms of communication.

With regard to the varying languages our technology now makes possible for us, can we identify not only the problems best suited for them, but also train in those languages directly, without using the mediation of verbal language (where the appropriate language is nonverbal)? Can we identify the relevant abstractions and rules and their order? Shall we teach the abstractions first and obtain immediate dimensional control, as we do in perception experiments? Or shall we allow the abstractions to emerge from stimuli in which they are intertwined with dimensional stimuli, as we do in human concept and many animal discrimination experiments? Or, as is probably the more profitable case, can we identify the conditions under which it is appropriate to use one procedure rather than the other, or some combination?

These control methods may also be used to establish insight, creativity, and self-control. That this is not really a paradox has been considered elsewhere by the author (Goldiamond, 1965a). We can, for example, utilizing the control procedures mentioned, train the student to "find out for himself," as in concept formation and animal discrimination experiments. In such research, we intentionally intertwine instructional and dimensional stimuli, pairing a presentation containing the dimension we are interested in with one or more presentations which do not. Both correct and incorrect presentations contain many other dimensions as well and may be programmed to differ in these in addition to the relevant dimension, in order to keep superstitious control from being developed by the wrong dimensions. This multiplicity of dimensions may be one of the sources of the power of words in various forms of learning.* Words can have many dimensions, including those of meaning, and hence may be systematically used as stimuli which intertwine instructional and dimensional control, in a program for the emergence of control by self-instruction; or in the establishment of discrimination along dimensions considered appropriate. We have

---

*Including psychotheraphy. See references to psychotherapy contracts with the Office of the Surgeon General, involving collaboration with Jarl Dyrud and Miles Miller, psychiatrists, to whom the author is indebted for suggestions and critical comments.

indicated that it is possible to treat these properties of words in the same way that we treat other stimulus dimensions, and thus apply to words the technology and procedures developed in these other areas. "Finding out for oneself" is often hazardous, since the failures involved can have drastic consequences. Are the failures and extinctions in the laboratory inherent in learning, or are they inherent in learning only when learning is equated with the trials-to-acquisition procedure? Current research suggests that we can, utilizing the fading-shaping procedures, establish instructional control (including self-control) without error. Can we define the necessary dimensions we must direct behavior away from, as well as along, and rationally program these into our errorless procedures? Can we extend shaping-fading into other elements of the operant paradigm, for example, reinforcers, and alter the value system? These, it would seem, are all legitimate questions for the laboratory. Although their exact relation to significant problems outside, and their exact translation, remains to be seen, recent results suggest that translation and extension are both possible and desirable (See Ref. Cohen, 1965, for programming a regular class of 250 sophomores). In the laboratory, learning the concept or rule assures the organism, so to speak, that it will obtain reinforcement when it encounters the dimensional stimuli. And through long histories of such payoffs from rules, abstraction may be reinforced, and may also reinforce and maintain the behaviors of which it is a consequence. So it would appear in the laboratory, and so, we expect, it is outside.

An Operant Analysis
of Problem Solving*

The behavior observed when a man solves a problem is distinguished by the fact that it changes another part of his behavior and is reinforced and strengthened when it does so. Two stages are easily identified in a typical problem. A hungry man faces a problem if he cannot emit any response previously reinforced with food; to solve it he must change either himself or the situation until a response occurs. The behavior which brings about the change is properly called problem solving and the response it promotes a solution. A question for which there is at the moment no answer is a problem. It may be solved, for example, by performing a calculation, by consulting a reference work, or by acting in any way which helps in recalling a previously learned answer.

Since there is probably no behavioral process which is not relevant to the solving of some problem, an exhaustive

*Preparation of this manuscript has been supported by Grant K6-MH-21,775 of the National Institute of Mental Health of the U.S. Public Health Service, and by the Human Ecology Fund.

analysis of techniques would coincide with an analysis of behavior as a whole. This paper is confined to the status and
function of the terms appearing in an operant formulation.

CONTINGENCIES OF REINFORCEMENT

Problem solving is concerned with the relations which
prevail among three terms: a stimulus, a response, and a reinforcing consequence. Many classical issues in human behavior have gone unresolved for a long time because some one of
them has been neglected.

When a response occurs and is reinforced, the probability that it will occur again in the presence of similar stimuli is
increased. This is simple operant conditioning. The process
no longer presents any great problem for either organism or
investigator. Problems arise when contingencies are complex.
For example, there may be no response available which satisfies a given set of contingencies. Or competing responses may
be evoked—among them emotional changes which weaken the
very response upon which reinforcement is contingent or de-
stroy the power of a reinforcer. Or the contingencies may be
satisfied only by a sequence or chain of responses, early members of which are too remote from the terminal reinforcer to
be strongly affected by it until conditioned reinforcers have
been set up.

Problems of this kind are exemplified by Thorndike's
classical puzzle box in which a hungry cat could escape from a
box and reach food only by turning a latch. In Thorndike's experiment the probability of turning the latch was at first quite
low. The box evoked conditioned and unconditioned escape

behavior, much of it incompatible with turning the latch. The close confinement probably elicited emotional responses which made the food less reinforcing when it was eventually reached. The terminal performance that satisfied the contingencies was a chain of responses: orienting toward and approaching the latch, touching the latch and turning it, orienting toward and passing through the opened door, and approaching and eating the food. Some links in this chain may have been reinforced by the food and others by escape from the box, but some could be reinforced only after other reinforcers had been conditioned. For these and other reasons the box presented a problem—for both the cat and Thorndike.

Thorndike thought he solved *his* problem by saying that the successful cat used a process of "trial and error learning." The expression is unfortunate. "Try" implies that a response has already been affected by relevant consequences. A cat is "trying to escape" if it engages in behavior which either has been selected in the evolution of the species because it has brought escape from dangerous situations or has been reinforced by escape from aversive stimulation elsewhere in the life of the cat. The term "error" does not describe behavior, it passes judgment on it. The curves for trial-and-error learning plotted by Thorndike and many others do not represent any useful property of behavior—certainly not a single process called problem solving. The changes which contribute to such a curve include the adaptation and extinction of emotional responses, the conditioning of reinforcers, and the extinction of unreinforced responses. Any contribution made by an increase in the probability of the reinforced response is hopelessly obscured.

Even in Thorndike's rather crude apparatus we could isolate the change resulting from reinforcement. We could begin by adapting the cat to the box until emotional responses were no longer important. By opening the door repeatedly (while making sure that this event was not consistently contingent on any response), we could convert the stimuli generated by the door into conditioned reinforcers which we could then use to shape the behavior of moving into a position from which the latch would be likely to be turned. We could then reinforce a single instance of turning the latch and would almost certainly observe an immediate increase in the probability that the latch would be turned again.

This kind of simplification is common in the experimental analysis of behavior. It eliminates the process of trial and error and disposes of the data which are plotted in learning curves. It leaves no problem and, of course, no opportunity to solve a problem. Clearly it is not the thing to do if we are interested in studying problem solving, or in *teaching* problem solving. It is because programmed instruction eliminates problem solving that some objections have been raised against it. Whether the programmer is interested in isolating a behavioral process for experimental purposes or in teaching a student to behave in a given way, he solves the learner's problems for him. How does he do so? What must he not do if he is either to study or to teach problem solving?

CONSTRUCTING DISCRIMINATIVE STIMULI

Consider a simple example not unlike Thorndike's puzzle box. You have been asked to pick up a friend's suitcase

from an airport baggage claim. You have never seen the suitcase or heard it described; you have only a ticket with a number for which a match is to be found among the numbers on a
collection of suitcases. To simplify the problem let us say that
you find yourself alone before a large rotary display. A hun-
dred suitcases move past you in a great ring. They are moving
too fast to be inspected in order. You are committed to selecting suitcases essentially at random, checking one number at a
time. How are you to find the suitcase?

You may, of course, simply keep sampling. You will almost certainly check the same suitcase more than once, but
eventually the matching ticket will turn up. If the suitcases are
not identical, however, some kind of learning will take place;
you will begin to recognize and avoid cases which do not bear
the matching number. A very unusual case may be tried only
once; others may be checked two or three times but responses
to them will eventually be extinguished and the suitcase eliminated from the set.

A much more effective strategy is to mark each case as
it is checked—say, with a piece of chalk. No bag is then inspected twice, and the number of bags remaining to be examined is reduced as rapidly as possible. Simple as it seems,
this method of solving the problem has some remarkable features. Simply checking cases at random until the right one is
found is of no interest as a behavioral process; the number of
checks required to solve the problem is not a dimension of behavior. It is true that behavioral processes are involved in
learning not to check cases already found to bear nonmatching
numbers, but the time required to find the right case throws no

useful light on them. Mathematicians, showing perhaps too much confidence in psychologists, often take this kind of learning seriously and construct theoretical learning curves and design learning machines in which probabilities of responding change in terms of consequences, but the changes actually occurring in the processes of extinction and discrimination can be studied much more directly. (In a recent article called "Learning in Some Simple Non-Biological Systems," H. D. Bloch (1965) argues that a learning curve which is "fairly typical of those found for biological organisms in general" can be traced to an "embarrassingly simple" mechanism the explanation of which becomes "utterly transparent." The *euphoria mathematica* is scarcely justified. Bloch is not analyzing a behavioral process at all.)

It is the use of the chalk which introduces something new. Marking each suitcase as it is checked is a kind of precurrent behavior which furthers the reinforcement of subsequent behavior—by reducing the number of samplings needed to find the right suitcase. Technically speaking, it is constructing a discriminative stimulus—an S^{Δ}. The effect on the behavior which follows is the only reinforcement to which making such a mark can be attributed. And the effect must not be neglected, for it distinguishes the chalk marks from marks left by accident. One could "learn" the Hampton Court maze after a fresh fall of snow simply by learning not to enter any path showing footprints leaving it; it is only when footprints have been found useful and, hence, when any behavior which makes them conspicuous is automatically reinforced that we reach the present case. A well-worn path over difficult terrain or through a

forest is a series of discriminative stimuli and hence a series
of reinforcers. It reinforces blazing or otherwise marking a
trail. Marking a *right* path is, technically speaking, constructing an "S^D".

It is much easier to construct useful discriminative
stimuli in verbal form. Easily recalled and capable of being
executed anywhere, a verbal response is an especially useful
kind of chalk mark. Many simple "statements of fact" express
relations between stimuli and the reinforcing consequences of
responses made to them. In the expression *Red apples are
sweet* for example, the word *red* identifies a property of a discriminative stimulus and *sweet* a property of a correlated reinforcer; red apples are "marked" as sweet. The verbal response makes it easier to learn to discriminate between sweet
and sour apples, to retain the discrimination over a period of
time, and, especially when recorded, to respond appropriately
when the original discrimination may have been forgotten.
(Whether one must describe or otherwise identify contingent
properties in order to form a discrimination is not the issue.
Lower organisms discriminate without responding verbally to
essential properties, and it is unlikely that man gave up the
ability to do so. He simply discovered the additional value of
constructing descriptive stimuli which improve his chances of
success.)

THE TRANSMISSION OF STIMULI CONSTRUCTED WHILE
SOLVING PROBLEMS

A constructed external mark has another important advantage: it affects other people. A stranger can follow a well-

worn path almost as well as the man who laid it down. Another
person could take over the search for the suitcase using our
marks--either after we had told him to ignore cases marked
with chalk (that is, after the chalk mark had been made an
effective discriminative stimulus through verbal instruction) or
after he had learned to ignore marked cases—in a process
which would still be quicker than learning to ignore all un-
marked cases. Two people could also search for the same case
using each other's marks. Something of the sort happens when,
for example, "scientists" are said to be working on a problem.

The stimuli which a man constructs in solving problems
can be helpful to other people precisely because the variables
manipulated in self-management are those which control the
behavior of men in general. In constructing *external* stimuli to
supplement or replace *private* changes in his behavior, a man
automatically prepares for the transmission of what he has
learned. His verbal constructions become public property as
his private discriminations could not. What he says in describing his own successful behavior *(I held the base firmly in my
left hand and turned the top to the right)* can be changed into a
useful instruction *(Hold the base firmly in your left hand and
turn the top to the right)*. The same variables are being manipulated and with some of the same effects on behavior.

The role of a public product of problem solving in the
accumulation and transmission of folk wisdom is exemplified
by a formula once used by blacksmiths' apprentices. Proper
operation of the bellows of a forge was presumably first conditioned by the effects on the bed of coals. Best results followed
full strokes, from wide open to tightly closed, the opening

stroke being swift and the closing stroke slow and steady. Such
behavior is described in the verse:

> *Up high, down low,*
>
> *Up quick, down slow —*
>
> > *And that's the way to blow*
> >
> > (See ref., Salaman, 1957)

The first two lines describe behavior, the third is essentially a
social reinforcer. A blacksmith may have composed the poem
for his own use in facilitating effective behavior or in discussing effective behavior with other blacksmiths. By occasionally
reciting the poem, possibly in phase with the action, he could
strengthen important characteristics of his behavior. By recalling it upon a remote occasion, he could reinstate an effective performance. The poem must also have proved useful in
teaching an apprentice to operate the bellows. It could even
generate appropriate behavior in an apprentice who never saw
the effect on the fire.

Much of the folk wisdom of a culture serves a similar
function. Maxims and proverbs describe or imply behavior and
its reinforcing consequences. The reinforcement is positive
in *A penny saved is a penny earned,* which may be para-
phrased *Not-spending, like earning, is reinforced with pennies.*
It is negative in *Procrastination is the thief of time,* where a
connection is described between putting things off at the moment and being unpleasantly busy later. Many maxims describe
social contingencies. The reinforcing practices of a community
are often inconsistent or episodic, but contingencies which remain relatively unchanged for a period of time may be described

in useful ways. *It is better to give than to receive* specifies two forms of behavior and states that the net reinforcement of one is greater than that of the other. (The golden rule is a curious instance. No specific response is mentioned, but a kind of consequence is described in terms of its effect on those who use the rule. In the negative form one is enjoined not to behave in a given way if the consequence would be aversive to oneself. In the positive form one is enjoined to behave in a given way if the consequences will be reinforcing to oneself. The rule may have been discovered by someone particularly sensitive to his effects on others, but once stated it should have proved generally useful.) Maxims usually describe rather subtle contingencies of reinforcement, which must have been discovered very slowly. They should have been all the more valuable in making such contingencies effective on others.

The formal laws of governmental and religious institutions also specify contingencies of reinforcement involving the occasions upon which behavior occurs, the behavior itself, and the reinforcing consequences. The contingencies were almost certainly in effect long before they were formulated. Anyone who took another's property, for example, would often be treated aversively. Eventually men learned to behave more effectively under such contingencies by formulating them. A public formulation must have had additional advantages; with its help authorities could maintain the contingencies more consistently and members of the group could behave more effectively with respect to them—possibly without direct exposure. The codification of legal practices, justly recognized as a great

advance in the history of civilization, is an extraordinary example of the construction of S^D's.

A well-known set of reinforcing contingencies is a language. For thousands of years men spoke without benefit of
codified rules. Some sequences of words were effective, others
were less so or not at all. The discovery of grammar was the
discovery of fairly stable properties of the contingencies maintained by a community. The discovery may have been made
first in a kind of personal problem solving, but a description of
the contingencies in the form of rules of grammar permitted
men to speak correctly by applying rules rather than through
long exposure to the contingencies. The same rules became
helpful in instruction and in maintaining verbal behavior in con-
formity with the usages of the community.

Scientific laws also specify or imply responses and their
consequences. They are not, of course, obeyed by nature but by
men who deal effectively with nature. The formula $s = \frac{1}{2}gt^2$
does not govern the behavior of falling bodies, it governs those
who correctly predict the position of falling bodies at given
times. As Ernst Mach pointed out, the scientific law may be
descended from the apprentice's rule (1893).

As a culture produces maxims, laws, grammar, and science, its members find it easier to behave effectively without
direct or prolonged contact with the contingencies of reinforcement thus formulated. (We are concerned here only with stable
contingencies. When contingencies change and the rules do not,
rules may be troublesome rather than helpful.) The culture
solves problems for its members, and it does so by transmit-
ting discriminative stimuli already constructed to evoke

solutions. The importance of the process does not, of course, explain problem solving. How do men arrive at the formulas which thus prove helpful to themselves and others? How do they learn to behave appropriately under contingencies of reinforcement for which they have not been prepared, especially contingencies which are so specific and ephemeral that no general preparation is possible?

PROBLEM-SOLVING BEHAVIOR

The question "Who is that just behind you?" poses a problem which, if the person is known by name, is solved simply by turning around and looking. Turning and looking are precurrent responses which generate a discriminative stimulus required in order to emit a particular name. One may also generate helpful stimuli by looking more closely at a stimulus which is not yet effectively evoking a response even though it is already in the visual field, and beyond "looking more closely" lie certain problem-solving activities in which a vague or complex stimulus is tentatively described or characterized. A stimulus is more likely to be seen in a given way when it has been described (and may then even be "seen in its absence"). A crude description may contribute to a more exact one, and a final characterization which supports a quite unambiguous response brings problem solving to an end. The result is useful to others if, in public form, it leads them to see the same thing in the same way. The reactions of others which are reinforcing to those who describe vague situations may shape their descriptions, often exerting a control no less powerful than the situations themselves.

Behavior of this sort is often observed as a kind of running comment on contingencies of reinforcement to which one is being exposed. A child learns to describe both the world to which he is reacting and the consequences of his reactions. Situations in which he cannot do this become so aversive that he escapes from them by asking for words. Descriptions of his own behavior are especially important. The community asks him: *What did you do? What are you doing? What are you going to do? And why?* and his answers describe his behavior and relate it to effective variables. The answers eventually prove valuable to the child himself. The expression *I grabbed him because he was going to fall* refers to a response (grabbing) and a property of the occasion (he was going to fall) and implies a reinforcement (his falling would have been aversive to the speaker or others). It is particularly helpful to describe behavior which fails to satisfy contingencies, as in *I let go too soon* or *I struck too hard.* Even fragmentary descriptions of contingencies speed the acquisition of effective terminal behavior, help to maintain the behavior over a period of time, and reinstate it when forgotten. Moreover, they generate similar behavior in others not subjected to the contingencies they specify. As a culture evolves, it encourages running comment of this sort and thus prepares its members to solve problems most effectively.* Cultures which divert attention from behavior to mental events said to be responsible for the behavior are notably less helpful.

*For the relevance of verbal self-stimulation to problem solving, see Skinner, 1957, pp. 438 and following.

It is possible to construct similar discriminative stimuli without engaging in the behavior. A piece of equipment used in the study of operant behavior is a convenient example of a reinforcing system. One may arrive at behavior appropriate to the contingencies it maintains through prolonged responding under them and in doing so may formulate maxims or rules. But the equipment itself may also be examined. One could look behind the interface between organism and apparatus and set down directions for behaving appropriately with respect to the system there discovered. The environment is such a reinforcing system, and parts of it are often examined for such purposes. By analyzing sample spaces and the rules of games, for example, we compose instructions which evoke behavior roughly resembling the behavior which would be generated by prolonged responding under the contingencies they maintain. Science is in large part a direct analysis of the reinforcing systems found in nature; it is concerned with facilitating behavior reinforced by such systems.

(When prescriptions for action derived from an analysis of a reinforcing system differ from prescriptions derived from exposure to the contingencies maintained by the system, the former generally prevail. There are many reasons for this. A system is usually easier to observe than a history. The behavior summarized in a running comment may not be the terminal behavior which most adequately satisfies a given set of contingencies. A terminal performance may be marked by permanent though unnecessary features resulting from coincidental contingencies encountered *en route*, and so on.)

Contingencies are sometimes studied by constructing a

model of a reinforcing environment. One may react to the model in simpler ways (for example, verbally) and acquire appropriate behavior more quickly. If rules derived from exposure to the model are to prove helpful in the environment, however, the contingencies must be the same, and a model is helpful therefore only if the reinforcing system has already been described. It is helpful simply in facilitating exposure to the contingencies and in studying the resulting changes in behavior.

Many instances of problem-solving behavior would be called *induction*. The term applies whether the stimuli which evoke behavior appropriate to a set of contingencies are derived from an exposure to the contingencies or from direct inspection of the reinforcing system. In this sense induction is not the deriving of a general rule from specific instances but the construction of a rule which generates behavior appropriate to a set of contingencies. Rule and contingency are different kinds of things; they are not general and specific statements of the same thing.

Deduction is still another way of constructing discriminative stimuli. Maxims, rules, and laws are physical objects, and they can be manipulated to produce other maxims, rules, and laws. Second-order rules for manipulating first-order rules are derived from empirical discoveries of the success of certain practices or from an examination of the contingency-maintaining systems which the first-order rules describe. In much of probability theory first-order rules are derived from a study of reinforcing systems. Second-order rules are discovered inductively when they are found to produce effective new first-order rules or deductively (possibly "tautologically") from an analysis of first-order rules or of the contingencies they describe.

Many rules which help in "solving the problem of solving problems" are familiar. "Ask yourself 'What is the unknown?'" is a useful bit of advice which leads not to a solution but to a modified statement to which a first-order rule may then be applied. Reducing the statement of a problem to symbols does not solve the problem but, by eliminating possibly irrelevant responses, it may make first-order problem solving more effective. Second-order, "heuristic" rules are often thought to specify more crea- tive or less mechanical activities than the rules in first- order (possibly algorithmic) problem solving, but once a heuristic rule has been formulated, it can be followed as "mechanically" as any first-order rule.

――― Solving a problem is a behavioral event. The various kinds of activities which further the appearance of a solu- tion are all forms of behavior. The course followed in moving toward a solution does not, however, necessarily reflect an important behavioral process. Just as there are almost as many "learning curves" as there are things to be learned (Skinner, 1963, p. 506), so there are almost as many "problem-solving curves" as there are problems. Logic, mathematics, and science are disciplines which are concerned with ways of solving problems, and the histories of these fields record ways in which particular problems have been solved. Fascinating as this may be, it is not a prime source of data about behavior. Strategies and in- stances in which strategies have actually been used have the same status whether a problem is solved by an individual, a group, or a machine. Just as we do not turn to the way in which a machine solves a problem for useful data in studying the electrical, mechanical, optical, or chemical principles on which the machine is constructed, so we should not turn to the way in which a man or a group solves a problem for useful data in studying individual behavior, communication, or coordinated action. This does not mean that we may not study individual, group, or machine behavior in order to discover better ways of solving problems or to reveal limits on the kind of strategies which may be employed or the kinds of problems which may be solved.

CONTINGENCY-SHAPED VERSUS RULE-FOLLOWING RESPONSES

The response which satisfies a complex set of contingencies, and thus solves the problem, may come about as the result of direct shaping by the contingencies (possibly with the help of deliberate or accidental programming) or it may be evoked by contingency-related stimuli constructed either by the problem solver himself or by others. The difference between rule-following and contingency-shaped behavior is obvious when instances are pretty clearly only one or the other. The behavior of a baseball outfielder catching a fly ball bears certain resemblances to the behavior of the commander of a ship taking part in the recovery of a reentering satellite. Both move about on a surface in a direction and with a speed designed to bring them, if possible, under a falling object at the

moment it reaches the surface. Both respond to recent stimulation from the position, direction, and speed of the object, and
they both take into account effects of gravity and friction. The
behavior of the baseball player, however, has been almost entirely shaped by contingencies of reinforcement, whereas the
commander is simply obeying rules derived from the available
information and from analogous situations. As more and more
satellites are caught, it is conceivable that an experienced
commander, under the influence of successful or unsuccessful
catches, might dispense with or depart from some of the rules
thus derived. At the moment, however, the necessary history
of reinforcement is lacking, and the two cases are of quite different kinds.

Possibly because discriminative stimuli (as exemplified
by maxims, rules, and laws) are usually more easily observed
than the contingencies they specify, responses under their
control tend to be overemphasized at the expense of responses
shaped by contingencies. One resulting mistake is to suppose
that behavior is always under the control of prior stimuli.
Learning is defined as "finding, storing, and using again correct rules" (Clark, 1963), and the simple shaping of behavior by
contingencies which have never been formulated is neglected.
When the brain is described as an "organ for the manipulation
of symbols," its role in mediating changes in behavior resulting from reinforcement is not taken into account. When a child
who has learned a language is said to have constructed "the
grammar for himself on the basis of his observation of sentences and nonsentences" (Chomsky, 1959), the effect of the
contingencies maintained by the verbal environment is

overlooked. In the same sense we should have to say that the outfielder who has learned to catch a ball has constructed the dynamics he needs to predict trajectories. Contingencies of reinforcement shape verbal behavior as they shape catching a ball—that is, without being formulated in rules.

Once the pattern has been established, it is easy to argue for other kinds of prior controlling entities such as expectancies, cognitive maps, intentions, and plans. We refer to contingency-shaped behavior alone when we say that an organism behaves in a given way with a given probability because the *behavior has been followed by a given kind of consequence in the past*. We refer to behavior under the control of prior contingency-specifying stimuli when we say that an organism behaves in a given way because *it expects a similar consequence to follow in the future*. The "expectancy" is a gratuitous and dangerous assumption if nothing more than a history of reinforcement has been observed. Any actual formulation of the relation between a response and its consequences (perhaps simply the observation, "Whenever I respond in this way such and such an event follows") may, of course, function as a prior controlling stimulus.

The contingency-specifying stimuli constructed in the course of solving problems never have quite the same effects as the contingencies they specify. One difference is motivational. Contingencies not only shape behavior, they alter its probability, but contingency-specifying stimuli, as such, do not do so. Though the topography of a response is controlled by a maxim, rule, law, or statement of intention, the probability of its occurrence remains undetermined. After all, why should an organism obey a law, follow a plan, or carry out an intention? It is not enough to say that organisms are so constituted that they automatically follow rules—as nature is said, mistakenly, to obey the laws of nature. A rule is simply an object in the environment. Why should it be important to an organism? This is the sort of question which always plagues the dualist. Descartes could not explain how a thought could move the pineal gland and thus affect the material body; Adrian acknowledged that he could not say how a nerve impulse caused a thought (1928). How does a rule govern behavior?

As a discriminative stimulus, a rule is effective as part of a set of contingencies of reinforcement. A complete specification must include the reinforcement which has shaped the topography of a response and brought it under the control of the stimulus. The reinforcements contingent on prior stimulation from maxims, rules, or laws are sometimes the same as those which directly shape behavior. When this is the case, the maxim, rule, or law is a form of advice.* *Go west, young man* is an example of advice when the behavior it specifies will be reinforced by certain consequences which do not result from action taken by the adviser. We tend to follow advice because previous behavior in response to similar verbal stimuli has been reinforced. *Go west, young man* is a command when some consequences of the specified action are arranged by the commander—say, the aversive consequences arranged by an official charged with relocating the inhabitants of a region. When maxims, rules, and laws are advice, the governed behavior is

*For a further discussion of this distinction see Skinner, 1957, pp. 38 and following.

reinforced by consequences which might have shaped the same behavior directly in the absence of the maxims, rules, and laws. When they are commands, they are effective only because special reinforcements have been made contingent upon them. Governments, for example, do not trust to the natural advantages of obeying the law to ensure obedience. Grammatical rules are often followed not so much because the behavior is then particularly effective as because social punishments are contingent on ungrammatical behavior.

Rule-governed behavior is obviously unmotivated in this sense when rules are obeyed by machines. A machine can be constructed to move a bellows up high, down low, up quick, and down slow, remaining forever under the control of the specifying rules. Only the designer and builder are affected by the resulting condition of the fire. The same distinction holds when machines follow more complex rules. A computer, like a mechanical bellows, does only what it was constructed and instructed to do. Mortimer Taube (1961) and Ulrich Neisser (1963) are among those who have recently argued that the thinking of a computer is less than human, and it is significant that they have emphasized the lack of "purpose." But to speak of the purpose of an act is simply to refer to its characteristic consequences (Skinner, 1963). A statement of purpose may function as a contingency-specifying discriminative stimulus. Computers merely follow rules. So do men who merely follow rules—such as the blacksmith's apprentice who never sees the fire, or the algorithmic problem solver who simply does what he has been told to do. The motivating conditions (for machines and men alike) are irrelevant to the problem being solved. (It

is the probability of the behavior, not its topography, which is
at issue here. There is no reason why a machine cannot be
constructed so that it is altered by the consequences of earlier
actions. Some have already been so constructed—we call them
men.)

Rules are particularly likely to be deficient in the sov-
ereignty needed for successful government when they are derived from statistical analyses of contingencies. It is unlikely
that anyone will ever stop smoking simply because of the aversive consequences associated with lung cancer, at least not in
time to make any difference, and it is therefore unlikely that
giving up smoking will be shaped by these consequences. The
actual contingencies have little effect on behavior under the
control of contingency-specifying facts or rules. A formal
statement of contingencies *(Cigarette smoking causes lung
cancer)* needs the support of carefully engineered aversive
stimuli involving sanctions unrelated to the consequences of
smoking. For example, smoking may be classified as illegal,
immoral, or sinful and punished by appropriate agencies.

Some contingencies cannot be accurately described. The
old family doctor was often a skillful diagnostician because of
contingencies to which he had been exposed over many years,
but he could not always describe these contingencies or construct rules which would evoke comparable behavior in younger
men. Some of the experiences of the mystic are ineffable in the
sense that all three terms in the contingencies governing his
behavior (the behavior itself, the conditions under which it
occurs, and its consequences) escape adequate specification.
Emotional behavior is particularly hard to bring under the

control of rules. As Pascal put it, "the heart has its reasons which reason will never know." Nonverbal skills are usually much harder to describe than verbal. Verbal behavior can be reported in a unique way by modelling it in direct quotation (Skinner, 1957). Nonverbal behavior is modelled so that it can be imitated but not as precisely or as exhaustively.

Rule-governed behavior is in any case never exactly like behavior shaped by contingencies. The golf player whose swing has been shaped by its effect on the ball is easily distinguished from the player who is primarily imitating a coach, even though it is much more difficult to distinguish between a man who is making an original observation and one who is saying something because he has been told to say it, but when topographies of response are very similar, different controlling variables are necessarily involved, and the behavior will have different properties. Operant experiments with human subjects are sometimes simplified by instructing the subjects in the operation of the equipment. The resulting behavior may resemble that which follows exposure to the contingencies and may be studied in its stead for certain purposes, but the controlling variables are different, and the behaviors will not necessarily change in the same way in response to other variables—for example, under the influence of a drug.

The difference between rule-following and contingency-shaped behavior may be observed as one passes from one to the other in "discovering the truth" of a rule. A man may have avoided postponing necessary work for years either because he has been taught that *Procrastination is the thief of time* and therefore avoids procrastination as he avoids thieves, or because he dutifully obeys the injunction *Do not put off until to-morrow what you can do today*. Eventually his behavior may come under the direct influence of the relevant contingencies—in doing something today he actually avoids the aversive conse-quences of having it to do tomorrow. Though his behavior may not be noticeably different (he continues to perform necessary work as soon as possible) he will now behave for different rea-sons, which must be taken into account. When at some future time he says *Procrastination is the thief of time,* his response has at least two sources of strength: he is reciting a memo-rized maxim and emitting a contingency-specifying statement of fact.

The eventual occurrence of a planned event works a sim-ilar change. Plans for a symposium on cognition are drawn up and followed. Eventually, almost incidentally it may seem, the symposium is held and certain natural consequences follow. The nature of the enterprise as an instance of human behavior has changed; in particular the probability that similar behavior will occur in the future has been altered. In the same way those half-formed expectancies called "premonitions" suddenly be-come important when the premonitored events occur. A similar change comes about when an actor, starting with memorized words and prescribed actions, comes under the influence of simulated or real reactions by other members of the cast, under the shaping effect of which he begins to "live" the role.

The classical distinction between rational and irrational or intuitive behavior is of the same sort. The "reasons" which govern the behavior of the rational man describe relations be-tween the occasions on which he behaves, his behavior, and its consequences. In general we admire the intuitive man, with his contingency-shaped behavior, rather than the mere follower of rules. For example, we admire the man who is "naturally" good rather than the merely law-abiding, the intuitive mathematician rather than the mere calculator. Plato discusses the difference in the *Charmides*, but he confuses matters by attributing our admiration to speed. It is true that contingency-shaped behavior is instantly available, whereas it takes time to consult rules and examine reasons; but irrational behavior is more likely to be wrong, and there is therefore an important sense in which we admire the deliberate and rational man. We ask the intuitive mathematician to behave like the calculator— to construct a proof which will guide others to the same conclusion even though he himself did not need it. We insist, with Freud, that the reasons men give in explaining their actions should be accurate accounts of the contingencies of reinforcement actually responsible for their behavior.

OTHER KINDS OF PROBLEMS

To define a problem, etymologically, as something explicitly put forth for solution (or, more technically, as a specific set of contingencies of reinforcement for which a response of appropriate topography is to be found) is to exclude instances in which the same precurrent activities serve a useful function although the topography of a response is already known. The distinction between contingency-shaped and rule-following behavior is still required. Sometimes the problem is not *what* to do but *whether* to do it. Problem-solving behavior is designed to strengthen or weaken an already identified response.

Conflicting positive and negative consequences, of either an intellectual or ethical nature, are especially likely to raise problems of this sort, as when a strongly reinforced response has deferred aversive consequences or when immediate aversive consequences conflict with deferred reinforcers.

A relevant problem-solving practice is to emit the questionable response in tentative form—for example, as a *hypothesis*. Making a hypothesis differs from asserting a fact in that punishment is contingent upon it if it is found to be wrong. The emitted response is nevertheless useful, particularly if recorded, when it enters into other problem-solving activities. For rather different purposes one acts verbally before acting in other ways by making a *resolution*. It is easier to resolve than to act; and the resolution, as a description of action under the control of many of the variables controlling the action itself, makes the action more likely to take place. (A *promise* specifies a response and creates social contingencies which strengthen it, and contingencies of social origin are invoked when one "promises oneself" to do something in making a resolution.) A *statement of policy* is also a description of action to be taken. (Resolutions and statements of policy are often made because action itself is at the moment impossible, but they are relevant here only when the action they strengthen or weaken is not under physical constraint.) A joint secret statement of policy is a *conspiracy;* it describes cooperative action to be undertaken by a group.

Like the rules and plans appropriate to problems in which the topography of the solution is not known, hypotheses, statements of policy, and so on, are not to be inferred in every instance of behavior. People act without making resolutions or forming policies. Different people or groups of people (for example, "capitalists" in socialist theory) act in the same way under similar contingencies of reinforcement, even cooperatively, without entering into a conspiracy. The conclusion to which a scientist comes at the end of an experiment was not necessarily in existence as a hypothesis before or during the experiment.

Sometimes the problem is to arrive at a less than maximal probability appropriate to intermittent reinforcement. A calculated probability, derived either by sampling a schedule of reinforcement or by directly inspecting the system maintaining such a schedule, controls an appropriate strength of response. But, again, a person is not always acting under the control of such a calculation or of any prior "felt" probability or sense of confidence, trust, or belief.

Sometimes the problem is to decide which of two or more responses to emit, the topographies of all alternatives being known. The concepts of choice and decision making have been overemphasized in psychological and economic theory. It is difficult to evaluate the probability that a single response will be made, but when two or more mutually exclusive responses are possible, the one actually emitted seems at least to be stronger than the others. For this reason early psychological research emphasized situations and devices in which only relative strength was observed (the rat turned right rather than left or jumped toward a circle rather than a square). Efforts to assess the separate probabilities of the competing responses were thus discouraged. Single responses were treated only as decisions between acting and not acting, within the time limits set by a "trial." The notion of relative strength is then practically meaningless, and "choose" simply means "respond." The problem of whether to act in one way or another differs from the problem of whether or not to act only because one of the aversive consequences of acting in one way is a loss of the opportunity to act in another. The same problem-solving activities are relevant. A decision announced before acting is essentially a resolution or statement of policy. The mere emission of one response rather than another, however, does not mean that a decision has been formulated.

The notion of a problem as something set for solution is even less appropriate when neither the topography of the behavior strengthened by precurrent activity nor its consequences are known until the behavior occurs. Artists, composers, and writers, for example, engage in various activities which further the production of art, music, and literature. (Sometimes they are required to produce works meeting quite narrow specifications, and their behaviors then exemplify explicit problem solving, but this is by no means always the case.) The artist or composer explores a medium or a theme and comes up with an unforeseen composition having unforeseen effects. A writer explores a subject matter or a style and comes up with a poem or a book which could not have been described or its effects predicted in advance. In this process of "discovering what one has to say," relevant precurrent behavior cannot be derived from any specification of the behavior to follow or of the contingencies which the behavior will satisfy. The precurrent behavior nevertheless functions by virtue of the processes involved in solving statable problems. For example, crude sketches and tentative statements supply stimuli leading to other sketches and statements, moving toward a final solution. Here again, it is a mistake to assume that the artist, composer, or writer is necessarily realizing some prior conception of the work he produces. The conditions under which Renoir was reinforced as he painted *The Boating Party* must have been as real as those under which a mathematician or scientist is reinforced for solving a set problem, but much less could have been said about them in advance.

THE PRODUCTS OF PROBLEM SOLVING AND THEIR DIMENSIONS

Problem solving is often said to involve the production of knowledge and thought (not to mention cognition). An operant formulation permits us to distinguish between some of the things to which these terms have been applied.

Knowledge. What is knowledge, where is it, and what is it about? Michael Polanyi (1958, 1960) and P. W. Bridgman (1959) have raised these questions with respect to the apparent discrepancy between scientific facts, laws, and theories (as published, for example, in papers, texts, tables of constants, and encyclopedias) and the personal knowledge of the scientist. Objective knowledge transcends the individual; it is more stable and durable than private experience, but it lacks color and personal involvement. The presence or absence of "consciousness" can scarcely be the important difference, for scientists are as "conscious" of laws as they are of the things laws describe. Sensory contact with the external world may be the beginning of knowledge, but contact is not enough. It is not even enough for "conscious experience." Stimuli are only part of the contingencies of reinforcement under which an organism distinguishes among the aspects and properties of the environment in which it lives. Responses and reinforcements are also required before anything can be seen.

The world which establishes contingencies of reinforcement of the sort studied in an operant analysis is presumably "what knowledge is about." A person comes to know that world and how to behave in it in the sense that he acquires behavior which satisfies the contingencies it maintains. Behavior which is exclusively shaped by such contingencies is perhaps the closest one can come to the "personal knowledge" of Polanyi and Bridgman. It is the directed, "purposive" behavior of the blacksmith who operates his bellows because of its effect on the fire.

But there is another kind of behavior which could be called knowledge of the same things—the behavior controlled by contingency-specifying stimuli. These stimuli are as objective as the world they specify, and they are useful precisely because they become and remain part of the external world. Behavior under their control is the behavior of the apprentice who never sees the fire but acts as he instructs himself to act by reciting a poem. So far as topography goes, it may resemble behavior directly shaped by contingencies, but there remains an all important difference in controlling variables. [To say that the behaviors have different "meanings" is only another way of saying that they are controlled by different variables (Skinner, 1957).]

The difference which Polanyi (1959) in particular seems to be trying to make is between contingency-shaped and rule-governed behavior rather than between behaviors marked by the presence or absence of "conscious experience." Contingency-shaped behavior depends for its strength upon "genuine" consequences. It is likely to be nonverbal and thus to "come to grips with reality." It is a personal possession which dies with the possessor. The rules which form the body of science are public. They survive the scientist who constructed them as well as those who are guided by them. The control they exert is primarily verbal, and the resulting behavior may not vary in strength with consequences having personal significance. These are basic distinctions, and they survive even when, as is usually the case, the scientist's behavior is due to both direct reinforcement and to the control exercised by the contingency-specifying stimuli which compose facts, laws, and theories.

The structure of thought. It has been argued [Skinner (1957), Ch. 19], that the term "thinking" should not be restricted to verbal behavior, to weak or covert behavior whether verbal or nonverbal, or to behavior which is effective primarily because it is self-stimulating. Instead, it may profitably be said to describe operant behavior in all its forms. Several distinctions are still to be made among its products, many of which suggest traditional issues.

The environment is presumably "what is thought about." It has a structure, and behavior has a corresponding structure because it has been shaped by environmental contingencies. The structure of the environment is thus reflected in the structure of thought. But contingency-specifying stimuli also correspond with environmental contingencies, and the structure of behavior under the control of such stimuli also reflects the structure of the environment—though at one remove. The kinds of correspondences which prevail among these various structures are part of the subject matter of an experimental analysis of behavior.

It should be possible to compose definitions of knowledge, thought, and cognition compatible with the present formulation, but the traditional functions served by terms of this sort have no place in an operant analysis. They belong, rather, in psychological speculations which restrict themselves to stimuli (as in the analysis of conscious content) and to responses (as in a psychology of action). The traditional view is that the organism is in contact with the environment at two points: the point at which the environment acts on the organism, and the point at which the organism acts on the environment. Information theory has clarified the formulation: there is input and output, and the problem is to relate one to the other. Knowledge, thought, and cognition are therefore invoked. Someone or something (somewhere) processes the information received, stores it, and retrieves it on appropriate occasions. This is done out of sight, if not out of mind. An operant analysis, often mistakenly identified with stimulus-response theories, goes beyond input and output to much more subtle and complex environmental arrangements. Psychologists in general are not aware of the intricacy of the contingencies of reinforcement now under experimental analysis. As the analysis grows more powerful, and hence more successful, there is less and less need to assume such inner activities as the processing, storing, and retrieving of information. Characteristics of behavior once traced to thought and to a memory store of knowledge, processed or not, are traced instead to environmental contingencies. The traditional terms may suggest problems for an operant analysis, but they cannot characterize its solutions, for they have the wrong dimensions.

10

ARTHUR W. STAATS
University of Wisconsin

An Integrated-Functional Learning Approach to Complex Human Behavior

The history of psychology is a history of separatism, of clashes of men and theories. Many of the various schools of psychology began as "rebellions." The field of learning has continued in this tradition; and even as it has been arrayed against other orientations, major efforts within learning have been expended in developing and maintaining separate experimental methods, separate general (philosophical) methodolcgies, and separate terminologies—even when the empirical referents involved the same principles.

More particularly there has been such separatism in learning approaches to the study of complex human behavior, the area of present concern. For example, there have been people interested in the operant conditioning of verbal behavior (see Krasner, 1958; Salzinger, 1959; Skinner, 1957; Staats, 1963) who often eschew the experimental results and conceptions of investigators of word meaning and semantic mediation (see Mowrer, 1954; Osgood, 1953; Staats, 1961). And, many times these latter investigators reject the importance of

operant conditioning in the area of language. A third approach
has focused upon verbal learning, including serial and paired
associate verbal learning (see Underwood and Schulz, 1960).
And this approach has ignored the findings of the former two
areas—an action that has largely been reciprocated. To continue with the example, another group has been concerned with
the mediational properties of word associates (see Russell and
Storms, 1955; Jenkins, 1963). Thus, even though these various
approaches spring from the same tradition, they have been
theoretical competitors rather than complementing a general
learning approach.

This state of affairs is a great disadvantage. The separate
growth of the experimental results and more importantly the
terminologies of the various approaches has retarded the development of a believable conception of human behavior in
learning terms. Simplistic learning approaches to human behavior, while productive in their own research realms, have
been vulnerable to criticism on general issues (see Chomsky,
1959; Miller, 1965)—it has been relatively easy to pick an example of behavior that the isolated approach could not handle.
Obviously, complex language (cognitive) behaviors cannot be accounted for solely on the basis of word associations, or word
meaning, or operant conditioning principles. Thus, the traditional learning approaches by themselves have been inadequate
for dealing with a wide range of human behaviors, and their
methods have not promoted the most rapid progress.

An integration of the various results and orientations
within the field of learning, put into a consistent terminological
convention, offers a more powerful conception of human be-

havior; a conception that is capable of dealing with the various areas of interest. The author, with help from his associates, has generalized his general conception in various areas of psychology and has made a number of theoretical and experimental analyses in the area of language learning (Staats, 1955, 1961, 1963, 1964*a*, 1964*c*, 1964*d*; Staats and Staats, 1963; Staats, et al., 1961*a*, 1962, 1964*a*). This paper will in general terms characterize and extend his approach and indicate some of its implications for the study of complex human behavior, especially that included under the cognitive terms "problem solving," "reasoning," "concept formation," and the like. In doing so some research results and research implications and methodologies will be described. First, however, several examples will be given of the need for an integration of learning principles in the study of complex human behavior. These examples will also indicate that an important part of an integrated learning theory is the elaboration and schematization of the ways that stimulus and response events may be combined in complex constellations—these S-R mechanisms then functioning in complex human adjustment.

COMPLEX BEHAVIOR REQUIRES AN INTEGRATED LEARNING ANALYSIS

The Operant Conditioning of Verbal Concepts

The first example that will be cited in this section involves the operant conditioning of verbal response classes. That is, it has been shown in a number of studies (see Krasner, 1958) that words in various verbal "concepts," such as *animal* words, *food* words, *nature* words, and so on, have a functional unity. That is, when a word in such a concept class is reinforced, other words in the class are also strengthened. An individual reinforced when he emits an animal word will begin emitting *animal* word responses with greater frequency.

This type of result has been interpreted within the framework of standard operant conditioning principles (Salzinger, 1959). A closer look at the type of behavior involved, however, suggests that a more complete analysis of such verbal concepts indicates more clearly why they can be operantly conditioned—and increases our knowledge of the formation of such verbal concept classes. Staats (1961) originally suggested that classes (or concepts) of words could be formed on the basis of classical conditioning principles. That is, if the members of a set of words were each paired with a similar stimulus object, a similar response should be conditioned to each word. This conditioned response would also in this process come to elicit each of the words as a response in the training of the child.

As a consequence, it was suggested that words that elicited a similar response, the common meaning of the words, should also operantly condition as a word class. That is, when the subject emitted a word in the operant conditioning situation, this being followed by reinforcement, the meaning response of the word would also be conditioned to the situation. The meaning response, however, would also tend to elicit the other members of the word class, thus increasing the probability of occurrence of each response in the concept class. Each reinforced emission of one of the words in the class would have this general strengthening effect. This hypothesis was supported in two experiments. In one, a class of positive evaluative meaning words, selected on the basis of semantic differential ratings, was operantly conditioned using an adaptation of an experimental method used by Cohen, et al., to operantly condition word responses (1954). Each word in the class was presented upon a card with three foil words. The subject had to select and read one of the four words. He was reinforced when he read one word from the class. Frequency of selecting this type of word increased in the group of subjects (Staats, et al., 1961*a*). This study was replicated using a class of negative evaluative meaning words (Staats, et al., 1961*b*). The results support the analysis which integrates the concepts of word meaning and response mediation with the results of the operant conditioning of word classes.

Both of these studies illustrate one type of S-R mechanism which, incidentally, would be called one type of verbal concept. That is, a number of word responses can come to elicit a common response, in one case the type of response elicited by positive reinforcing stimuli, in the other by aversive stimuli. In addition, the stimulus of the common response (see Staats, 1961) also comes to elicit the individual word responses. This S-R mechanism, as will later be described, can function in producing further learning and problem solving in ways other than shown in the present studies.

There are additional possibilities for demonstrating the advantage of an integrated learning approach using the example of the operant conditioning of word concept classes. For example, on the basis of implicitly elicited sequences of verbal responses (see Russell and Storms, 1955), it would be expected

that any serial chain of word responses would demonstrate concept characteristics in the operant conditioning situation. The
author and associates (see Staats, 1963) have shown that serial
chains of nonsense word responses, previously learned in
paired associate training, will operantly condition as a class
of word responses. Furthermore, the greater the paired associate habit strength, the more strongly will the concept class
of nonsense words operantly condition.

The study thus illustrates another type of verbal concept,
and another type of S-R mechanism. The S-R mechanism involves the acquisition of sequences of verbal responses. The
author has suggested that many of our adjustive behaviors are
based upon having acquired many such mechanisms (Staats and
Staats, 1963). As one example, Judson, Cofer, and Gelfand (1956)
have shown that problem solving may depend upon such verbal
response sequences.

In addition to this type of verbal concept class (S-R
mechanism), any words which occur frequently in contiguity
with each other in our language experience should function as a
class. Take, for example, the word associates to a stimulus
word in word-association norms. Many of them are interasso-
ciated. For example, in the word responses to MUSIC there
are SWEET and SOFT, but SWEET and SOFT also elicit MUSIC.
In addition, the word LOUD, although not elicited by MUSIC, is
elicited by SOFT. Thus, LOUD would tend to occur as a response
to MUSIC, since it is mediated by the response SOFT. Now LOUD
as a stimulus word has as its associates a number of responses
which are also direct associates to MUSIC, as well as the word
MUSIC itself. If complete word-association norms were avail-

able for these words, additional interassociations would be seen.

Based upon the previous analysis, such a group of words should also form a verbal concept and operantly condition as a class. This was tested (see Staats, 1963), using the methods of operant conditioning already described, for the word associates to MUSIC. It was found that reinforcing the individual members of the class of MUSIC-associates had a general strengthening effect upon the concept class of word responses. This study illustrates another type of S-R mechanism, or, in other terms, another type of concept.

Thus, it is suggested that there are a number of different types of S-R mechanisms that the individual acquires and which function in his adjustive behaviors. Many of these mechanisms are commonly called concepts, especially when verbal responses are involved. This analysis thus suggests that there are many different types of concepts, a suggestion that will also be made in the context of problem solving. Furthermore, the findings on the acquisition and function of these concept (word) classes were based upon an integration not only of learning principles but also learning methods—operant conditioning procedures, serial learning methods, semantic measurements, as well as the use of word association norms.

Communication

Another area of study that requires an integration of learning principles is that of communication. In a classic paper, Mowrer suggested that communication may be considered as higher-order classical conditioning (1954). In this analysis the predicate word in a sentence may be considered to be a conditioned stimulus that reliably elicits a conditioned meaning response. When this word follows the subject of the sentence the meaning response it elicits will be conditioned to the subject word, and to the meaning response elicited by the subject word.

Mowrer discusses communication as the transfer of "meanings from sign to sign," that is, the higher-order classical conditioning of a response elicited by one word to another word. According to this view, a new word could become meaningful through this process. Let us say that the word EVIL is unknown to the child and meaningless, although the child has been conditioned to respond to the word BAD. That is, in the past the child has been punished while being told he was BAD, thus making BAD a conditioned stimulus for various internal responses. Now when the child asks what EVIL means and is told EVIL MEANS BAD, this constitutes a conditioning trial. Each time he repeats the phrase he provides an additional conditioning trial. In this way EVIL will come to elicit the responses which BAD already elicits and thus EVIL will come in this sense to be meaningful.

It may also be suggested that an analogous process takes place upon the basis of operant conditioning. Let us say, for example, that the word CLOSE has become an S^D for the child such that it controls a "closing motor response." When presented with the verbal stimulus CLOSE THE DOOR the child makes the appropriate movement.

Let us also say that the word SHUT has never before been presented to the child and is, in essence, a nonsense syllable.

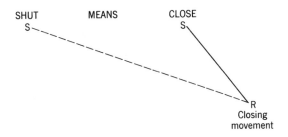

Fig. 1: When a word stimulus which controls a motor response is paired in a sentence with a meaningless word, in this sense, the meaningless word will also come to control the motor response. In this example, the new word SHUT becomes a controlling stimulus for the closing response through being paired with CLOSE in the sentence SHUT MEANS CLOSE. (From Staats, 1964c, pp. 193-194.)

It would be expected that if the child was told SHUT MEANS CLOSE that SHUT would come to control the response which CLOSE already controls. In the future if the child is told SHUT THE DOOR, he will respond appropriately. This is depicted in Fig. 1.

While this hypothesis was rationally derived, the author also tested the hypothesis with his four-year-old daughter. That is, she was first told WUG MEANS CLOSE. This was repeated several times. Then she was told WUG THE DOOR, and she promptly got up and closed the door. This analysis suggests that once a verbal stimulus has come to control a motor response, even though the principles involved were those of operant conditioning and not classical conditioning, simple contiguity of that verbal stimulus with another word will result in the new word also coming to control the response. Thus, the contiguous pairing of the two words resulted in the communication. That is, the word CLOSE already elicited the motor response. When CLOSE was paired with the new word WUG the new word also came to control the response.

It is because paired-associate learning, as well as verbal learning in general, takes place through the *contiguous* presentation of two-word stimuli that the process has been said to involve classical conditioning. This suggestion has been enhanced because there is no manipulation of reinforcement in verbal learning studies. However, the responses involved in this type of learning are not acquired through classical conditioning. There are no unconditioned stimuli that originally elicit word responses. Word responses are acquired through the principle of reinforcement, and these responses are brought under the control of discriminative stimuli according to operant discrimination principles. Paired-associate learning may be considered to involve the presentation of two discriminative stimuli, each of which elicits a vocal response. When this occurs frequently enough, the first vocal response comes to elicit the next. Many sequences of verbal responses are formed in this manner.

These are but examples, but they do suggest that although the classical conditioning conception of communication is important it may be considered only a part of what is called communication. Operant conditioning principles and complex S-R mechanisms are also involved. The present author (Staats, 1964a; Staats and Staats, 1963) has suggested that this type of human behavior may generally be more fully accounted for by an integration of learning principles.

Verbal Reinforcement

There is another area of study in the area of cognitive behavior, related to the previous discussion, that profits greatly from an integrated learning approach. Thus far, with few exceptions, conceptions of word meaning as a conditioned mediating response have been strictly separate from conceptions of the way that operant conditioning principles apply to language. Yet there are many indications that suggest a needed integration.

For example, there are many indications that words can serve as reinforcers. Most of the studies of the operant conditioning of word classes have been accomplished through the use of verbal reinforcers, such as GOOD, FINE, VERY GOOD, CORRECT, and so on (see Krasner, 1958). On the other hand there are a number of experiments that show that words may function as conditioned stimuli and come to elicit meaning responses as shown by semantic rating procedures (see Staats, 1961). Furthermore, investigators now generally agree (even those of an operant orientation) that conditioned reinforcers are formed through being *paired* with other reinforcers—in a process of classical conditioning. These are the elements with which to make a unification of the concept of word meaning as an implicit response with the concept of conditioned reinforcement as established through the process of classical conditioning.

The account may be summarized as follows. When a neutral stimulus is paired with a reinforcing stimulus, the neutral stimulus also acquires reinforcing value. It becomes a conditioned reinforcing stimulus, and it may be suggested, as Hull

(1943) similarly suggested, that this occurs because the conditioned reinforcing stimulus has come to elicit the same response as does the other reinforcing stimulus. Now, not all stimuli that elicit responses are reinforcing stimuli. Thus, it would be expected that not all conditioned stimuli that came to elicit responses would also have in the process acquired reinforcing value. Only stimuli paired with other reinforcers would come to be both conditioned stimuli for some response as well as conditioned reinforcers in an operant sense. Conditioned reinforcers, however, should be able to strengthen the behaviors they follow in the same manner as do primary reinforcers, and that is apparently the case (see Zimmerman, 1957).

Now, it has been suggested also that words may function as conditioned stimuli and come to elicit responses. Staats, et al. (1962), for example, have shown that a word paired with aversive stimuli (shock and loud noise) would come to elicit a conditioned response, a GSR. In addition, this word also acquired in the process a negative evaluative meaning, that is, the subjects so conditioned would rate the word as having an unpleasant meaning. Additional evidence of the commonality of these two responses was shown by the significant correlation between the amplitude of the conditioned GSR and the intensity of the conditioning negative meaning.

This analysis, even briefly stated here, suggests that certain words come, as they are conditioned to elicit responses, to also acquire a reinforcing function. That is, some words are systematically paired with environmental stimuli that are either positive or negative reinforcers. Because of this process it would be expected that the words would come to elicit the same response the environmental stimuli elicit. As a consequence, the words should also come to be either positive or negative reinforcers.

In the experiment cited just above, the word paired with the shock and noise should have come to be a negative conditioned reinforcer, as well as a conditioned stimulus, for shock and noise are both negative primary reinforcers. It would be expected that the experimental effect on the semantic rating which was shown was also indicating that conditioned reinforcement value had been acquired by the word in the conditioning process. That is, in general it is suggested that semantic rating scales such as used by Osgood and Suci (1955) actually index the *reinforcing properties of words,* as well as the conditioned stimulus value of the words. Words with positive meaning ratings should have positive reinforcing value, and words with negative meaning ratings should have negative reinforcing value.

Based upon this rationale an experiment (Finley and Staats) was conducted to test the hypothesis that words that have positive evaluative meaning will function as positive reinforcers, that words that have negative evaluative meaning will function as negative reinforcers, and that words of neutral meaning will have no reinforcing effect.

The study was conducted as follows. A group of positive evaluative meaning words, a group of negative evaluative meaning words, and a group of words without evaluative meaning were selected on the basis of semantic differential ratings of sixth-grade children. Then other sixth-grade children were used as subjects in a situation where the task was to press either a right-hand button or a left-hand button when a light in front of the subject was illuminated. After a preconditioning period to tabulate the frequency of the two responses, the positive, negative, or nonevaluative meaning words were presented contingent upon each left-hand response. For one group of subjects each left-hand response occasioned the auditory presentation of a positive meaning word, for another group a negative meaning word, and for a third group a nonevaluative meaning word. [A large class of each type of word was used so that a word was used only once. Examples of positive meaning words are *holiday, laughter, blossom, dollar, America, vacation,* and *supper.*] Over six blocks of ten trials (the first block was preconditioning) of making one or the other response, the subjects increased in their rate of emission of the left-hand response when the response was followed by positive evaluative meaning words. When the negative evaluative meaning words were presented contingent upon the response, the response decreased in frequency. The words without evaluative meaning, although they were meaningful in other ways, did not systematically increase or decrease the strength of the response.

The results showed that words with positive evaluative meaning function as positive reinforcers, words with negative evaluative meaning function as negative reinforcers, and words without evaluative meaning, although otherwise meaningful, do not function as reinforcers. [The effects of the three types of verbal reinforcers, each with a different group of subjects, are shown in Fig. 2.] In the light of the previous treatment of word meaning as respondently conditioned, these results support [the] contention that conditioned reinforcement value is respondently

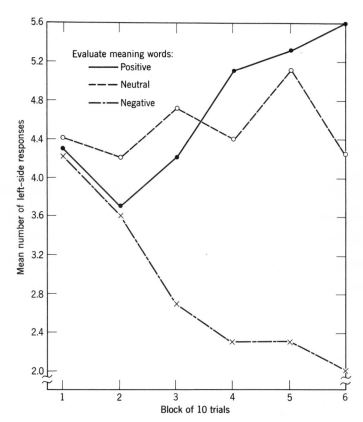

Fig. 2: Strength of response as a function of reinforcement with positive, negative, and neutral evaluative
meaning words.

conditioned and that it depends upon the conditioned response.
Furthermore, the experiment helps integrate the study of word
meaning and the semantic rating of words with the principles and
findings of operant conditioning. It also suggests that semantic
differential rating scales can be used to measure the reinforcement value of stimuli, that is, the extent to which stimuli will
shape and maintain human behavior. This suggestion has a good

deal of significance since the study of psychological measurement, as one example, concerns to a large extent the assessment of the reinforcing value of stimuli, as in tests of interests,
values, attitudes, and personality (Staats, 1964d, pp. 210-211).

In terms appropriate to the present conference, it could
be said that we learn a verbal "concept of reinforcement." In
common-sense terms it could be said that many words have,
or express, a positive or negative concept. The "verbal reinforcement concept" may be seen to involve the functioning of an
S-R mechanism consisting of a large class of word responses
each of which elicits a common emotional (or reinforcing) response. Because they elicit a common response, the words can
have a common function in promoting further learning or problem solving. That is, there are many words that have the ability
to shape new motor learning when applied in a response contingent manner, because of the meaning that these words acquire
for people in our language culture. This may be seen as one of
the most important functions of language, and an integration of
learning principles thus offers a more powerful conception of
this central type of human behavior.

Novel Sentence Generation

A frequent criticism of learning approaches is that they
cannot account for novel behavior. Miller (1965, p. 18) has recently presented such a challenge to learning analyses in the
context of the study of language. He states, for example, "Since
the variety of admissible word combinations is so great, no
child could learn them all. Instead of learning specific com-

binations of words, he learns the rules for generating admissible combinations."

This, however, is a critique of fragmented, simplistic, learning theories. There is nothing in principle that suggests a learning approach is not capable of accounting for novel sentence generation, as well as other novel behavior—*based upon the past learning of the individual.* Actually with the concepts of response hierarchies, word associations, and complex environmental stimulus control, the way in which past learning produces novel sentence generation can easily be seen. The following simple example will suggest how a child could have learned specific S-R connections, and on this basis emit entirely novel combinations of words in generating a sentence.

Let us say that the child has been reinforced for saying MAN in the presence of different "man stimulus objects" and such a stimulus has come as an S^D to control the vocal response MAN. Let us also say that the child has also had the same experience with respect to the vocal response RUNNING. That is, in the presence of a running dog, a running boy, a running girl, and so on, the child has been reinforced for saying RUNNING. This response, however, has never been reinforced in the presence of a man running.

Let us also say, however, that the child sees a man who is running. Under these circumstances the child would be likely to say MAN RUNNING or RUNNING MAN. The total response would be entirely novel, since the child would never before have emitted the sequence. A study that illustrates this type of original behavior in the context of a different type of learning will be described later.

It may be suggested that a complex stimulus composed of components can elicit *original* behavior when the component stimuli each control a separately learned response. The originality consists of the emission of the behavior in a new configuration.

A somewhat more complex example will illustrate the principle more fully and demonstrate the role of word association S-R mechanisms in such original behaviors. Let us say that a child has had experience with the statement GIVE HIM HENRY'S PAPER. This experience, among other things, would be expected to form the word association $\underset{\text{GIVE}}{R}$ S - - - - - - - - - - - $\underset{\text{HIM}}{R}$ S. This would occur whether the child was told the sentence by someone else or read it himself. Let us also say that the child has experience with IT WAS IN HIM THAT I PUT MY TRUST, forming the word association $\underset{\text{HIM}}{R}$ S - - - - - - - $\underset{\text{THAT}}{R}$ S. From the sentence THAT BLUE BALL IS MINE the word association $\underset{\text{THAT}}{R}$ S - - - - - - - - - $\underset{\text{BLUE}}{R}$ S would be formed. And, finally, let us say that the sentence I WOULD LIKE TO HAVE A BLUE CAR results in the formation of the word association $\underset{\text{BLUE}}{R}$ S - - - - - - - $\underset{\text{CAR}}{R}$ S.

Let us also say that the child has also been trained to say each of the above words in the presence of the appropriate stimulus circumstances. With these givens, resulting from specifiable training conditions, it would come as no surprise that in the presence of two other small children, one of whom has just taken a toy blue car from the other, the child in the

present example would look at the aggressing child and emit the
original sentence $R_{\overline{GIVE}}$S-----$R_{\overline{HIM}}$S-----$R_{\overline{THAT}}$S-----
$R_{\overline{BLUE}}$S-----$R_{\overline{CAR}}$S. Never having said this before, the sentence would be entirely novel, but it would have been based upon
the word associations and vocal responses under environmental
stimulus control which the child had previously learned.

The function of the above child's original word associations could have been evidenced in other ways than in the above
situation. Having the word association structure, for example,
the child would be able to remember such a sentence more
easily than if he had not had the subsidiary training. Or, the
same sequence of previously learned responses could enable
the child to answer a grammar test item correctly. That is,
asked to underline the correct statement, the child would select
GIVE HIM THAT BLUE CAR rather than GIVE HE THAT BLUE
CAR. He could also select correctly among new items such as
GIVE HIM A BALL versus GIVE HE A BALL.

It should be indicated here that we actually have hierarchies of responses at each step of our learned sequences of
verbal responses—formed by our past conditioning experiences.
Just by virtue of the training the child in the preceding example
had, the word response hierarchies depicted in Fig. 3 would
have been formed. Both convergent hierarchies, where various
stimuli come to elicit one response, as well as divergent hierarchies, where one stimulus comes to elicit various responses,
as shown in the Figure, must be considered to be formed and to
function in complex cognitive behaviors.

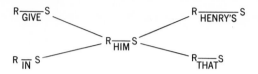

Fig. 3: The above S-R mechanism
involves a convergent mechanism
where the two-word stimuli converge
on the response HIM. In addition, a
response hierarchy mechanism is involved in which the word HIM tends to
elicit two other responses.

Thus, it must be concluded that upon the basis of the
child's experience with language through reading, being spoken
to, being prompted to repeat things, through being reinforced
when he says certain things and not others, and so on, the child
acquires word associations that yield sequences of hierarchies
of responses. These are important types of S-R mechanisms in
cognitive behavior and general adjustment. Under suitable environmental conditions, or verbal conditions (as in tests), the
child will emit the one appropriate sequence from the various
possible combinations—simply on the basis of his past training.
As the author has indicated (Staats and Staats, 1963, pp. 169-
178), this analysis may serve to indicate how the child learns
grammatical word orders, as well as to indicate how original
sequences of language behavior occur.

Novel Problem-Solving Behavior

The author has also suggested (Staats and Staats, 1963)
that the principles involved in the preceding analysis have im-

plications for understanding even complex cases of original problem solving. Several examples were presented and the following excerpt is taken from this account. It deals with an "original proof" in geometry and attempts to show the types of experiences upon which such novel behavior might be based.

First, the following verbal response may be considered to be a complex sequence under the control of appropriate stimulus objects and events: QUANTITIES EQUAL TO THE SAME QUANTITY ARE EQUAL TO EACH OTHER. This response sequence might have been acquired, for example, in a situation where each of two bags of sugar were successively balanced with the same weight and then with one another, and the individual tacted the situation as IF THE TWO BAGS BALANCE WITH (EQUAL) THE SAME WEIGHT, THE BAGS EQUAL EACH OTHER. Further training would bring the verbal sequence under the control of many analogous stimulus situations involving numbers, angles, lengths, and so on.

Another verbal response, IF EQUAL SUMS ARE SUBTRACTED FROM EQUAL SUMS THE REMAINDERS ARE EQUAL, could also come under the control of appropriate stimulus situations through procedures comparable to those described above. Finally, a third verbal response can also be considered a complex sequence learned to certain objects, in this case to certain lines and angles: THE SUM OF THE ANGLES ABOUT A POINT ON ONE SIDE OF A STRAIGHT LINE IS EQUAL TO 180°.* This verbal response, just as the other two

---

*In these examples, the complex verbal response sequences are probably composed of simpler individual responses. The response SUM is a word under the control of multiple stimuli which can be responded to

described, might have been acquired through experience in many diverse situations.

On the basis of these complex verbal responses, each of which is itself under the control of complex stimulus situations, the development of an even more complex language structure might be considered, that is, Thales' demonstration that vertical angles of two intersecting straight lines are equal (Shute, Shirk, and Porter, 1960). This example is clearly one of "originality" in verbal behavior but may be considered in terms of a number of previously acquired complex verbal response sequences that are controlled by specific situations and are emitted together in a novel manner when the individual is confronted with a complex situation that simultaneously tends to elicit all of them.

Figure 4 illustrates the problem, showing the intersecting lines and the angles produced.

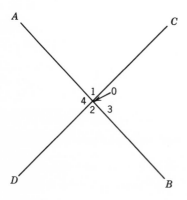

Fig. 4: Illustration used in demonstrating that when two straight lines intersect, the vertical angles in pairs are equal. (From Staats and Staats, 1963.)

---

singly or as a group, usually by making an arithmetic response. The response ANGLES is also a verbal response under the control of multiple "angle stimuli." The same is true for POINT, STRAIGHT LINE, EQUAL, and 180°.

To demonstrate that when two straight lines intersect the vertical angles in pairs are equal, Thales was given two straight lines, AB and CD intersecting at 0, forming the vertical angles, $\angle 1$ and $\angle 2$, and the vertical angles, $\angle 3$ and $\angle 4$. Since AB was given a straight line, and since the sum of the angles about a point on one side of a straight line is equal to 180°, Thales knew that $\angle 1 + \angle 3 = 180°$. Similarly, since CD was given a straight line, he knew $\angle 3 + \angle 2 = 180°$. Applying the axiom, quantities equal to the same quantity are equal to each other, Thales obtained the equality: $\angle 1 + \angle 3 = \angle 3 + \angle 2$. Thales next applied the subtraction axiom by subtracting $\angle 3$ from both sides of the equation to get the equality: $\angle 1 = \angle 2$. In like manner, Thales proved that $\angle 3 = \angle 4$. Thus Thales proved that vertical angles in pairs are equal (p. 25).

The following is a brief account of the "derivation" of the final statement in terms of the behavioral principles that have been discussed. Figure 5, which depicts the possible S-R processes involved in this example, is simplified for purposes of illustration and some steps have been omitted to conserve space.

The first S^D in the chain of reasoning might be part of the geometric form: Line AB is a straight line intersected at point 0 producing the Angles 1 and 3, and producing another line OC. As S^D_1, this complex stimulus might control the verbal response sequence R_1, THE SUM OF THE ANGLES ABOUT A POINT ON ONE SIDE OF A STRAIGHT LINE IS EQUAL TO 180°. This response sequence could then be considered S^D_2, in the chain eliciting the writing response R_2: ANGLE ONE PLUS ANGLE THREE EQUALS 180°. Line CD with the line 0B emanating from point 0 is also a stimulus (S^D_4), which elicits R_4, the same verbal response elicited by S^D_1, and thus the analogous writing responses with respect to Angles 2 and 3, that their sum equals 180°.

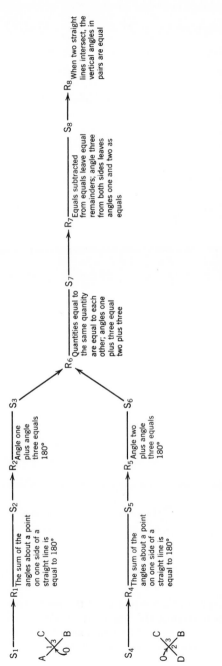

Fig. 5: An S-R sequence illustrating the elicitation of previously acquired responses to specific situations that, when elicited together in a situation that simultaneously tends to elicit all of them, results in a novel or "original" behavior. (From Staats and Staats, 1963.)

The stimuli produced by the next two written responses (S_3^D and S_6^D) combine because of the past history of training to elicit the verbal response sequence (R_6) QUANTITIES EQUAL TO THE SAME QUANTITY ARE EQUAL TO EACH OTHER; ANGLES ONE PLUS THREE EQUAL TWO PLUS THREE. This verbal response sequence produces S_7^D, which then elicits the next verbal response (R_7) EQUALS SUBTRACTED FROM EQUALS LEAVE EQUAL REMAINDERS; SUBTRACTING ANGLE THREE FROM BOTH SIDES LEAVES ANGLES ONE AND TWO AS EQUALS. This response might then be the S^D that would elicit the final statement WHEN TWO STRAIGHT LINES INTERSECT, THE VERTICAL ANGLES IN PAIRS ARE EQUAL. It thus seems conceivable that such types of original reasoning could be based upon S-R processes acquired individually through the individual's past experience and that without such previously acquired response sequences, the novel response could not occur.

In this example, the response sequences described could be called "original" reasoning because the extended sequence of responses that emerges has never occurred before. Each of the components as described, however, had been conditioned to a more simple stimulus, but in the presence of a more complicated stimulus the first response sequence produces stimuli which, in conjunction with the complex stimulus, elicits the next response and so on, until the final novel response occurs.*

---

*For simplicity, the stimulus of the geometric figure is not shown in Fig. 5 at each step of the chain. It should be remembered, however, that the geometric figure could remain an S^D at each stage and might be quite important in eliciting the appropriate R.

The final sequence might then become an even more complex verbal response sequence to the geometric stimulus.

Thus, it may be suggested that it is possible to consider even complex cases of originality in terms of the past learning of the individual. In doing so, however, one must be prepared to utilize the various principles of conditioning and to look for the complex ways that stimuli and responses can be organized into S-R mechanisms, on the basis of the principles.

Conclusions

These are examples showing that "monolithic" learning approaches to various aspects of complex human behavior are inadequ
The author (see Staats, 1964; Staats and Staats, 1963) has also given other examples in the areas of grammatical speech generation, problem solving, originality, intelligence, human motivation, social interaction, various types of child learning, and so on. As these suggest, an integration of learning principles can be considered to be the necessary model for dealing with the complex behaviors ordinarily included under the term cognitive behavior. In addition, the theoretical model must include an elaboration and schematization of the ways the principles can yield complex S-R mechanisms. The next section will sketch some of the outlines of such an integrated learning theory.

AN "INTEGRATED" LEARNING APPROACH

The Notation System

Part of the task of presenting an integrated learning approach involves the use of a terminological convention that reflects the integration. One of the basic splits in the area of learning involves the fact that investigators tend to work either with operant or classical conditioning. Perhaps as a consequence, separate conventions have developed for the depiction of the S-R principles involved in each type of conditioning— with little indication of the points of overlap.

Thus, a separate symbolic convention has been developed for operant conditioning consisting of S^D's, or discriminative stimuli, S^R's, or primary reinforcers, and S^r's, or conditioned reinforcers. This convention has remained separate from the symbols which depict classical conditioning, that is, UCS for unconditioned stimuli, and CS for conditioned stimuli. The separate terminology for the two types of learning fails to indicate the overlap or interaction which occurs between operant and classical conditioning. Although the responses involved in the two types of conditioning are largely separate (motor responses in operant conditioning, versus visceral responses in classical conditioning) there is overlap in the *functions* that a particular S can have.

A stimulus can have multiple functions both within one of the types of conditioning as well as between them. That is, one stimulus can be both an S^D as well as an S^r. It is also the case that one stimulus can be a CS, S^r, and S^D, as an example. Perhaps the most important overlap between the two types of conditioning resides in the fact that a stimulus acquires reinforcing value, becomes an S^r, in the process of becoming a conditioned stimulus, a CS. Thus, at a very basic level operant and classical conditioning appear to be related, and the symbolic convention should reflect this.

The fact that one stimulus can have multiple functions has been suggested for operant conditioning. For example, Keller and Schoenfeld (1950), while incorrectly suggesting that a stimulus must be a discriminative stimulus before becoming a conditioned reinforcer, did indicate that one stimulus can have these two functions. It is suggested that when conditioning principles are applied to other areas of complex human behavior, a notation system that shows the relationship of the reinforcing, eliciting, and controlling (discriminative) functions of stimuli is very advantageous. These are the symbols with which an S-R theorist does his thinking. The following simple convention is thus suggested.

All stimuli regardless of function should be depicted by an S. The functions of the stimulus should be depicted by super-prefixes, a more convenient method for S-R diagrams than the more commonly used suffixes.

(1) A stimulus that elicits a response with no training is called an unconditioned stimulus, or ^{UC}S.

(2) An S that will not elicit such a response will come to do so, will become a ^{C}S, when contiguously presented with a ^{UC}S.

(3) Some ^{UC}S also have another function. When they are presented following a motor response they will later have a strengthening or weakening effect on that response. These stimuli should be depicted as ^{UCR}S, for unconditioned reinforcing stimuli, with a positive sign, $^{UCR^+}S$, for the strengthening function and a negative sign, $^{UCR^-}S$, for the weakening function.

(4) An S paired with a ^{UCR}S will acquire two functions.
It will become a ^{C}S and elicit the same response as
the ^{UCR}S. Presumably because of this acquired
eliciting function, the stimulus will also become a
^{CR}S, a conditioned reinforcing stimulus that is capable of affecting the strength of any motor behavior.

(5) When a ^{CR}S is paired with a new S, as in higher-order
classical conditioning, the new S will also become
both a ^{C}S as well as a ^{CR}S. The way in which a
stimulus can acquire reinforcing value through higher-
order conditioning, especially in the realm of language, is an important elaboration and requires
further attention.

(6) As mentioned, when a $^{UCR+}$S or $^{CR+}$S is presented following a motor response the response will be increased in strength. When a response is reinforced
in this manner, but only in the presence of a particular stimulus, that stimulus will become a ^{D}S, a discriminative stimulus. That is, presentation of the
^{D}S will increase the frequency of the response, and
the ^{D}S can thus be said to control the response.

(7) Furthermore, this process will also make the ^{D}S a
^{CR}S since in this process of discrimination training
the stimulus involved is paired with a ^{UCR}S or ^{CR}S.
Thus operant discriminative learning gives the
stimulus involved both ^{D}S and ^{CR}S functions.

(8) It should also be noted that a stimulus can acquire
^{D}S value for a response by being contiguously presented with another ^{D}S. This implication, as some

of the others, requires additional research, although
as suggested in the section on communication it appears to occur in language learning.

(9) Finally, it may be concluded that any particular
stimulus may have all the functions mentioned. A
stimulus could be a ^{UC}S for one response and a ^{C}S
for another classically conditioned response, which
could also make the stimulus a ^{CR}S. If the latter conditioning took place in an operant discrimination task,
the stimulus would also become a ^{D}S for a motor response. One stimulus would thus be a $^{UC \cdot C \cdot CR \cdot D}S$.

The author has found this notational system to be effective
pedagogically, helping clarify the confusion that arises when
operant conditioning principles and classical conditioning principles are discussed with different notational conventions. Difficulties occur, for example, when in describing classical conditioning food is mentioned as a UCS and later in the context of
operant conditioning as an S^{R+}. Further complications occur
when it is stated that the stimulus paired with food becomes a
CS, and in a later description, in the context of operant conditioning, the same stimulus is said to become an S^{r+} through the
same process of being paired with food. Notwithstanding, the
usual notation system does not acknowledge the relationship of
the two stimulus functions.

More importantly, however, the notation system has
heuristic value and aids one's thinking in extending learning
principles to the area of complex human behavior. As one example, as has been described, words have been shown to be ^{C}S

and have been considered widely as such (Staats, 1961; Mowrer, 1954). The above type of analysis suggests, furthermore, that words that elicit certain meaning responses may also be expected to be reinforcing stimuli, or ^{CR}S. Thus, the various things we know about classical conditioning should apply to the formation of verbal reinforcers, for example, the principles of higher-order conditioning. This aspect of the integration alone indicates an important area of research.

S-R Mechanisms

An important aspect of an integrated learning theory, however, involves the presentation of the general ways that stimuli and responses can be formed into complex constellations. It is suggested that although the basic principles must be separated to distinguish and study them, in actual life the principles function in concert. Furthermore, although the conditioning principles themselves are simple, the S-R mechanisms that are formed in real life consist of exceedingly complex arrays and constellations of the S-R mechanisms. Critics of learning approaches are customarily aware only of the basic principles, not of the complex S-R mechanisms that can be formed on the basis of the principles. Many of the S-R mechanisms have been shown to operate in experimental circumstances, and some of them can be abstracted from analyses of naturalistic observations of human behavior.

Except for the assumption that either classical or operant conditioning principles are involved, the manner in which the stimulus comes to elicit the response is not of primary importance in this section. Rather, the ways that S-R elements can occur in complex constellations are of concern. Thus, some of the S-R mechanisms to be illustrated here will not show whether operant or classical conditioning principles are involved, although this is implied in some cases by the type of response involved in the example. Thus, the stimuli to be depicted could in many S-R mechanisms be eliciting classically conditioned responses or operantly conditioned responses. In addition, the S-R mechanisms to be illustrated will not differentiate between responses that occur overtly and those that occur covertly.

The simplest S-R mechanism is one where one stimulus comes to elicit one response. Most basic experiments attempt to isolate such occurrences. The basic principles of classical conditioning and operant discrimination learning may be considered as examples.

Most human behaviors, on the other hand, involve complicated stimulus events and complicated response events, combined in complex ways. The first elaboration to be made is that single S-R events may be combined into *sequences* on the basis of conditioning principles. That is, responses can be thought to have stimulus properties. Muscular responses activate nerve cells in the muscles and tendons. Vocal responses produce auditory stimuli. Many visceral responses have sensory qualities, and so on. Thus, a response can be conditioned to the stimulus produced by a preceding response. When this occurs a sequence of responses occurs like that depicted in Fig. 6. Such sequences may be of great length and contain many members. Language behavior is replete with such examples.

In addition, however, more than one response may come

R_1—S_1————————R_2—S_2————————R_3—S_3————————R_4—S_4

Fig. 6: A response sequence exists when the stimulus produced by one response tends to elicit another response. Sequences can involve various numbers of responses.

under the control of a particular stimulus, as Hull (1943) showed with rats. Thus, when the stimulus occurs it will tend to elicit the various responses that have been conditioned to it. These responses may be competitive, that is, only one or the other can occur. When this is so, the particular response that occurs may also depend upon the other stimuli present in the situation that tend to elicit one or the other response. A man hurrying toward his office when passing an acquaintance will tend to (1) stop and talk, (2) hurry by, (3) greet the individual but state he must be on, (4) nod and continue walking. Which of the responses under the control of the social stimulus will actually be emitted will depend upon other stimuli, such as whether the acquaintance looks at him, looks down, what the clock on the building states, and so on. This type of mechanism is depicted in Fig. 7.

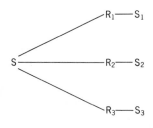

Fig. 7: An S-R mechanism in which one stimulus has come to elicit several different responses.

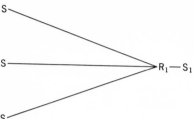

Fig. 8: An S-R mechanism in which several stimuli have come to elicit the same response.

Conversely, different stimuli may come to elicit the same response, as Hull (1943) has also suggested. Different words as stimuli, as one example, may all elicit the same word responses. Thus, the Russell and Jenkins norms (1954) indicate that the words BED, DREAM, COMFORT, and DEEP as stimuli tend to elicit the word associate SLEEP. This type of mechanism is depicted in Fig. 8.

Moreover, these mechanisms may combine into even more complex mechanisms. Thus, a sequence of responses may actually be a sequence in which the stimulus produced by one response controls more than one following response, with more than one such stimulus controlling any particular following response. Thus, in our language culture the stimuli of the word response GIVE will be followed in the child's experience by the personal pronouns HIM, HER, and ME and acquire tendencies to elicit those responses, among others. This will also be true of the word responses THROW and PUSH. A relatively simple sequence of these multiple S-R mechanisms which everyone in our language culture would have acquired through his language experience is depicted in Fig. 9.

Mediated generalization studies have also discovered an important type of S-R mechanism. The studies indicate, in gen-

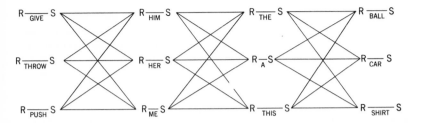

Fig. 9: A complex S-R mechanism consisting of a sequence of convergent stimulus mechanisms and response hierarchy mechanisms.

eral terms, that two different stimuli will become functionally the same if the stimuli each come to elicit the same response. That is, two "dissimilar" stimuli are those which are not functionally the same in terms of primary stimulus generalization. A response conditioned to one will not be elicited by (generalize to) the other—which is the index of similarity. However, if two such stimuli are first made to elicit the same response, then any further experience (conditioning) the individual has with one *will* generalize to the other. As an example, let us say that two people, a man and a woman, are dissimilar stimuli. Let us say, however, that the child is trained to call each of them DOCTOR. In addition, however, the child is later taken to one of them over a period of time and is given a series of painful shots. Each such experience would condition negative responses to the word DOCTOR. This conditioning would then generalize to the other person, and in fact to all people called DOCTOR. This general process is schematized in Fig. 10. As Staats has indicated (see Staats and Staats, 1963) verbal responses made to problem-solving objects can be of primary importance in cases where they mediate the problem-solving behavior. The

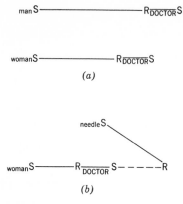

(a)

(b)

Fig. 10: (a) The child has previously been trained to call the man and woman (otherwise "dissimilar" stimuli) by the common response DOCTOR. (b) When the child has unpleasant treatment from the woman, another response, R_2, is conditioned to the response DOCTOR. (c) Since the man also elicits the response DOCTOR, the response R_2 learned to the woman will generalize to the man.

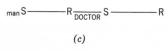

(c)

experiment by Judson, Cofer, and Gelfand (1956) illustrates this mechanism in the context of problem solving and additional examples will be given later on.

Thus, this type of mechanism, response mediated generalization, has additional implications. Words come through conditioning also to be functionally the same as the environmental stimuli with which they are paired. That is, if a word is systematically paired with a certain aspect of the environment it will come to elicit the same responses as does the environmental stimulus with which it is paired (see Staats, 1961). Since the word and the environmental stimulus both elicit the same response, further experience with one will generalize to the other. When this mechanism has been formed experience the individual has with the word will generalize to the environmental stimulus. Direct experience with the environmental stimulus is then not necessary for the individual to learn further how to respond to the environmental stimulus. This, of course,

is one of the powerful types of human learning. The human need
not have direct experience: words perform the same function—
and an S-R account can handle this type of phenomenon.

Another similar aspect of cognitive behavior may be considered in terms of verbal responses (or the stimuli they produce) coming to control motor responses. It is suggested that
the individual through operant discrimination training acquires
a very large repertoire of motor responses and motor skills
under the control of verbal stimuli. Because of this training,
when the verbal stimulus is presented it controls the appropriate motor response. An individual with such a verbal-motor
response repertoire can then acquire new motor skills simply
on the basis of contact with verbal stimuli. This process may
short-circuit what might have taken centuries for the motor
skill to develop. Many years, for example, have gone into the
development of the present-day motor skill of high-jumping.
However, the young athlete today does not have to go through
the various steps involved in this development. A coach presents instructions (verbal stimuli) that control the appropriate
behaviors. Much perfection of the final motor skill by the
athlete is still necessary. However, the main skill can be im-
parted on a verbal level. This process requires, of course, that
the verbal stimuli have come to control the correct responses.
Thus, an important S-R mechanism that accounts for much
human behavior involves series of verbal stimuli that when
presented individually control motor responses. Although at
first the motor responses may depend upon the verbal stimuli
for elicitation, if the motor responses occur in sequence a number of times through the verbal control, the motor responses

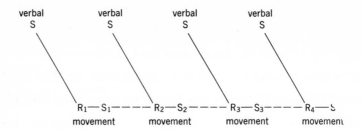

Fig. 11: When a series of verbal stimuli are
presented, each of which controls a particular
movement, and this process is repeated, the
stimuli produced by each movement will come
to control the next movement. In this way a new
complex movement sequence can be established
by language means. (From Staats, 1964*a*.)

will be conditioned in a sequence and will occur under their own
control! At this point the verbal instructions are no longer
necessary. Such a mechanism is depicted in Fig. 11.

It is also true, as already mentioned, that verbal responses (or the stimuli they produce) can also elicit emotional
(reinforcing) responses, either of a positive or negative kind.
This has a good deal of significance for understanding certain
aspects of human reasoning, including social reasoning. Sequences of verbal behavior are many times elicited that are
relevant to future events. The student is asked to accompany
a friend to a show and this and other stimulus circumstances
elicit a long sequence of verbal responses. He says, let us say,
IT IS A VERY FUNNY PICTURE, HOWEVER, I HAVE NOT
STUDIED FOR MY EXAM TOMORROW AND IF I DO NOT I
WILL FAIL THE COURSE. The word stimuli VERY FUNNY
are positive conditioned reinforcers, for the individual with the

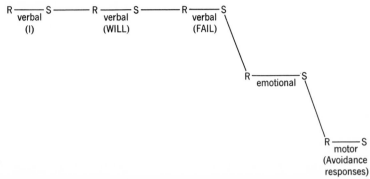

Fig. 12: A sequence of verbal responses elicits an emotional response which in turn elicits a motor avoidance or withdrawal response.

appropriate conditioning history, and would tend to control the approach behaviors of attending the movie. The word stimuli FAIL THE COURSE, on the other hand, will control conditioned negative emotional responses in the individual with the appropriate conditioning history, and these emotional (reinforcing) responses will in turn control behaviors that avoid the proposed activity.

What the individual does in this problem situation will be influenced by his sequence of verbal behaviors *and* their reinforcement value. An oversimplified depiction of verbal behaviors controlling emotional responses that in turn control motor responses is depicted in Fig. 12.

The scope of the present paper will not allow the presentation of the various S-R mechanisms that are important to understanding complex human behavior. Those presented herein may be considered only as examples that characterize the present approach. One additional example will be given, however, because it is so appropriate to the consideration of higher cognitive behavior, or abstract thinking. The mechanism, stated simply, is that many important types of human behavior involve sets of related verbal responses *under the control of other sets of related verbal responses.* That is, the stimuli produced by a set involving a large number of verbal responses can come to be the stimulus "objects" that control a more "abstract" set of verbal responses that are far fewer in number. Sequences of the abstract set of verbal responses can then act as very general "rules" which can then mediate appropriate sequences in the much larger, lower-level class of verbal responses. This may sound very arcane; illustrations, however, may be used to suggest the possibilities more clearly.

A previous section of this paper suggested that a child can be trained according to operant discrimination principles to make a verbal response to both a man and to the stimulus events produced by a running mammal. Such a child will respond to the relationship of the two events by saying MAN RUNNING. Well, verbal stimuli are also stimulus objects. The individual trained to verbally respond to verbal stimulus objects will also be able to respond to such verbal stimulus objects in new combinations. Thus, it would be expected that a child who had been trained to respond to any number with a literal number response, let us say a, b, or c, would be in position to emit certain novel literal number responses when presented with various addition problems (verbal stimulus objects). That is, the child after training on a number of problems of the sort $2 + 4 = 6$, $1 + 3 = 4$, $7 + 8 = 15$, and so on, might respond with the new sequence $a + b = c$. Literal numbers, as one example, may be considered to consist of a related set of verbal

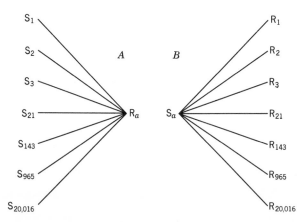

Fig. 13: Part A of the figure represents a hierarchy of specific number stimuli, each of which tends to elicit the literal number response a. In addition, a as a stimulus comes to elicit a class of arithmetic number responses. This is depicted in Part B. (From Staats and Staats, 1963.)

responses. The *concept* of the literal number, it may be suggested, involves both of the types of concept mechanisms previously described in Fig. 7 and Fig. 8. That is, the learning of a literal number would depend upon the various number stimuli coming to elicit a literal number response, and the literal number response in turn coming to have tendencies to elicit each of the number responses. This mechanism is depicted in Fig. 13. In learning literal number responses, the child is actually learning a language about (or under the control of) another language.

The products obtainable from creating a whole set of literal number response statements is very evident of course. In teaching a child, for example, the more simple literal number sequences can be presented and they will mediate the much larger number of actual number statements. Furthermore, the individual who has acquired the literal number response statements to the point of fluency could be expected to emit such statements (general rules) that have never before been seen with actual numbers. Thus, we have discoveries in mathematics, the more abstract verbal response repertoire, that were not observed in the empirical world but which have implications for the empirical world. Thus, negative numbers were derived from the more "abstract" number sequences. A grammar, or the descriptive statements of linguists,may also be considered to be "abstract" verbal responses, in the sense discussed, that have come to be made to other verbal responses. The author has more fully described examples of sets of verbal responses learned under the control of other verbal stimuli (see Staats and Staats, 1963). Because such abstract verbal behaviors are not under the control of environmental events, but rather other verbal responses (stimuli), original abstract verbal behavior more readily gives the impression that mental events are involved that are over and above what the individual could have *learned*.

In concluding this section it may be suggested that learning theory, certainly in the area of complex human learning, now requires an integration of empirical conditioning principles in concert with an elaboration of the various types of S-R mechanisms. This section thus outlines an integrated learning theory based upon a notation system for integrating operant and classical conditioning principles. Part of the theoretical body for dealing with complex human behavior also includes the manner in which more complex S-R combinations develop on the basis of the higher-order (more general), basic principles. It is suggested that these S-R mechanisms, including their pictorial representation, constitute an important part of a learning theory of complex human behavior. The other, more basic, part of the theory consists of the various principles involved in the study of classical and operant conditioning.

It is also suggested that although the basic principles are simple, their possible combination into constellations of multiple stimuli and multiple responses of various kinds provides a theory that includes all the potential flexibility and discovery that we see in complex human behavior. Moreover, because the theory is based upon empirical principles, an analysis of human cognitive behavior in the terms of this theory will suggest empirical hypotheses for research as well as hypotheses for dealing with problems of human behavior.

Although in the past the tendency has been to be separatistic rather than to produce a comprehensive theory, it is to be expected that a learning theory, like other scientific theories, that can encompass the most findings, other things equal, is the most powerful. The events to be encompassed by the basic laboratory principles and their extension into S-R mechanisms are the actions and interactions of man. When the principles of a science are relevant to actual problems of the world, one of the criteria for evaluating the worth of the principles is in the extent to which they are validated in the context of those problems. The more representative the sample of problems dealt with in the research is to the universe of actual problems, the more important the validation. One aspect of the present learning approach is the validation of its principles in the context of complex human behavior. The next section will deal with some of the implications of the necessity of this type of validation for the study of complex cognitive behavior.

LEARNING AS A THEORY OF HUMAN BEHAVIOR

"Functional" Learning Theory

The title of this paper includes the terms "integrated" and "functional." The first part of the paper gave examples supporting the need for an integrated learning theory. This section of the paper will suggest that we also need to study better samples of behavior in the areas presently called concept formation, problem solving, reasoning, originality, and other areas of human behavior as well.

The field of problem solving within psychology did not arise primarily with research by learning oriented investigators. For the most part the early investigators interested in problem solving were Kohler, Duncker, Wertheimer, Maier and other Gestalt or "semi-Gestalt" psychologists. Many times the work in problem solving was actually antagonistic to a learning interpretation and was conducted primarily as a challenge.

However, the field of learning has had and still has a characteristic of building part of its generality upon the empirical findings of its critics, and that process has been quite evident in the field of problem solving. It will prove helpful to glance at examples of the progress that has been made in a learning interpretation of problem solving, before making suggestions for further lines of study.

Maier, in studying problem solving in humans, devised several problem-solving tasks that have been frequently used in later learning-oriented investigations. One of them has been called the two-string problem. Two strings are suspended from the ceiling too far apart for the subject to reach and tie together —which was the solution. The subject is given several objects to reach a solution, only one of them (a pliers) being of sufficient weight to tie to one of the strings and swing it, allowing the subject to grasp one string as he holds the other. Staats (1955) suggested that subjects that could readily verbalize use of the problem-solving tool as a weight would solve the problem more quickly. Subjects' verbal responses to the problem-solving objects were obtained before they participated in the problem task. Maltzman (1959) improved upon the procedure by having one group of subjects try the problem with no prior verbalization and another group after they had read various uses of the problem-solving objects. The latter group solved the problem more readily. Judson, Cofer, and Gelfand (1956) also showed that if they had subjects learn a sequence of verbal responses that included $R\overline{}S$-----$R\overline{}S$-----$R\overline{}S$, the subjects would solve the problem more readily. These studies suggested that learning principles were involved and that verbal responses to the problem-solving objects could play an important role in problem solving.

Kendler and Kendler (see 1961) and their associates have conducted a series of studies which also suggest that verbal responses to problem-solving stimuli can be important to the solution of the problem. Their task consists of developing a discrimination to stimuli that differ in two dimensions, like color and size. Thus, one stimulus could be large and black, another small and black, one large and white, another small and

white. If largeness is reinforced the subject will come to respond to that stimulus dimension. Then, in the crucial part of
the method, the correct stimulus dimension is changed; either
the opposite of the stimulus dimension, in this case smallness,
is reinforced, or the other stimulus dimension, for example,
blackness, is reinforced. Apparently, children react differently
to the second discriminations, depending upon whether or not
they have verbal responses to the problem-solving objects.

Verplanck (1962) has reported experiments in which he
also makes explicit the verbal nature of aspects of problem
solving, and demonstrates that these verbal responses function
according to reinforcement principles. The task he uses is a
card sorting task in which backs of playing cards were used.
The cards had great variety, allowing the experimenter to reinforce complex stimulus attributes of the cards. Thus, for
example, one problem-solving task could be to place cards with
two objects to the right, others to the left. The subjects had to
state the rule they were following in making their placement,
and they also had to place the cards. Verplanck and his associates found that if the verbal "rule" statement itself was reinforced it could be strengthened independently of the actual motor
"problem-solving" behavior of placing the card. Conversely,
reinforcement of the card-placement behavior strengthened this
behavior independently of the verbal rule statement. In terms
of the present analysis, the results clearly indicate the verbal-
motor response mechanism involved in the problem-solving
task, and showed how the S-R mechanism could be manipulated.

Two other types of experimental tasks will be described,
as well as the learning studies that have used them. First,

Adamson (1959) has shown that an anagram solution of a particular type, for example, where the words must be rearranged
in a 2-3-4-1 order, may be considered a response that functions
according to learning principles. That is, when a particular
order has been reinforced on an intermittent reinforcement
schedule, it is more difficult for the subjects involved to solve
new anagram problems that require a different order than it is
for subjects that have been reinforced for the original order on
a continuous reinforcement schedule. This difference in the
"rigidity of problem-solving set" would be expected on the basis
that intermittent reinforcement makes a response more resis-
tant to extinction.

Finally, Long and Holland (see Skinner, 1961, p. 90) have
worked on a teaching machine program that is described by the
term "inductive reasoning." They have shown that when series
of visual stimuli are presented that have changed in a certain
systematic way, the subject can indicate what the next stimulus
in the series is. Moreover, these systematic changes can be
made increasingly difficult and if the subject is gradually introduced to more difficult problems requiring response to additional stimulus features, the subject can come to solve very
difficult problems. Presumably the term inductive reasoning is
used because the subjects respond to the regular change, the
"rule," of the stimulus series. The S-R repertoires involved in
this type of reasoning will be suggested in a later discussion.

Besides the support these various studies give to a learning interpretation of problem-solving behaviors, the results also
support the suggestion given herein that different types of behaviors (for example, verbal behaviors and motor behaviors)

can be joined into S-R mechanisms on the basis of learning principles and can function in complex behavior.

Need for Representative Research Samples of Complex Behavior

The preceding studies, as examples, are important demonstrations that the principles of learning do apply to complex human behavior, including verbal behavior in problem-solving types of situations. As such the studies are an important part of the advancement of the science of learning. That is, the first step in the development of the science was the discovery and specification in the laboratory of the basic principles. At this stage investigators were limited by the need for good experimental control largely to research with simple organisms, simple behaviors, and simple situations. However, the progress of the science has also included the extension of the principles to the study of simple behaviors of humans, child and adult. Furthermore, the principles and methods have been extended into areas of more complex behaviors, or behaviors more unique to man, again with success. The extension of the principles into the study of problem solving (and other areas) suggests that even the most complex cognitive behaviors of man may involve the functioning of such learning principles. This verification encourages us to look further; to extend the principles and methods more widely.

However, it is important to realize what the nature of this advance is, as well as some of the characteristics of the task that lies ahead. Thus, although we have confidence in our principles in the context of complex human behavior, we are still a long way from dealing with adequate samples of the behavior we variously call problem solving, reasoning, or concept formation, and the like. Ultimately, we must study problem solving in its lifelike complexity, dealing with functional behaviors important to the individual's adjustment.

That is, it is suggested that the aspects of learning that deal with human behavior meet their final evaluation in the extent to which they are able to compete with other approaches to the study of and dealing with actual complex human behavior. This means the extent to which such behavior can be predicted and desirable behaviors produced (scientific prediction and control). When the principles of a science are relevant to practical events, although the science can grow in the basic lab, it cannot be restricted to this type of progress. The principles and methods of the science must also eventually show superior ability to deal with those practical events. To extend the science of learning toward this ultimate assessment, it is suggested that we must begin to work with samples of behavior that are more representative of the behaviors in which we are actually interested —the functional behaviors we see in everyday life.

Previous research in such areas as problem solving, even learning-oriented studies, has almost seemed to assume that there is a "faculty" of problem-solving ability, a more or less unitary process. At least this has been implied by the fact that any type of problem task was accepted as a representative sample of problem-solving behavior. Thus, one could speak of problem solving whether the study involved the Maier two-string problem, the Luchins water-jar problem, anagram solution, card sorting, or complex discriminations. However, problem solving, as well as concept formation and reasoning, may not be

considered to be a unitary process, or a unitary type of behavior. Different problem situations call out behaviors learned via
different principles, and involving different types of behavior
combined into different S-R mechanisms.

One is forced to ask what actual problem-solving behaviors
of real life are sampled by the two-string problem, by anagram
solution, card sorting, and selecting the next stimulus in a series.
What, for example, is the relationship of the inductive reasoning
task of Long and Holland to the inductive reasoning that occurs
in various scientific problems? It may be said that some of
these various studies demonstrate the working of complex S-R
mechanisms. But in what way are the problem tasks samples of
complex human problem solving, and how do the principles and
findings generalize to the universe of actual problem-solving behaviors in which we are ultimately interested? The best experimental and statistical control goes for naught if the behavior we
sample in our experiment is not a sample of the universe of behaviors in which we are interested. Thus, attention to this type
of sampling becomes crucial when one is interested in an aspect
of complex human behavior.

The question of representative behavior sampling is generally pertinent to much of the field of human learning. Take the
field of verbal learning, to illustrate the point more fully, although the points to be discussed apply equally well to problem
solving, concept formation, and reasoning research. Verbal
learning research originally stemmed from an interest in an
aspect of complex human behavior. The hundreds of experiments
in paired-associate and serial verbal learning have shown the
relevance of the principles and procedures to this type of human

learning. A necessary avenue of advance, however, is to begin to deal with better and better (more and more representative) samples of the behavior we ultimately wish to generalize back to. However, there seems to be little conscious effort to do this. The field of verbal learning has had little contact with the events of complex human behavior for many years, and many hundreds of experiments. As the situation now exists in the field of verbal learning, the research has largely ceased obtaining lifelike samples of complex human behavior, the experiments stem solely from other experiments. It may be suggested that experimental fields can also stray away from the events in which they were originally interested.

One of the criteria by which to assess the worth of the scientific principles and methods of verbal learning will ultimately be in the extent to which they give a better understanding and control of actual verbal learning. Grammatical speech production, much of mathematical learning, reasoning, reading, writing, and communication are examples of complex behaviors that appear to involve the establishment and function of word response sequences (word associations). What, one may ask, can the science of these events tell us about how the child learns such S-R mechanisms and how they function in his adjustment. These are legitimate demands upon the field. Presumably, the principles obtained by the research must ultimately refer back to the events of original interest. However, this cannot be done without experiments to relate the basic methods and principles to those events.

Does this mean that the task is now to study the most complex of human behaviors, which are certainly beyond the present capacities of the present knowledge of learning? This is not suggested. However, there are several suggestions that can be made in accomplishing the task of gradually moving toward more representative research samples of complex human behavior.

Study of the Original Learning of Complex Behaviors

First, it may be suggested that being a good reasoner or problem solver in the fields in which we are interested involves the acquisition of a tremendous repertoire. Rather than thinking of problem solving or reasoning as internal abilities, it is suggested that we consider these aspects of behavior to involve the functioning of the complex S-R mechanisms the individual has acquired—especially in the realm of language behavior.

Thus, the theoretical physicist's problem solving, as one example, is dependent upon a vast prior training. It begins with original language learning, the original learning of reading, counting, writing, arithmetic, verbal response sequences, and so on. Now, although we cannot at this point subject the reasoning of the physicist to controlled laboratory study, it *is* now feasible to systematically study the basic behaviors, the original learning, that leads to successful reasoning with, and solving of, the problems of physics.

It has not in the past been possible to study complex human behavior, even with the more simple original learning of children. The first task in getting better samples of human behavior waited upon the development of procedures with which to make this study. A major point in this is the ability to work with the learning of children over long periods of time—for complex behavior requires long-term training. An experimental procedure that provides the possibility for the study of complex, basic learning in children will be described in the context of a research project to study the original learning of reading.

In following the rationale that has been developed herein, the author began the systematic analysis of the original acquisition of reading in pre-school children. Reading is an important, functional, complex human behavior. It was felt that an important part of developing a learning theory of human behavior would depend upon the demonstration that such complex human behaviors could be more profoundly studied through the use of learning principles; and that the findings of the learning analysis could be applied in the solution of some of the problems involved in training children to read.

A complete analysis of reading in learning terms cannot be given herein. It may be suggested, however, that an important aspect of reading learning involves bringing word vocal responses under the control of visually presented word stimuli. This may be considered as operant discrimination learning. If the vocal response is reinforced as the child looks at the stimulus, the stimulus will come to control the response. This is essentially what happens in reading training. In addition, of course, the child has to acquire reading units in smaller "chunks" than whole words. Syllables and individual letters have to come to control parts of word responses. When this has occurred the child can respond to successive letters and thus sound out new words on which training has not been received. The first step in the research was to create a laboratory situation to verify the applicability of the general analysis and to begin the development of methods to work with this type of behavior and with the

population of subjects involved. The first study to be reported
will summarize this development.

The aim of the beginning aspect of the learning analysis
of reading was to construct a laboratory procedure within which
reinforcement principles could be studied objectively with young
children over long periods of time, where the verbal stimuli
were presented in a controlled manner. The reading stimulus
materials devised for the experimental work were selected to
fulfill certain criteria. While the task was chosen to be a reading task, to produce good laboratory control the materials were
selected to be as simple and as homogeneous as possible. Since
words and sentences are of different lengths and difficulty, single
vowels and consonant-vowel pairs were selected.

In addition, to obtain good experimental control, an apparatus was constructed in which the phonetic letter stimuli could be
displayed systematically. The apparatus is schematized in Fig.
14. The stimulus presentation apparatus consists of the panel
with four plastic-covered windows. One of the windows is cen-
tered above the other three. Pressure on any of the plastic
covers activates microswitches which lead to various experimental contingencies.

The verbal stimuli are presented to the child in a discrimination procedure. The top stimulus is "matched" by one
of the three stimuli in the bottom row of windows. The task of
the child is to select the stimulus that matches the one in the
top window. In the procedure the stimuli are presented, and the
experimenter, who is not visible to the child, "names" the top
stimulus. The child must repeat the name and then press the
plastic cover over the top window. Then he must select the

matching stimulus from among the bottom windows, press the plastic cover, and again "name" the phonetic stimulus. When this response occurs, and the match is correct, the child is automatically and immediately reinforced. If the child correctly "names" the stimulus before the experimenter does so, that is, "anticipates" the correct name, reinforcement immediately follows (it is then not necessary to go through the matching task).

A problem with the study of child learning over long periods of time has been with construction of a reinforcer system that will maintain voluntary participation. One of the things we see on the basis of naturalistic observation, however, is that tokens, like money, become excellent reinforcers for people—even without states of deprivation of primary reinforcers. Taking this tip from everyday life, a reinforcer system following the same principle was developed. This consisted of tokens backed up by various items which the children had previously selected—the ratio of tokens to back-up reinforcers dictated by the capacity of the tube in which the tokens are deposited (see Fig. 14). One class of reinforcers, the small edibles and trinkets, may be exchanged for the token on a 1:1 ratio. Small toys are exchanged for 10 tokens, larger toys (or toys of higher quality) for 35 tokens, yet larger toys for 80 tokens; and the largest toys for 150 tokens. None of the toys are expensive; each token averages about one cent in value. The toys are hung in the experimental room (see Fig. 14), each above a plastic tube. The size of the plastic tube indicates the number of tokens required to obtain the reinforcer. The child may thus "work" for any of the back-up reinforcers; he may obtain an edible or a trinket by depositing the token in the funnel-shaped opening in

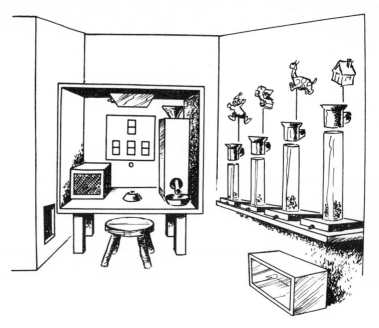

Fig 14: The laboratory apparatus for the experimental study of
reading behavior. The child is seated before the center panel
within easy reach of the various manipulanda which are involved
in the reading response sequence. Letter stimuli appear in the
small plexiglass windows in front of the child whenever he activates the pushbutton on the table before him. If a correct reading response sequence then occurs, the marble dispenser located at the child's near-right drops a marble into a tray posi-
tioned at its base. To the child's left is an open bin in the Universal Feeder cabinet into which are delivered trinkets, edibles,
or pennies, whenever the child deposits a marble in the funnel
located atop the marble dispenser. A marble may also be "spent"
for toys displayed at the child's far-right. Whenever the plexiglass tube beneath a toy is filled with marbles the child receives
that toy. An intercom speaker at the child's left allows his vocal behavior to be monitored from the outside the experimental
chamber. The light at the top of the center panel was not used
in this study. (From Staats, 1964b.)

the right upper corner; he may consecutively deposit 10 tokens in the smallest plastic tube and obtain the reinforcer above it, and the same with the other plastic tubes; or he may work for several different back-up reinforcers at the same time. As soon as he obtains a toy, another that he has previously selected from the same class is placed on display so that he always has a choice among four "for which to work."

Whenever the child's response was correct in all aspects, a marble reinforcer would be delivered. The mechanism would then be turned off until the child had deposited the marble in one of the possible alternatives and had put away any back-up reinforcer that he might have received. Each correct response was recorded automatically with standard cumulative recording equipment. That is, the record consisted of a pen that moved from left to right at a constant speed. Thus, time constituted the baseline of the diagrams representing the child's rate of reading performance. Each time the child made a response, the pen would take a graduated step upwards. The more rapidly the child responded the more steeply would the line slope upwards. The steepness of the slope of the line thus indicates how rapidly the child is reading. Markers were also used to indicate when the child was reinforced with a marble and when he received a back-up reinforcer, as well as what it was. These cumulative records constituted the main results of the first studies that are to be summarized.

The next step in the experimental analysis of reading acquisition was to test the combined apparatus and procedure. While each phase of developing the laboratory facility involved pilot work, it was important to determine whether the entire system would maintain the child's behavior for a long enough period of time to study significant variables in the learning process, to see if the stimulus materials and apparatus produced control of attentional responses, to establish the feasibility of cumulative recording, and to note the sensitivity of the records, and so on. The learning curves of two children run for 40 daily twenty-minute training sessions under conditions of continuous reinforcement will be presented (Staats, et al., 1964b). The first child's record is one of great consistency following the preliminary training sessions (see Fig. 15). For this child the tokens appeared to immediately constitute strong and invariant reinforcers. That is, this child customarily deposited his tokens in the tubes for the larger toys, which meant that several times his behavior was maintained for as many as three daily sessions with no back-up reinforcers—only tokens. The second child's working behavior in the reading training was more variable, including pauses of various intervals (see Fig. 16), with consequent changes in the child's rate of reading as indicated by the varying steepness of slope of the record.

Thus, the results for these children indicated that the various procedural developments were functional in producing a laboratory situation within which to study the complex human learning of a reading repertoire. Long-term studies now appeared to be possible as each of these two children emitted about 1,500 reading responses in the 40 days of training.

Although this study demonstrated the effectiveness of the use of the reinforcement system in maintaining arduous learning behavior of the children, it did not do so in an experimental fashion. That is, the reinforcement was not manipulated during

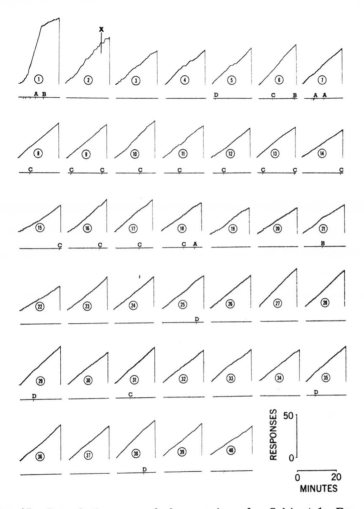

Fig. 15: Cumulative records by sessions for Subject 1. Responses made prior to point X in Session 2 are those occurring during various pretraining phases. Point X marks the beginning of the actual reading task. The slash marks located on the line below each curve represent the presentation of various back-up reinforcers. A indicates that a $.10 toy was exchanged for 10 marbles; B marks the presentation of a $.35 toy in exchange for 35 marbles; the child's exchange of 80 marbles for a toy is denoted by a C; D marks the exchange of 150 marbles for a toy; unlettered slash marks indicate that the child deposited a marble for some item from the Universal Feeder. (From Staats, 1964b.)

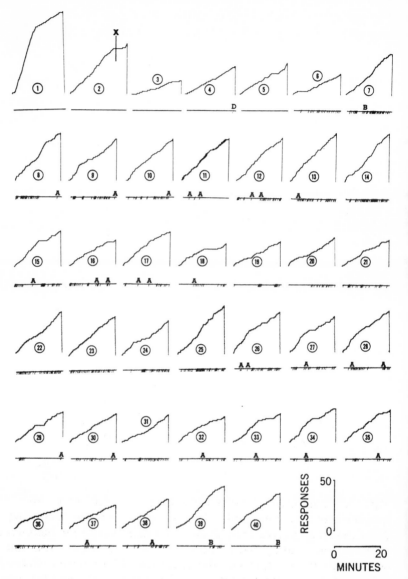

Fig. 16: The cumulative records by sessions for Subject 2. The sequence of pretraining tasks occurs until point X, at which time the reading program was introduced. The occurrence of back-up reinforcers is indicated below each curve as on the previous subject's records. (From Staats, 1964b.)

the study to see the effect that its presence and absence would
have on the behavior of the children. This would be necessary
to more firmly show the importance of this variable in the original learning of small children. Thus, the next step in the systematic analysis of reading was to use the laboratory facility to
begin to assess variables important to the acquisition of reading.
As part of this, also, there was the need to test the extent to
which the facility was well enough controlled to be sensitive to
the manipulation of important independent variables.

The next study (Staats, et al., 1964a), using additional
children, was oriented toward this question. Two different
schedules of reinforcement were applied to each subject,
and rates of response under each schedule were
compared. The procedure was that of discrimination learning:
the child was reinforced in one manner under one room-light
condition and in another manner under another room-light condition. These light-reinforcement conditions were alternated
during each training session in a manner which has been referred
to as a multiple schedule (Ferster and Skinner, 1957; Orlando
and Bijou, 1960).

The first child was run under continuous reinforcement
for one light condition and under extinction (no reinforcement)
for the other light condition. We would expect a discrimination
to develop such that the reading behavior would occur under
the appropriate light condition, but much less so under the other
light condition. That is what occurred. By the sixth session the
discrimination began to form and thereafter became even more
pronounced. The stimulus conditions (in this case the light)

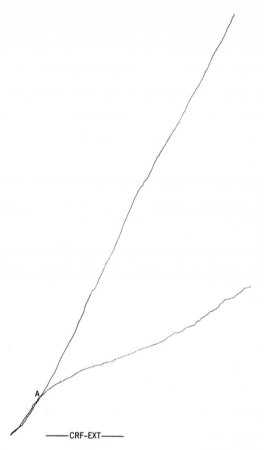

Fig. 17   Composite record for the *mult* CRF-EXT subject. In
order to make a comparison between an S's response rates for
the two experimental conditions the records for reinforcement
schedules were separated and recombined to yield an individual
curve for each condition according to daily session sequence.
All records commence with the introduction of the reading program. The composite records for the four S's are directly comparable; however, the size of each record is determined by S's
response rate. This figure shows that for the *mult* CRF-EXT S
the EXT rate was initially the higher rate, but at point A it de-
clined and crossed the CRF curve. The CRF response rate was
relatively rapid and stable throughout the experiment. (From
Staats, 1964*b*.)

which were correlated with response-contingent reinforcement assumed control over the working behaviors of the child. That is, when the light came on which was correlated with reinforcement, the child immediately began responding more rapidly. When the light condition changed, reading behavior deteriorated. The dramatic nature of the discrimination is shown clearly in Fig. 17, where the responses under each reinforcement condition are pieced together so that the high rate under reinforcement can be compared to the low rate under extinction over the 30-session training period. The records of the next two children to be described will also be of this type.

The second subject was run in a similar manner under continuous reinforcement and variable-ratio reinforcement—in the final training sessions the variable-ratio schedule had reached an intermittency of one reinforcer for an average of five responses. Higher rates of response were produced under the intermittent schedule—using, of course, fewer reinforcers (see Fig. 18). The third child's results include responding under continuous reinforcement and variable-interval reinforcement where the first response the child made after an average of two minutes had passed was reinforced. As would be expected, the child's reading response rate was lower under the variable-interval condition than under continuous reinforcement (see Fig. 19).

These studies show clearly the importance of reinforcement in the context of this important type of learning. When the child is reinforced his participation is enthusiastic, interested, hardworking. When reinforcement for the behavior is not forthcoming the child's reading learning becomes desultory, disin-

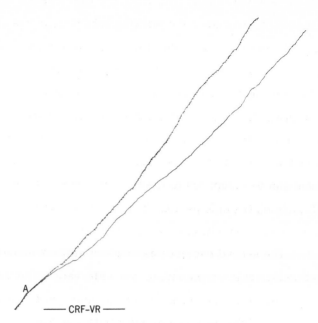

Fig. 18: Composite record for the multiple continuous-variable ratio reinforcement (mult CRF-
VR) subject. The VR curve (shown with slash
marks on the record) was initially lower than the
CRF curve. However, from point A the VR rate
is the more rapid of the two. (From Staats, 1964b.)

terested, and other behaviors occur which are antithetical to
learning.

In addition, finer reinforcement principles were demonstrated. That is, it was also possible to increase the vigor of
the children's reading behavior through the use of partial or
intermittent reinforcement schedules. In any event, the basic
principles of reinforcement learning may be considered to have
been supported in these laboratory studies. The results and the

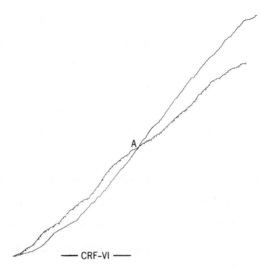

Fig. 19: Composite record for the multiple continuous-variable ratio reinforcement (mult CRF-VI) subject. The VI
curve (with slash marks) is depicted
above the CRF curve until point A on the
record, at which point it becomes the
lower of the two curves. (From Staats,
1964*b*.)

preceding analysis, however, open up further lines of study in
the systematic analysis of this type of learning. The next study
to be summarized (Staats, et al., 1962) will indicate not only
that reinforcement is important in maintaining the attentional
and working behaviors of the child, but also that reinforcing
these behaviors results in the actual learning of a reading repertoire. This study is a step on the way to transposing the find
ings in the laboratory study of reading to actual procedures
for training children to read.

For this study a small group of words was arranged in a program in which words were presented singly as well as in sentences and in short paragraphs. The child was prompted to say a word as he looked at it, and was reinforced with small edibles, trinkets, or tokens backed up by small toys. Eight 40-minute training sessions were presented to the children and the number of new words the children learned to read was tested after each training session.

Three 4-year-old children were introduced to the training without extrinsic reinforcement—they were given social reinforcers (i.e., approval) but not the other reinforcers. This was continued until the child requested discontinuance of the activity, which was only 15 minutes for two of the children and 15 minutes into the second session for the other child. At this point reinforcement was instated and in each case the child's reading behavior was strengthened and maintained for the remainder of the training. The records of these children are shown in Fig. 20. These children acquired 16-, 17-, and 18-word reading vocabularies respectively, in the eight training sessions.

Three other children were given the opposite treatment. That is, they were started under the reinforcement condition and after two training sessions were switched to no-reinforcement. As the figure shows they learned words readily under reinforcement, but when it was "cut off," their learning behaviors extinguished. After three or four sessions of no-reinforcement each child requested discontinuance and the condition was changed to reinforcement. In two cases the reading behavior was reconditioned, and learning "picked up" again. The records of these children are presented in Fig. 21.

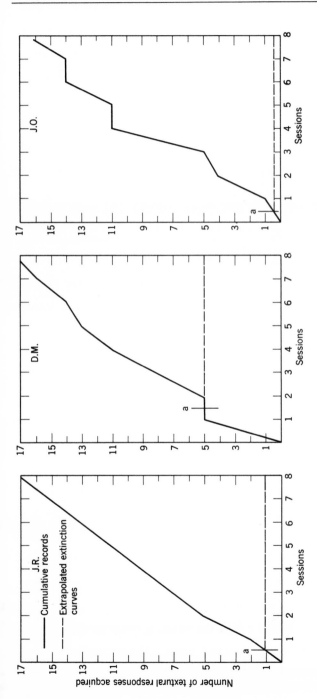

Fig. 20: The curves shown here were generated under a beginning period of no "extrinsic" reinforcement. When S would no longer remain in the experimental situation, reinforcement was instated as indicated by the mark on the curve. The dotted line commences at the point S would no longer remain in the experiment, and indicates the curve which would have resulted if reinforcement was not introduced. (From Staats, et al., 1962.)

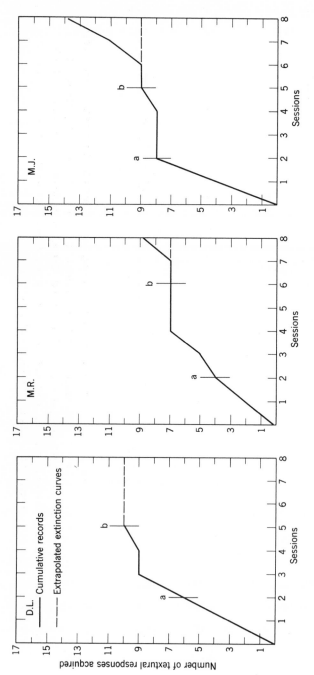

Fig. 21: For these S's, the first condition included reinforcement which was discontinued at the point of the first mark on the curve. When S would no longer remain in the experimental situation, reinforcement was reinstated, as the second mark on the curve indicates. The dotted line commences at the point the S would no longer remain in the experiment and depicts the curve which would have resulted if reinforcement was not reinstated. (From Staats, et al., 1962.)

The results of this study support and extend the findings of the previously described studies. That is, when the attentional and working behaviors of the children in the reading task were reinforced these behaviors were maintained in good strength. Without such reinforcement, however, the behaviors weakened and other competing behaviors that were not relevant to the task became relatively stronger. Furthermore, when the attentional and working behaviors of the children were strong they learned new reading responses rapidly; the converse was true when the behavior was not reinforced. The observations of the children's behavior in the learning situation as well as the recorded results indicated that basic to learning to read are the minute-to-minute attentional and working behaviors of the child. When the child attends to the material and works at a high rate, he rapidly learns to read. The major variation in learning seems to be a function of these basic behaviors. Thus, it would appear that under more appropriate conditions of reinforcement, even very young children are capable of sustained work activities and can learn complex verbal skills.

The next step in applying principles from the learning model to a significant human behavior would be to conduct long-term studies in which children were actually trained to a reading repertoire. Actually, the author had begun working on the development of such procedures with his young daughter while the other studies were being conducted. The procedures established in this study have more recently been generalized to other pre-school children in the areas of writing, number, and reading concept learning, and these and other results are now being prepared for book publication. It is not possible to summarize the many results herein; however, it may be said that the research provides an empirical basis for a theory of these types of complex behavior.

Furthermore, additional steps have been taken on this research project to progressively obtain more and more representative samples of the behavior involved—while staying within the context of laboratory experimentation and learning principles. For example, the theoretical analysis developed for original writing, reading, and number concept learning is now being tested in an experimental nursery school group in a public school—maintaining the experimental control of the laboratory.

In addition, the theoretical analysis of reading acquisition and the reinforcement procedures have been extended to remedial reading training. A 14-year-old, Mexican-American, delinquent boy, who had a long history of school failure and misbehavior and second grade reading achievement, was given 40 hours of reading training which extended over a 4-1/2 month period. S.R.A. reading materials were adapted for use in conjunction with a token system of reinforcement. During the training S's attention and participation were maintained in good strength by the reinforcers, he made many reading responses and learned and retained 430 new words, his reading achievement increased to the 4.3 grade level, he passed all his courses for the first time, and his misbehaviors in school decreased to zero. This research is being extended to additional subjects.

These studies actually sample significant, adjustive, complex behaviors and in so doing extend and elaborate the integrated-functional theory of learning. It is more generally suggested, however, that the present studies (see Staats, 1964; Staats and

Butterfield, in press; Staats, et al., 1962, 1964) describe experimental procedures that constitute a general method with
which to study complex learning in children. With this experimental method the children's behavior may be studied over a
long period of time during which it is possible to produce the
repertoire in which the investigator is interested and to test
the function of this repertoire in other types of activities. It
should be pointed out that when we study problem solving, or
concept formation, we are studying the "function" of behaviors
the individual has already acquired—usually over long periods
of training—even though the problem-solving situation itself may
result in further learning (Staats, 1957).

It must be concluded that the problem-solving ability of
the physicist depends upon his previously learned basic repertoires, his mathematical verbal response sequences, and the
like. Certainly the best experience we could recommend for a
child at the present time, if we wanted to produce an original
problem solver, would be a good education in the field containing the problems. It would be safe to say that a child would
learn more about being a good problem solver from learning to
read, to count, to emit arithmetic and mathematical behaviors
appropriately than he would from card sorting, anagram problems, or even from completing an inductive reasoning program
involving visual stimuli. Although we are not yet capable of experimentally studying the behavior of an Einstein, it is suggested
that we are ready to study the basic behaviors that make up such
complex types of reasoning. It is suggested that the study of
these basic, but complex, human behaviors will as progress occurs yield information about problem solving itself, as well as

other cognitive behaviors. The samples of behavior that can be studied in this way may actually approach more closely to the cognitive behavior in which we are interested than do some of the more artificial experimental tasks that are called by the names problem solving, concept formation, and so on.

Thus, in summary, one way of getting simplification in the study of complex behavior is to use children in their original learning tasks. In the experimental example given, the original learning of reading was used. In such circumstances one can pump in the repertoire that one wants to deal with, thus maintaining good assurance that there are not unknown sources of variance. In addition, dealing with the original learning of children has other features for gaining the simplification necessary for laboratory study. For example, the literary creation of a novelist may be too complex to bring into the laboratory for systematic study. However, the original language learning of the child, such as original reading and writing learning, are not. After we have gained a detailed knowledge of the principles involved in this behavior, we will with this knowledge be able to advance to even more complex cases.

Additional Suggestions for Representative Behavior Samples

The summary of this research, while it contains general methodological suggestions, is not recommended as a single prototype of future research in problem solving, originality, or concept formation. It is not suggested that the study of these complex behaviors be *restricted* to samples of basic child learning in the areas described. The same methods and S-R principles could be used in the context of behaviors even more repre-

sentative of original cognitive behaviors. As an illustration, in
an earlier section, an example was given of Thales' proof that
the vertical angles in pairs of two intersecting lines are equal.
It would seem possible to experimentally test the suggestion that
this is a type of original behavior resulting from stimulus combination, where each stimulus controls a separate response.
Why could not a child or a group of children be trained to the
type of separate responses involved in the geometric proof and
then arrange the circumstances so the stimuli are combined?
The possible emergence of the original behavior could then be
observed. Such a demonstration would be a dramatic example
of producing a significant creative behavior in the laboratory.
This type of experiment would of course demand the detailed
S-R analysis and the long-term research already described.

The possible functioning of other complex S-R mechanisms
in the area of problem solving should be similarly tested to obtain more representative laboratory samples of behavior. Thus,
when a child is trained to make more "abstract" verbal responses
to other verbal stimuli, as in the example concerning literal
numbers, will the child under appropriate stimulus circumstances
emit sequences in the more abstract verbal response system which then lead him to make original responses in the less
abstract system? It would not be difficult to compose tasks,
based upon the analysis, that were close samples of the actual
behaviors in which we are interested. And the methodology of
working with a child for a long period of time, as demonstrated
in the previously described research, provides the experimental
methodology for dealing with complex, long-term learning.

One further example will be given. The author has suggested the following with respect to certain aspects of scientific behavior.

> The important point here, which might also be significant for understanding "originality" in the extension of scientific theories, is that verbal responses which may be developed . . . through experience with environmental stimuli may produce new verbal responses which have no known environmental counterparts but which may lead individuals to look for environmental events not previously seen, and so on. . . . An illustration of the possibility of discussing some of the functions of scientific theories in terms of behavior principles may be useful here.
>
> In a science area a possible example might be the periodic table of elements in chemistry. As [verbal responses] to environmental events a table of the weights of different elements was formed, let us say. The table itself, however, may be considered to have stimulus characteristics that can be . . . described. The new set of verbal responses, let us say, [described] the systematic nature of the table, with weights increasing in a certain fashion from element to element, even though there were gaps in the table. These verbal response sequences might then have elicited the final sequence that perhaps there were elements, yet unobserved, which would fill in the gaps. This verbal response sequence might then have controlled the behavior of making further observations, leading to the discovery of new elements, filling in the table, and so on (Staats and Staats, 1963, p. 244).

This is an example of one type of complex combination of S-R events (a complicated S-R mechanism). The account suggests that the original table is formed by the elicitation of verbal responses under the control of environmental stimuli. These verbal responses themselves then elicit further, more "abstract, verbal responses that are descriptive of the first verbal responses (the table), and these abstract verbal responses then elicit the motor behaviors of looking for further elements. It would seem that a more simplified counterpart of this type of learning could be established in the laboratory, using stimuli with systematic characteristics like the relationships occurring with atomic weights. Verbal responses could be trained to the stimulus elements and it could be observed if those verbal responses would elicit further verbal responses that resulted in further investigations.

A more simplified example of this type of reasoning, for better controlled laboratory purposes, could be constructed using a task like that used in Long and Holland's program. In one such reasoning problem, for example, a series of five stimuli is presented to the child, the stimuli of which vary in a systematic fashion. Thus, the first stimulus might be a bottle-shaped figure on its side, the next would be upright, the next on its side, the next upright, and the final bottle on its side. The child must then select from alternatives what the position of the next bottle in the series would be. Although Long and Holland do not specify the nature of the S-R mechanisms involved, and thus why the task is a sample of inductive reasoning, the S-R mechanisms that mediate problem solution may be suggested and then the similarity to other types of reasoning may be seen.

That is, it may be suggested that the child responds to the stimuli in the series with vocal responses, by saying something like the following: THE FIRST BOTTLE IS SIDEWAYS, THE SECOND IS UP, THE THIRD IS SIDEWAYS, THE FOURTH IS UP, THE FIFTH IS SIDEWAYS. This would represent the first set of verbal responses, elicited under the control of the environmental stimuli. In addition, however, the subject might then respond to these verbal responses with additional verbal responses, for example, by saying THE FIGURE'S POSITION IS ALTERNATED, WHEN ONE IS SIDEWAYS THE NEXT ONE SHOULD BE UP. On this basis he solves the problem by the motor response of selecting the correct alternative, or by some other means in another type of problem.

On the basis of this type of S-R analysis of this and other problems, it is suggested that similar types of problems could be set up in which the verbal behaviors necessary to problem solution were manipulated through training to find what the determinants of such abstract reasoning are. Thus, to solve the problem used in the above example, it might be necessary that the child have (1) learned to look at series of stimuli in sequence from left to right, (2) learned to make counting verbal responses to series of objects, and (3) learned the verbal responses SIDE-WAYS and UP, and (4) that he had learned to describe appropriate stimulus events as ALTERNATING. It is suggested that such an analysis in terms of the S-R mechanisms involved, as well as an experimental demonstration of the analysis, would then have generality and would suggest research on still more complicated problems that were even closer to the real problem-solving behaviors in which we are ultimately interested.

The crucial point here is that if we are interested in a type of complex human behavior the first step is to make a detailed analysis of the behavior in terms of the S-R mechanisms involved. When this has been done it is possible to produce an analogue of the S-R mechanism in simplified form. The simplified S-R mechanism can then be subjected to laboratory experimentation. In this way the analysis and the research methods can be developed with which to advance to more representative samples of behavior that involve a similar S-R mechanism.

Calling an experimental situation concept formation or problem solving does not in itself guarantee generalization of

the conclusions to actual behaviors that are considered in those
terms. One of the sources of unreliability of experiments resides in the nature of the behavior sampled, and in this sphere
improvement in sampling is one line of progress. Thus, it has
been suggested that we need progressively to get better samples
of complex behaviors—and that we must self-consciously attempt to make progress in this direction.

In summary, several examples have been cited to illustrate possibilities for this type of progress. These examples
contained several general points. (1) In obtaining more representative samples of complex behavior it is necessary to develop
laboratory procedures within which the behavior can be experimentally investigated over long periods of time. Most complex
human behaviors involve long periods of training. Adequate
samples of such training cannot be reproduced in short-term
studies in which the subjects participate for a few hours at
most. (2) Based upon S-R analyses, it is now feasible to experimentally study the original learning of children in a number of
different areas of behavior. Many times these behaviors are
actually samples of adult behaviors in which we are interested,
and many times they consist of behaviors that must first be acquired before the complex behaviors of the adult can be learned.
(3) Furthermore, it is suggested that more complex samples of
actual problem solving may be studied by first selecting a sample of such behavior and analyzing it in terms of the S-R mechanisms involved. Then an experimental situation may be composed to test the analysis. When the principles and S-R mechanisms have been verified in this simplified context, it is then
possible to move on to more complex samples of behavior that

involve the S-R mechanism. This approach may be contrasted to the more usual strategy of defining what we mean by concept formation, or problem solving (or other psychological construct), and then composing the experimental situation on the basis of the definition of the construct. If concept formation or problem solving were a unitary process, this latter strategy might be more appropriate. It would seem, however, that problem solving and concept formation are not unitary but instead involve different types of behavior and thus different types of S-R mechanisms.

One additional point should be made. The recommendation made herein that learning must be extended to complex behavior is not the same as the simple injunction to deal with significant behaviors (see Sanford, 1965). It is one thing to extend already established basic principles back to naturalistic occurrences. It is quite another to attempt to discover the basic principles in naturalistic circumstances where there are complex interactions and counteractions between the determining events—and where the investigator can do little to simplify, manipulate, and record these events. Although our interest begins with real life events, and we wish to work back to them, the path involves a sojourn in the laboratory, where basic, analytical principles may be found through the artificial simplicity of the laboratory. Here events may be isolated and less complex samples of these events may be obtained. *After* these basic principles have been found, we may then use naturalistic observations to test the principles and to elaborate the theory. The applications to the real-life situation then constitute part of the progress of the science.

CONCLUSIONS

It is suggested that to present an adequate learning theory of human behavior, it is necessary to integrate classical and operant conditioning principles as well as to elaborate the ways in which these principles function to produce complex S-R mechanisms. When this is done the resulting theory has the potential complexity and flexibility that is demonstrated in complex human behavior, including the possibility of accounting for original or novel behavior. The latter is crucially important to an adequate account of human cognitive behavior and general cultural advancement.

In this sense it may also be suggested that the resulting learning theory, as a conception of human behavior, has all the characteristics of true theory. The higher-order, most general, principles or propositions, the principles of classical and operant conditioning, in combination yield lower-order principles, which constitute the various S-R mechanisms. And from these S-R mechanisms in turn can be derived lower-order (less general) hypotheses concerning various types of complex human behavior. Moreover, in the best traditions of a science, the basic propositions have confirmation in the laboratory, as do many of the propositions concerning the S-R mechanisms. Many of these confirmations have involved simple organisms, simple behaviors, and simple situations. But one of the lines of development that must be consciously begun is the extension of the principles into more and more complex areas of human behavior. Thus far, the extensions that have been made have met with considerable success. Systematic integration of the basic principles and S-R mechanisms suggest further extensions.

Thus, an important part of the development and generalization of the theory is its extension into areas of more complex
human behavior. It is suggested that this extension is crucially
involved in the development of the theory. One of the necessary
developments in this task is obtaining more representative
samples of human behavior with which to test the relevance of
the propositions of the theory. As one line of development, it is
necessary, and now possible, to begin the study of behaviors
basic to the actual human behaviors of problem solving, reasoning, concept formation, and the like, as we know them in actual
life. That is, it is now possible to study the basic behaviors of
language development, reading, counting, arithmetic and mathematical sequences, writing, and the like, with laboratory methods
and the principles of learning. In addition, as another line of development, it is suggested that it is now possible to study the
various behaviors we call problem solving, concept formation,
reasoning, and other aspects of original behavior, in tasks that
better sample the behaviors as they actually occur in life. This
extension depends upon S-R analyses of the various types of cognitive behaviors. On the basis of such analyses, experimental
tasks can be designed that will better sample the behavior of
ultimate interest. An important aspect of both types of study will
be the ability to work with subjects in an experimental situation
for long periods of time since the type of learning to be involved
will ordinarily be complex.

It is not suggested that basic studies that isolate and demonstrate the formation and function of various S-R mechanisms
have been completed. Further research of this type is still

necessary. In addition, however, extensions of the various S-R mechanisms to more representative samples of complex human behaviors can be seen as a central path of present-day psychology. This extension can be expected to lead to further development of the integrated-functional learning theory of human behavior as well as to practical programs for dealing with the problems of human behavior.

11 D. E. BERLYNE
University of Toronto

Discussion of Papers by I. Goldiamond, B. F. Skinner and A. W. Staats

We have been privileged to hear three exceptionally meaty papers. In the time available, it will not be possible for me to do justice to them by taking them in turn and discussing the vital questions that each raises. The best that I can do is to consider things that all of this morning's three speakers have said or implied and things that all of them have omitted.

All three share a strong conviction that the study of the phenomena to which we refer by such terms as "problem solving," "cognitive" processes, and "thinking" must be rooted in the study of learning, and, in particular, in the study of the simplest kinds of learning that are found in animals as well as in human beings. This is a position with which I find myself in full agreement. There are a number of reasons for holding it. First, thinking and other intellectual processes are forms of learned behavior, and the overt behavior that results from them is a form of learned behavior. Secondly, there are ample grounds for believing that, both phylogenetically and ontogenetically, intellectual processes have grown out of functions belonging to lower levels of adaptation and that they are likely to

341

have more to do with acquired response patterns than with response patterns that are fixed by heredity. Thirdly, even if intellectual processes belonged to a different order of existence from simple learned behavior, we should not be fulfilling the aims of science until we had completed a thorough comparison of the two. Fourthly, as the history of other branches of science shows, it is desirable to use what is known about simpler phenomena as a starting-point when approaching the study of more complex phenomena, since only in this way can the nature of the complexities that separate the two be brought into focus and seen in perspective.

One of the most critical problems of research strategy facing the study of intellectual processes is how to strike a balance between the need to concentrate on the peculiarities of these processes and the need to integrate this area of inquiry with the theory and experimental study of learning in general. The kind of approach exemplified by this morning's speakers is an important one, but it is not the only one that we require at the present time. We must have people who follow other approaches but constantly keep an eye open for linkages between what they are finding and what is known about learning. All those who spoke during the last two sessions seem to have been doing just this in manifestly fruitful ways.

The balance is, however, not always struck, and undesirable extremes are not always avoided in contemporary psychology. For example, some of our contemporaries have spotted phenomena within the domain of intellectual processes that existing accounts of learning are unable to handle adequately. Under the apparent influence of a simple logical fallacy, which goes "A is different from B, therefore A is not like B," some not only deny the possibility of a synthesis between what has been newly discovered and what has come out of previous decades of research on learning but even advocate the dismissal of existing theoretical structures and methods of investigation from the areas for which they were originally designed. One trembles to think what would happen if the example of some of our psychological contemporaries were followed in the commercial world! One would have thought that the exponents of planned obsolescence had gone as far as they could, but they could evidently learn a great deal from some of our colleagues. Everybody would then be called upon to trade in his car whenever room for improvement were found in an ashtray—not, let it be noted, for a new car, but for a new ashtray! This would be particularly mortifying when it turned out that the ashtray with which fault was found belonged to a model of car that had been out of production since the 1920s!

On the other hand, those of us who believe in maintaining close contact between the study of learning and the study of thinking must not go to the opposite and equally undesirable extreme. We must not slur over the profound differences between simple learned behavior and behavior governed by intellectual processes, even if we expect many of these differences to be recognizable eventually as quantitative differences and differences in degree of complexity. We must not allow lines of research that happen to have become established among specialists in learning to dictate what aspects of thinking shall occupy our attention. We must rather consider first what are the salient characteristics of intellectual functioning that raise problems and, only after we have done this, search for possible starting-points amid the findings and ideas that have emerged from efforts to elucidate learning. We must, above all, establish as much communication as possible with those who have been pursuing other approaches to the psychology of intellectual functions, even when their concepts and terminology are uncongenial.

All three of our speakers have sought the essence of "problem solving" in situations where a response is controlled by discriminative cues in conjunction with other factors, such as Professor Goldiamond's "instructional stimuli" and Professor Skinner's "precurrent responses." There is a great deal to be said for this way of going about the task. Behavior under intellectual or, as we often say, "rational" regulation, is behavior determined jointly by the external environment of the moment and by symbolic processes going on within the organism that can, in their turn, be traced back to exposure to other external stimuli and performance of other responses on past occasions.

Nevertheless, I detect in all three of this morning's papers some influence of what seems to have been one of the great impediments to progress in this area of psychology, namely the legend that the royal road to thinking is through concept formation. Concept formation is, of course, merely discrimination learning of a greater or lower order of complexity. Like many other processes, concept formation can be aided by thinking, and thinking makes use of the products of prior concept formation. But this does not mean that the two can be identified. On the contrary, the typical concept-formation

experiment deflects our attention from some of the most conspicuous and perplexing attributes of thinking.

Some of these attributes have not received as much consideration from this morning's speakers as one might have
wished, although the beginnings of an attack on them are in evidence here and there.

First of all, the overt behavior that results from thinking
generally consists not of a single response but of a protracted
and complex sequence of responses, all of which must be performed in the right order and at the right time for the final reinforcement to be forthcoming. This is the principal lesson of
Köhler's work on insight in chimpanzees. It has sometimes
been thought that the essence of insight is the immediate appearance, without prior trial and error, of the behavior con-
stituting a solution to the problem. But a look at Köhler's protocols or at the reports of the somewhat similar experiments
done under Pavlov's auspices in the 1930s shows that the solution is often found after several errors have been made and
abandoned. The main point about the behavior is that it consists of a chain of responses that would have been extremely
unlikely to occur, with or without prior trial and error, if
representational processes had not intervened. The components of the chain must, of course, consist of, or resemble,
responses that the subject has learned to perform in different
contexts in the past. But how do representational processes
cause them to be fitted together in the required pattern?

Secondly, in everyday human life, the processes that
supplement the external stimulus, including what Professor
Goldiamond has called "instructional stimuli" and Professor

Skinner has called "precurrent responses," themselves take the form of elaborate sequences. Once again, the elements must already have been part of the subject's repertoire of behavior, but the precise combination will often be unprecedented for him. Much of the hard work of thinking goes into the construction of an appropriate combination of "mediators" or "thoughts" for the first time. How is the combination arrived at? Of the three speakers, Professor Staats has offered suggestions pertaining to this question, and it will be interesting to see how his continuing work develops this line of investigation during the next few years.

There are many indications that sequences of mediating symbolic responses depend for their effectiveness on the manner in which their components are concatenated, more than on anything else (Berlyne 1965, Ch. 5). As indicated by a number of writers of differing orientations, including Sechenov, Selz, and Piaget, directed thinking—that is, thinking aimed at problem solution—depends on sequences of implicit responses representing transformations. The transformations may stand for physical processes that are capable of turning one natural phenomenon into another, but they are likely to have originated in our experience of effecting changes in the external world through our motor responses. It is interesting to see in some of Professor Goldiamond's experiments illustrations of the way in which relations between stimulus patterns are handled by regarding one pattern as the product of a transformation applied to the other and how children may be helped to cope with problems of this nature by allowing them to implement the transformations through their own actions.

Thirdly, a mediating formula (a chain of properly con- catenated symbolic responses) evidently has effects on behav- ior that none of its components would have alone or even that the same combination of components would not have if pieced together in a different way. In other words, we have an in- stance of what Hull called "patterning," whose importance also emerges clearly from Selz's writings. The pattern of mediators will, more often than not, be one to which the subject has never been exposed before, as has already been pointed out. Yet it influences behavior in its peculiar, and quite possibly unique, way. How does this come about? It is undoubtedly a conse- quence of previous learning but of previous learning that in- volved different stimuli and different responses from those that are at work now. This is the kind of problem that some of our contemporaries have attempted to handle, or perhaps sometimes to circumvent, with the help of terms like "rule" or "principle." Those of us who are distrustful of recourse to such terms must nevertheless confront the problem and look for some more adequate way of dealing with it.

Fourthly, mediators, symbolic responses, thoughts, in- structional stimuli, precurrent responses, or whatever one wishes to call them, reflect in some way external stimulus conditions that are at present inaccessible, forms of behavior that the subject would be well advised to perform, or rein- forcement contingencies. But how exactly are they related to these? To call them "descriptions" is hardly enough. They may not be descriptions in any strict sense of the term, and in any case, what is a description? In order to answer questions like this, the language of information theory is indispensable.

It is imperative to determine both where information contained in the mediating pattern originates and to what processes
it will be further conveyed. A comparison of the distribution of
information among the elements of what is represented and its
distribution among the elements of the representational process
is also required if several of the long-standing problems that
concern thinking are to be handled in a way that is compatible
with modern behavior theory (Berlyne 1965, Ch. 7).

Lastly, and most important of all, there are what some
of us call "motivational" questions. These questions concern
the role of the psychophysiological processes that are associated with the dimension of arousal, which, it is clear, have
much to do with thinking as with so many other facets of behavior. They concern the changes in the organism's state that are
brought about by what Professor Goldiamond has called "instructional stimuli" and similar factors. They concern, above
all, the sources of reward or reinforcement that are at work
in behavior dependent on thinking and the nature of any aversive conditions whose removal might supply reinforcement.
Many ingenious experiments, including ones for which all three
of this morning's speakers have been responsible, show how
judicious scheduling of conventional, extrinsic rewards can
work wonders in the modification of behavior. It is conceivable
that other kinds of reward might be still more efficacious, and,
in any case, most real-life thinking is, it would seem, not controlled by such rewards as food, toys, or marks of social distinction. On the contrary, there is good reason to believe (Berlyne 1960; 1963; 1965, Chs. 9-11) that the rewards that are at

work in the situations in question are most commonly self-administered and internal.

One of our distinguished contemporaries (Miller, 1965) has expressed disappointment with "attempts to characterize human language in terms derived from behavioristic investigations of conditioning and learning in animals." One of the reasons he gives for his disenchantment is that "the kind of reinforcement schedule a child is on when he learns language is very different from what we have used in experiments on discrimination learning. No one needs to monitor a child's vocal output continually and to administer 'good' or 'bad' as rewards and punishments."

There is, however, no need whatever for a behavior theory that leans heavily on the concept of instrumental or operant conditioning to confine its attention to external events, like the words "good" or "bad" or like pieces of candy or cuffs over the head, as sources of reinforcement. The notion of internal reinforcement has been available for a long time. Years ago, Thorndike (1932) spoke of a "confirming reaction" as essential to what we now call reinforcement. For quite some time, Russian researchers (e.g.,Figurin and Denisova 1929) referred to some forms of exploratory behavior ("orienting-investigatory activity") as "self-reinforcing." We often speak of such forms of behavior, as well as of playful behavior and of thinking, as carried on "for their own sake," by which we must mean that they are carried on for the sake of their internal rewarding consequences. The study of avoidance learning, especially when a trace-conditioning procedure or the Sidman procedure is used, has provided further examples of reinforcing conditions,

in this case safety signals or fear-reductions, that are internal
and dependent on some reaction of the animal. More recent research has turned up a much wider variety of self-administered,
internal aversive conditions and rewards that are applicable to
a wide range of learning processes, including apparently some
instances of discrimination learning (see Berlyne 1964).

Let us take another quotation from the same author
(Miller 1962) to indicate further a direction in which existing
behavior theories could profitably be extended, although he
himself seems more inclined to regard the phenomenon in
question as grounds for abandoning them altogether. In his
foreword to Weir's book, documenting the way in which a two-
year-old child practices talking to himself in his crib and apparently perfects thereby his own pronunciation and grammar.
Miller writes "Among psychologists in the United States there
has been general agreement that language learning is much like
any other kind of learning. That is to say, we have usually assumed that language learning depends critically upon a supporting environment that will respond to the child's vocaliza-
tions, that will approve or correct, that will reinforce suc-
cesses and extinguish failures until the proper stimulus-response connections are established." The phenomenon is certainly an instructive one. Something of the sort will be familiar to anybody who has tried to master a foreign language.
After being exposed to a fair sample of, say, written or spoken
French, he can react to something that he himself has uttered
by saying "No, that sounds wrong! That is not how a Frenchman
would put it!" and then try again, until he can say to himself,
"Yes, that sounds right! That sounds very French!"

Several conclusions can be drawn:

1. The infant or the would-be polyglot pronounces sentences to himself, and maybe repeats them over and over again, because the consequences, auditory, or proprioceptive, or neural, of these responses determine which verbal formulae will be retained and which will be rejected. So we have a clear case of instrumental learning with reinforcement dependent on consequences of the response.

2. Which responses are retained and which are rejected depend clearly on previous learning, since the criteria will vary with the linguistic community to which the child has been exposed. The information that is needed in order to distinguish which utterances are correct and which incorrect has come from the external environment. The main difference between what happens here and what happens in the usual instrumental-conditioning experiment is that it does not come from the external environment of the moment but has been stored within the subject after being deposited by past external environments.

3. The reinforcement or non-reinforcement of a particular response pattern depends on a comparison of its consequences with some kind of trace left by previous learning experiences. In other words, processes going on within the subject's nervous system (in this case, one process consisting of feedback from his present responses and the other of a revived trace of previous

learning) can be related either in a harmonious way, which results in reinforcement of the response pattern, or in a disharmonious way, which acts as an aversive condition and impels the subject to resume his search for a more successful response pattern.

In other words, we have a process that fits the paradigm of trial-and-error learning admirably, the principal difference between this and familiar animal-learning situations being in the kinds of motivation and reward that are at work. Yet the hypothesis that certain configurations of internal processes can be aversive and that other configurations can be rewarding is being thrust on our attention from an amazing variety of directions. In different forms, it is emerging from studies of attitude change (Brown 1962), child development (Piaget 1957), exploratory and aesthetic behavior (Berlyne 1960), humor and play (Berlyne 1966). Above all, we are compelled to consider it as soon as we face the much neglected motivational aspects of thinking (Berlyne 1965).

All these developments thus indicate deep affinities between intellectual processes including language, on the one hand, and other forms of learned behavior, on the other, rather than demonstrating the uniqueness of the former. What we call "problems" are generally situations in which the makings of conflict are discernible, and what we call "solutions" are conditions that relieve conflict. Thinking, it seems, is commonly motivated by such conditions of conflict between implicit responses as we call "uncertainty," "perplexity," "bafflement," and "puzzlement." These conditions are assuaged when we acquire, whether from an external source or from a symbolic pattern of our own construction, the information from whose lack we were suffering. As work with computers has shown, recognition of "match" or "mismatch" between the outcome of operations performed so far and a representation of what is required determines whether the machine will terminate its search or continue it, as well as indicating the direction in which the search should proceed next (Newell and Simon 1961).

There are certainly times when the problems that we seek to solve are crassly practical ones and the rewards that crown our efforts are blatantly tangible. Nevertheless, the factors that motivate the most "disinterested" search for truth are likely to be at work, mixed up with other factors, even in the most mercenary and self-preservative intellectual efforts. Their elucidation is surely needed before our understanding of problem-solving activities can make much further headway, and it is one on which many brands of research can fruitfully converge.

12 | GARLIE A. FOREHAND
Carnegie Institute of Technology

Epilogue: Constructs and Strategies for Problem-Solving Research

In the mid 1960s, research on thought processes is in either an early stage of a renaissance or the midst of a fad. The volume of research on the topic, its academic respectability, its attractiveness to psychologists and other behavioral scientists of diverse backgrounds and theoretical viewpoints all stand in marked contrast to its status in, say, the early 1950s. The beginning of the upsurge may be roughly dated. Green, in this volume, places it in the mid 1950s when information processing models began to provide a new language for talking about processes and when behaviorists began serious analysis of mediating processes. Hebb, in 1960, suggested to American psychologists that "the serious analytical study of the thought process" —the second phase of the American psychological revolution— "cannot be postponed any longer." But Hebb was observing as well as predicting; the impetus for and the outline of the developments that he foresaw were discernible in the lines of research that he reviewed. Whatever the date of origin of the phenomenon, the evidence indicates that the trend is accelerating rather than abating.

Does the new emphasis on cognitive process signify psychology's long-promised involvement in the detailed study of complex, integrated, nonartificial human behavior? Or is it the excitement of the moment, feeding upon itself and building a rickety structure of poorly defined concepts and unsupportable assumptions? Is it renaissance or fad? Several signs encourage the renaissance interpretation. First, the major approaches have developed out of time-tested traditions of research and theory, inheriting the facts, methods, and languages of their forebears. Secondly, the traditions are several; scholars working on diverse problems from diverse points of view find themselves led by the development of their research programs to ask similar questions. Thirdly, the resulting studies bear the earmarks of maturity: disciplined interplay among hypothesis, theory, method, and data. With respect to problem solving, the papers in this volume document the last point. The first two provide a context for these contributions.

Current research in problem solving stems from several different historical streams of thought. As a result, there are distinguishable traditions in such research, and if they have not congealed into mutually uncommunicative "systems," they do reflect, in method and concept, their respective patrimonies. Most contemporary studies of problem solving can be classified into four such approaches.

The oldest of the contemporary approaches is that developing from classical Gestalt psychology. While other approaches came to their interest in cognition by way of related concepts, such as learning or intelligence, the Gestalt approach has remained adamantly devoted to the analysis of internal process. Proponents of this approach have been diligent in their demonstrations that a simplistic explanation of the mind (most especially a behavioristic one) is not sufficient to account for observable phenomena. However, the holistic postulate that guided these investigations also prevented very much in the way of detailed analysis of cognitive events to supplant the S-R mechanisms so vehemently rejected. If S-R mechanisms were too simple an explanation, unanalyzed concepts of insight, fixation, and cognitive organization were certainly too vague. Contemporary representatives of this approach, while retaining the holistic postulate, have sought to develop more rigorous concepts of cognitive functioning. A result has been numerous studies of the nature of cognitive organization, of its developmental origin, and of its influence on covariation of traits. A number of contemporary research programs stemming from this tradition are outlined in the papers edited by Constance Scheerer (1964).

A second tradition of studying problem solving has been the psychometric. The classic concern of this approach has been to understand the nature of intelligence, and its most characteristic method has been the attempt to discover and interpret additive components of general mental ability. The factors thus defined are, in effect, theoretical constructs derived from statistical relationships among the end products of problem-solving activity. The major concern is with traits and the approach has had little to say about processes of or conditions for problem solving. The study of intellectual traits, however, must concern itself to some extent with the nature of problem solving *per se*, at least in the initial (item construction) and final (factor interpretation) phases. It seems likely that the measurement emphasis of the psychometric approach can be combined profitably with experimental techniques and theoretical concepts from other traditions. Proposals for such combinations have been made by Guilford (1961) and Green (1964), but work on these proposals is just beginning.

The third contemporary approach to problem solving has grown out of the laboratory study of learning. Of all pervasive interests of psychologists, the study of learning has been the most distrustful of mentalistic speculation, the most insistent upon external referents for the terms used in explanation, and, in general, the most sympathetic to behaviorism. It was the dominance of behavioristic analysis of learning in the psychological research of this country that led to the long hiatus in analytical study of thought that Hebb observed. Learning theory never denied the reality or importance of the phenomena termed problem solving, conceptualization, and the like; instead it maintained that the phenomena can be accounted for most efficiently by means of constituent elementary relationships among stimuli and responses, and that premature invention of nonoperational concepts is a hindrance rather than a help to the development of the desired explanations. As learning theorists have established elementary principles and developed their laboratory techniques, they have moved toward attempting the promised analyses of complex processes. In doing so, they have, in general, remained faithful to their heritage by postulating internal processes cautiously, and, when doing so, by expressing them as mediating S-R processes, obeying the same laws as elementary behavioral processes.

Finally, the youngest of the major approaches to problem
solving is the information-processing approach. This approach
derived much of its impetus from a source outside traditional
psychology—the programming of computers to solve complex
problems. Examining the programming techniques required to
accomplish such "artificial intelligence," some psychologists
postulated that programs might serve not only to supplement
human cognitive processes but also to provide theoretical
models of them. Thus a new technique, computer simulation,
came into being. Computer models provided a method for detailed and rigorous specification of postulated cognitive processes, and a built-in "sufficiency test" of the specifications.
The mechanics of programming facilitated the statement of
cognitive processes in terms of the vicissitudes of information
in a processing system—its coding, storage, retrieval, and
transformation. This conception found kinship with certain
ideas within Gestalt psychology, notably those of Wertheimer
(1945) and Duncker (1945), and with the European systems
summarized (and represented) by de Groot in this volume.
From the combination has developed a lively new information-
processing approach to psychology (Feigenbaum and Feldman,
1963; Bruner, Goodnow, and Austin, 1956). Like behaviorism, this
approach is elementistic as opposed to holistic, and is insistent
upon discipline and detail in theory statement. Like Gestalt
psychology, it accepts the validity of complex internal events,
and eschews the assumption that such processes obey the laws
of classical and operant conditioning.

This volume presents detailed contemporary statements

from representatives of two of these traditions: the learning-psychology tradition, as represented by Goldiamond, Staats, and Skinner, and the information-processing approach, as represented by Hayes, de Groot, and Paige and Simon. In addition, it presents, in the Gagné paper, an examination of the phenomena confronting the student of problem solving, and the requirements of a theoretical explanation. The other traditions are not ignored: Gestalt psychologists will find much of relevance to their concepts in a number of the information-processing analyses and in Goldiamond's analysis of the relation between perception and conceptualization. The psychometric approach is alluded to in relation to information processing by de Groot, and is discussed explicitly in relation to individual differences by Gagné. But the bulk of the volume is devoted to the contributions of behaviorism and information processing to the study of problem solving. This particular juxtaposition has proved beneficial in two ways. The presentation of the two approaches in the same volume offers the reader an opportunity to compare and contrast them. Perhaps more importantly, the fact that they were presentations on the same topic made from the same platform encouraged the authors to communicate with one another and to respond to challenges posed by different points of view. Although some of their disagreements are real and fundamental, others stem from differences in emphasis on different parts of the domain of problem solving, or on terminological variations. These papers offer an unusual opportunity to sort out the differences, to identify points of contact between the approaches, and to assess their potential contributions to an understanding of problem solving.

Gagné categorizes and discusses the phenomena to be
understood and accounted for in the study of problem solving,
and hence defines targets for theoretical argument. He explicitly draws the distinction that underlies much of the strategic
variation and most of the theoretical controversy of the other
papers in the volume: the distinction between external and internal events in problem solving. The external events which he
describes as instructions and verbal directions are the focus
of analyses by Goldiamond and Skinner, both of whom pose the
question of what, precisely, instructions are in an operant
analysis. Concerning the third category of external events,
stimuli, Gagné raises the problem of the transition between
external and internal events—the problem of encoding. This
problem is a prepotent one for information-processing theorists, and receives much of their attention, as manifested most
explicitly in this volume by de Groot.

The problem of dealing with internal events demands a
strategy for inference. The strategy that is perhaps most
widely used nowadays is model building. The model is an abstract description of a system that is regarded as analogous to
the processes of concern. The psychologist's problems are to
develop realistic (and therefore, generally complex) analogies,
to discover implications of them, to translate the implications
into properties of mental process, and to invent ways of testing
the empirical validity of these inferences. As Gagné points out,
many kinds of languages are available for expressing models;
the language of information processing well serves several
contributors to this volume. The Gagné model describes problem solving as occurring in a temporal sequence of stages,

including recall of subordinate rules, search and selection combining subordinate rules, and verification. A problem of the model builder, and of the empiricist, is to specify the rules of linkage of the stages and the condition governing the transition from one stage to another. Newell takes issue with Gagné in regard to the usefulness of a stages model, and Green reviews reasons why historical attempts to develop stages models have proven sterile. The point of issue seems to be whether the stages as the model defines them serve as rigidly bounded segments of the processing sequence. Does the model builder expect to be able to draw brackets around the events occurring during any particular time period and say that during that time period combining-subordinate-rules and nothing else occurred? Newell argues rather convincingly that a model based upon such a premise would be too rigid either to simulate human thinking or to solve problems very effectively. But it would appear that Gagné proposes a more flexible and more defensible stages model. He might suggest drawing brackets around a particular time sequence and saying that during this time period subordinate rules got combined, and that that was the main result of that segment of processing. The stage is a convenient way of summarizing the results of a (perhaps arbitrary) segment of the process. One implied question here is: At what level of abstraction does a model describe a process? Does one describe the process itself or results of a process? This question is a pervasive one for model builders, and we shall encounter it again.

Gagné's third category of phenomena in problem solving, individual differences, raises questions which need to be dealt

with by proponents of the various systems of cognitive research.
When one sets out to study problem solving, he must either begin with completely naive subjects, as the behaviorists seem to
suggest, or recognize that each of his sophisticated subjects
has developed his own unique processing system. An attempt
to model process in general will never be precisely accurate
in particular; and if one models *an* individual, as information-
processing theorists sometimes suggest, he must face the issue
of identifying *which* individual and saying how his processes
differ from those of other individuals. Gagné approaches the
problem via psychometrically defined abilities that determine
variations in outcomes of each of the stages of problem solving.
Another approach is to look for variations in the process itself;
such an approach is needed both for testing process models and
for understanding the nature of intellect. In his empirical comparisons of processing systems of highly skilled and unskilled
problem solvers, de Groot contributes to these goals, and suggests that taxonomies of processes developed in model-based
studies ought to be systematically related to statistical results
of trait-oriented research. As Taylor points out in his com-
mentary, the diverging conceptual frameworks of the two approaches present barriers to straightforward extrapolation
from one to the other. In particular, processes used in solving
complex problems may not be discoverable in the short and
simple problems usually subjected to factor analysis, and the
linear model underlying factor analysis may not be sufficient
for expressing relationships among such processes. But while
the two approaches differ in method, they share a concern with
understanding the nature of intellect. Green (1964) has explored

possible relations among them in more detail.

The major distinction between behavioristic and information-processing approaches to problem solving is perhaps best
made by referring to Gagné's definition of problem solving as
a change in behavior that results in a novel generalizable rule,
and to his classification of external and internal conditions of
problem solving. Behavioristic approaches generally emphasize the external conditions for the acquisition of the rule. Information-processing approaches are more concerned with describing the precise nature of the rule and the internal events
that constitute its acquisition, application, and generalization.
The differences between the two approaches are well revealed
by their choice of models. Information-processing approaches
look toward the computer program as the model *par excellence*
for representing internal processes in all their complexity
without sacrifice of specificity. Goldiamond, on the other hand,
proposes the animal experiment as a useful model for research
on human problem solving precisely because the experimenter's
inability to provide verbal instruction to the subject forces
maximum emphasis upon precisely controlled external events
when constructing an explanation. Each of the approaches,
therefore, has its own special strengths within the domain of
the study of problem solving, and each is confronted by challenges from the other. In this volume, both sides have responded to those challenges.

The challenge to information-processing psychology is to
relate its detailed conceptions of cognitive processing to observable events, to meet the classic demand to define its concepts operationally via the behavior of organisms. All three

representatives of this approach have emphasized this problem
in their presentations. In contrast to many previous treatments,
the concern of these papers is with information processing by
men rather than by computers. The shadow of the computer is
never far away: Paige and Simon's study of the way students
solve algebra word problems is guided by a program that
solves such problems; de Groot considers simulation to be a
goal toward which his projects work; Hayes has developed special problems that are eminently programmable, and are designed to elicit human processing analogous with that performed by the machine. But the emphasis is on data rather
than models, on discovering processes used by humans rather
than inventing ones to be used by the machine.

The classic method for studying human information processing is protocol analysis. All three of these papers make
extensive use of it, and de Groot outlines a program of study
to improve the precision of protocol analysis. He identifies the
principal tasks of protocol analysis—translation of statements
into behaviors, reconstructing chronology, coding responses
into subordinate processing mechanisms, and developing an
abstract statement of the sequence of events so identified.
Both de Groot and others refer to research in progress designed to supplement and clarify the results of protocol analysis, including the recording of eye movements, and linguistic
analysis of subjects' statements.

These psychologists have not been content with subjective
analysis of protocols, however. Each of the projects reported
here used ingenious techniques for bringing the covert thought
processes of subjects into the open.

Paige and Simon suggest that the power of a model lies in its capacity to guide empirical inquiry. Once a set of operations sufficient to solve a class of problems has been defined, an experimenter can ask to what extent subjects employ those operations. Observed differences between the performance of a model and that of subjects suggest modification of the model, and the modified model in turn poses new questions about behavior. In their contribution to this volume, Paige and Simon emphasize the phase of comparing a running model with performance of subjects. For this purpose, they have devised new techniques for observing and communicating features of the processing performed by subjects. Three features of their techniques facilitate the making of such observations: the class of problems chosen for study, the form in which problems are presented, and the behavioral outcomes elicited.

The problems chosen for study (algebra word problems) are well suited for investigating a question that both Newell and Gagné cite as central to the study of problem solving: the nature of the problem solver's internal (conceptualized, coded) representation of the problem to be solved. Algebra word problems are designed to require a translation from the problem as stated in natural language to a new problem that can be solved by algebraic manipulation. The problem expressed in algebraic terms is a result of a considerable amount of processing that has already occurred. One may ask a number of questions about the representation and the processes that produced it. Translations can sometimes be based upon purely syntactic properties of the problem statement, for example, by substituting symbols representing unknowns for certain nouns and operators for certain verbs, identified by conventional syntactic cues. (For example, "twice the number of bliks plus 8" can be translated into "$2x + 8$," whatever "bliks" might be.) On the other hand, the problem solver may (and may need to) introduce auxiliary information from his knowledge of the tangible objects referred to in the problem, making use of the semantics of the problem statement. In addition to protocols, Paige and Simon use two experimental techniques to provide behavioral evidence concerning properties of the subject's representation of the problem: having subjects set up an equation for the problem and having them draw a diagram. To distinguish between representations stemming from syntactic and semantic information, they constructed special "illogical" problems for which equations can be defined in terms of syntactic properties of the problem statement, but whose algebraic solutions "make no sense" in terms of the meanings of the words in the problem. (For example, the unknown might turn out to be a negative number while the concept identified with the unknown is length; the solution is algebraically permissible, but semantically contradictory.) If the problem-solving process is halted with the setting up of the equation, the contradiction may or may not be noticed. There is evidence that the type of representation is a consistent property of a subject's processing: subjects who set up equations representing the verbal statement also diagram properties of the verbal statement; subjects whose equations represent the physical objects described also tend to diagram the physical situation, sometimes translating the problem into a "logically" soluble, but verbally misinterpreted one. Those subjects whose representations contain physical (semantic) concepts are more likely to notice the contradictions in the problem. On the basis of these and similar findings, the authors conclude that provision for processing of auxiliary semantic information must be made in a computer model that will successfully simulate human performance on algebra word problems.

A similar concern for objective evidence of information processing is characteristic of the Amsterdam studies reported by de Groot. In the highly significant extensions of de Groot's own pioneering work on thought processes in chess (1965), a number of experimental and quantitative hypothesis testing techniques are employed. An analysis of uncertainty reduction by one-bit position guessing by chess masters yielded the surprising finding that masters are not substantially superior to either weak players or mechanical application of empirical first-order probabilities (that is, probabilities computed in ignorance of the likelihood of prior positions). This result tentatively rules out the hypothesis that knowledge of probabilities in chess will account for the superiority of chess masters. This conclusion is supported by comparing master and weak players with respect to their ability to *guess* the positions of a given set of pieces and to *reproduce* the positions after a five-second exposure. The curves plotting accuracy (percent correctly located pieces) against successive reproduction trials indicate again that master players' initial guessing of positions is not superior to that of weak players, or to empirical probabilities. The difference between master and duffer shows up in the differences between their respective reproduction and guessing curves. For masters, initial re-

productions are more than 91% accurate, and rapidly approach
100% over a few trials; for weak players, reproductions are
only slightly better than guesses, regardless of the number
of trials. These results, along with interpretations of protocols
suggest to de Groot that the superiority of master players resides in perceptual achievement, to be described in terms of
their coding systems. Thus, a question of how expert problem
solvers differ from weak ones has been refined: the question
is now posed not in terms of differences in general knowledge
of the structure of the problem, but in terms of differences in
the way in which perception of a complex stimulus array is
encoded and retained.

The experimental techniques used by Hayes are constructed on close analogy with information processing by a
computer. A list containing objects and relations between objects is stored in memory, and problems are presented which
require discovery of implications of the relations by successively operating on objects, the operations defined by the
stored relations. Having stored information by having the
subject memorize a list, Hayes can construct experimental
variations (for example, the amount of processing required,
the number of blind alleys in the problems, and the existence
of subgoals), operational definitions of dependent variables
(for example, solution time per problem), and distinct entry
points for protocol analysis. The power of using such problems
is illustrated by the experimenter's ability to define subject
variables using a combination of protocol and objective data.
For instance, Hayes' most intriguing findings are based on a
series of variables that can be generally described as time

(objectively measured) per step of analysis (inferred from protocols). Several analyses based on such measures suggest that rate of progress accelerates as a goal is approached, and that this effect depends upon the number of steps yet to be taken rather than the number already taken.

These methods also permit empirical explorations of processes postulated by information-processing models. Examples of such variables investigated by Hayes are forward versus backward (that is, beginning with the goal) processing, sequential list searching versus direct accessing as means of gaining access to a particular entry on a list, and organization of memory by means of intra-list relationships ("chunking" or "packaging" of information).

The experimental techniques employed by de Groot, Paige and Simon, and Hayes, in contrast to those characteristically used in the laboratory study of learning, focus upon subjects solving complex problems with minimal experimenter-imposed restriction. They are characteristically developed out of the study of protocols, with restrictions introduced slowly as probing devices to elicit more specific evidence about processes hypothesized in the process of interpreting protocols and writing programs. As a consequence, these techniques lack both the rigorous environmental control and the standardized procedures of, for example, the methodology of operant conditioning. The anticipated return for this cost is the ability to identify complex processes that are both rigorously specified and empirically verifiable.

If the challenge to information-processing theory is to subject its concepts to objective observation, the challenge to

the psychology of learning is to deal in a realistically complex
fashion with the events that intervene between S and R during
complex behavior. Berlyne has posed the challenge by citing
five "conspicuous and perplexing attributes of thinking" that
have been subjected to comparatively little explication by
learning theorists: the sequential nature of overt behavior that
accompanies problem solving, the sequential nature of "processes that supplement the external stimulus," the patterning
of mediating response sequences, the dependence of internal
processes upon goals ("stimulus conditions that at present are
inaccessible"), and intrinsically reinforcing properties of
thought processes. Attempts to handle such questions within
the psychology of learning have gone in two general directions:
the development of mediation theories, and operant analysis.
In this volume, the former approach is represented by Staats,
the latter by Skinner and Goldiamond.

Staats has attempted to deal with complex behavior by
means of an "integrated learning approach," which applies
the basic principles of classical and operant conditioning in
complex combinations. He conceptualizes internal events in
terms of a mediation model: a response (overt or covert) to a
stimulus becomes a stimulus for a following response. The
sequence of such S-R events is governed by complex S-R
mechanisms, the component links of which are determined by
the individual's past reinforcement history.

Staats' examples of how a mediation mechanism might
work in original problem solving provide an opportunity for
comparing this model with information processing. In his
analysis of the process of proving a geometry theorem, Staats

postulates the prior acquisition of verbal responses, such as
"quantities equal to the same quantities are equal to each
other." Each of these verbal responses has been constructed
from simpler responses (for example, "equal"), and, as a
unit, is under the control of particular discriminative stimuli.
As problem solving begins, a diagram and instructions provide
the first S^D of the chain, the response to which is a previously
learned verbal response sequence (a statement of an "implication"). This response serves immediately as a second S^D,
and produces a further response, the statement of another fact
about the geometric situation. Two verbal statements might
combine into a longer string to form a single discriminative
stimulus. This process continues until the problem solver has
emitted the verbalization that elicits as a response the statement *quod erat demonstrandum*.

This analysis suggests a straight line of reasoning from
the diagram to the solution. At a particular state in the problem-solving process, the next "response" is under the control
of present stimuli. There is no means-end analysis (comparison of desired result and present state), selective searching
of available alternatives, or use of heuristic decision criteria
for narrowing the range of alternative next steps. Such processes have been found effective for constructing sufficient
models for solving geometry problems (Gelernter, 1959), and
for logical reasoning in general (Newell & Simon, 1963).
Furthermore, there is much evidence to show that they do in
fact operate, evidence from protocols of subjects solving logical problems—most immediately in the protocols quoted by
Paige and Simon in this volume. Staats and the information-

processing psychologists have adopted different scientific strategies for constructing explanations of internal events, the one striving for simplicity, the other for sufficiency. The first question that information-processing theorists ask about their models is: Is the set of operations thus defined sufficient to achieve a solution that might be achieved by a human problem solver? The questions of the necessity of a model's components and whether it is, in fact, descriptive of human cognitive activity become relevant only when its sufficiency is established (that is, the program runs). Staats attempts to minimize the risk of postulating too many internal processes. In exchange for this parsimony he postpones the construction of a set of operations sufficient to describe any particular sequence of problem-solving processes.

This difference in methodological strategy also influences what the theorist sees when he peers into the black box. In attempting to understand a process, a continuous sequence of events, too complex and undifferentiated to be seen in its entirety, observers might select different features upon which to focus their attention. One may look for relatively short, unambiguously linked segments of the process. Staats terms these segments complex S-R mechanisms; information-processing theorists might call them chunks, nodes, or subprograms, depending on their specific functioning in a given instance. On the other hand, one might concentrate upon the processes governing the linking of these segments, making inferences when necessary from the few features of the process that he can glimpse. Staats takes the former approach. While he suggests by his examples that he expects S-R principles to be sufficient for describing process, his empirical emphasis is on the subject's repertoire of S-R mechanisms. The experiments that he reviews and the research that he outlines attempt to identify S-R mechanisms in the repertoires of subjects, and the conditions for their acquisition. One strategy based on this approach is to study original learning in children. This permits observation of the acquisition of a larger portion of the repertoire than does the study of sophisticated adults. The program of research on original learning now being conducted by Staats includes plans for longitudinal studies in which significant portions of the child's instruction is conducted and observed under controlled laboratory conditions. Such an approach offers a significant potential advantage: an opportunity for a researcher to know significant features of the content of a problem-solving subject's memory.

Skinner's "operant analysis" of problem solving does without the postulation of any events that occur "out of sight if not out of mind," be they implicit S-R mechanisms or operations on information. In developing this approach, Skinner challenges the sufficiency criterion: the sequence of operations that *can* solve a problem, though useful and interesting in itself, is not a behavioral event, and the sequence of behavior that *does* solve a problem is specific to the problem, and thus "not a prime source of data about behavior." Identifying a sample of behavior as problem solving says something about the environment in which it occurs and its effects on the environment. It does not imply that the emission of the behavior is to be accounted for by principles other than those governing any other kind of behavior.

A problem is defined when a reinforcing event is contingent upon something, either a property of the response or a property of the environment. Problem solving is the behavior that brings about the condition under which reinforcement will occur. Certain kinds of behaviors may be distinguished by the particular roles they play in problem solving. Problem solving may be hastened by the presence in the environment of discriminative stimuli which specify the contingencies of reinforcement. Constructing discriminative stimuli is a behavior that alters the situation in such a way as to facilitate solution. Such stimulus-constructing behavior is an example of a precurrent response, which is defined as a response that supplements solution. Precurrent responses include such behaviors as turning and looking, stating rules and drawing diagrams— responses which alter the stimulus situation. They also include statements of plans, resolutions and policies, which create new reinforcements.

The problem solver need not construct all of his own S^D's. He responds to many which are transmitted to him by his culture, usually but not necessarily, via verbal language, and often in the form of maxims, rules, or laws. Much problem-solving behavior can be described as rule-following, as opposed to contingency-shaped—that is, it is under the control of contingency-specifying S^D's, rather than a history of shaping through direct experience with contingencies. Many of the "processes" of problem solving may be described as rule-following precurrent responses—induction, deduction, hypothesis statement, and heuristic analysis, for example. For the operant analyst, however, description of the processes is

not a sufficient analysis of rule-following behavior. One must
specify the reinforcing circumstances under which the behavior
comes under the control of rules. Problem-solving behavior is
thus to be understood through thorough control of complex reinforcement contingencies, and the understanding will be manifested by tracing characteristics of behavior to environmental
contingencies.

A particular form of problem-solving behavior is examined in detail from an operant point of view by Goldiamond.
Goldiamond focuses upon concept attainment or abstraction.
The concept which he makes central to his analysis is the rule
that binds together a group of disparate stimuli. He suggests
that perceptual matching is a limiting case of conceptualization, in which the rule is one of equality. When the rule is
different from equality, its acquisition and application becomes
a phenomenon to be accounted for. Goldiamond proposes such
an accounting by defining a rule as an instruction and an instruction as a discriminative stimulus. The instructional discriminative stimulus is discriminative because reinforcement
of a response is contingent upon its presence. It is instructional as opposed to dimensional: if the concept to be attained
is "all red objects," the dimensional stimulus is color, with
red as the positively reinforced value, and the instructional
stimulus is that which informs the subject that color is the
relevant dimension. If the subject is adult and human the instruction process can be short-circuited by instructing the
subject to pay attention to color. In a conceptualization experiment the subject may have to induce the instruction from
successive trials. In operant-conditioning experiments, in-

structions and dimensional stimuli are usually intermingled, but they can be separated, as Goldiamond showed in an experiment in which subjects were verbally given one set of instructions, but another was reinforced. This experiment produced "insight curves"—sudden jumps from chance to near-perfect responses—with the jump occurring at the point at which the instructional shift was made by the subject.

The task of the psychologist studying problem solving then is to understand how the rule is acquired, how behavior comes under the control of the instructional discriminative stimuli. Goldiamond's operant approach to this task is in contrast with both information processing and mediation strategies. Rather than postulate internal S-R mechanisms, or develop an abstract model of the processing that the perceived stimuli undergoes, Goldiamond strives to bring the processing out into the open and under the experimenter's control. His applications of fading and shaping procedures are designed to bring about the attainment of the concept through errorless trials, by presenting the "mediations" overtly in the form of test stimuli that progress successively from simple perceptual matches to general instances of the concept. In effect, he is programming a mechanism—the subject—whose internal operations are poorly understood. The resulting program, or sequence of steps required to accomplish errorless acquisition, is a description of the process of acquiring the concept.

The "programs" of operant analysis and information-processing theory provide a basis for comparing the two approaches. The information processing theorist attempts to infer the cognitive processes of sophisticated subjects, and his programs serve as detailed specifications of his inferences. The operant analyst strives to control the processes of unsophisticated subjects, and his programs describe the environmental manipulations by which he accomplishes that end. If one's theoretical position is that "internal" events have nothing to do (or have everything to do) with the study of problem solving, one might conclude that the two approaches are diametrically opposed and have no joint contribution to make. But if one concludes that understanding of intervening events and precise knowledge of external events are both necessary conditions for solving the problem of problem solving, the approaches can be considered complementary rather than antagonistic. For example, one phenomenon that most of the contributors to his volume seem to consider contral in problem solving is that of perceptual encoding. An analysis of this phenomenon will require precise specification of stimulus input, a kind of specification that operant-analysis procedures are well designed to provide. An ultimate understanding of the phenomenon will require in addition a biological description of events occurring in the central nervous system. But it will also require translation from the language of stimulus specification to that of neurological functioning to that of overt responding, a description of results of neurological functioning expressed in terms of properties of the problem and the solution. Such descriptions are the promise of information-processing models.

The theoretical controversy in this volume is tripartite. Mediation theory and operant analysis on occasion present a common behavioristic front, notably in their joint insistence on the central role of reinforcement in determining problem-

solving (or any other) behavior. But at least as often as they
are at odds with one another, while each wages its own battle
with information-processing theory. The confrontation between
information processing and behaviorism has taken a somewhat
surprising turn. So thoroughly have the two points of view
responded to the challenges of one another that information-
processing psychologists, who generally champion the merits
of model and theory, stress experimentation and empirical results, while the behaviorists, unrivaled partisans of hard data,
engage in abstract discussion and generalization. We are permitted to observe the thought processes of the behaviorists and
the behavior of the process theorists. In part because of this
willingness to beard the lions in their respective dens, we can
occasionally detect latent agreements lurking under the different
vocabularies. Skinner grants that problem-solving process
("the course followed in moving toward a solution") is a behavioral event (and therefore, presumably a legitimate one for
psychological study), although he immediately concludes that it
"does not, however, necessarily reflect an important behavioral
process." On the other side, Paige and Simon report an extensive series of studies of precurrent responses (drawing diagrams and setting up equations) elicited by manipulated discriminative stimuli (problem statements), although they treat
them as means to the end of drawing inferences about the subjects' processes.

There are other unvoiced agreements hidden within these
papers. Indeed, it would be surprising if careful observers did
not discover similar phenomena, even if they choose to describe them differently. But the tone of the confrontation re-

mains dialectic, and it is probably more profitable to attempt to identify dimensions of controversy than to seek out instances of agreement.

One of the dimensions of controversy is the treatment of sequences of behavioral events. The operant analysts suggest that it is the constituent behaviors of such sequences that is of primary scientific interest. Their occurrence in sequence may be useful for describing contingencies of reinforcement, but the primary scientific objective is to describe the environmental circumstances in which a specified response will reliably occur. Mediation theory posits a mechanism governing the sequence of responses: a given response serves as a stimulus which controls the next response. But the mediation approach presented by Staats in this volume seems to agree with the operant analysis position that, however interesting a long string of responses may be, the basic phenomenon to be explained scientifically is the elementary S-R connection. For the information-processing psychologist the sequence itself is of major interest. The objective of the scientific study of thought is to understand the sequence as a process with laws governing the progression from one state to another.

A second point of disagreement is the role of internal events. There is frequent comment, sometimes sharp, about the advisability of postulating internal events. None of the authors discusses specifically his conceptions of neurological functioning and its relation to behavior, but it seems clear that all would agree that such functioning, at least, occurs in the black box. The question is: What should the psychologist do about it? The operant analysts would answer, "leave it alone," at least until one is ready to seek data about detailed correlation between neurological and behavioral processes. Construction of abstract concepts of internal functioning is dangerous, and, if precise control of complex environmental conditions is achieved, unnecessary. Mediation theorists propose that, whatever the specific biochemical events, they can be viewed behaviorally as stimuli evoking responses, and hence, described by the same stimulus-response laws as overt behavior. Information-processing psychologists make a less specific assumption about the nature of neural activity. They argue only that it is dynamic, that it, like behavior, occurs in sequentially linked processes. The function of a model is to describe a process in some way analogous to the presently inaccessible neural functioning. The model's language may be at varying levels of abstraction from the neurological events. It may have as elements components directly linked to neurons, synapses and nerve impulses, or it may describe relations among products of neural activity. The languages used thus far in problem-solving models are of the latter type. The criterion for a language that purports to describe the interrelationships is that it be useful for learning about and describing events that result from neural functioning. Thus, the events postulated in such models are not "mentalistic" in the sense that they refer to some reified entelechy storing and processing data. Rather they are descriptions, at a particular level of abstraction, of postulated outcomes of neural activity.

Frequently when the behavioristic and information-processing approaches clash, it is over the proper strategy for scientific inquiry. The operant analyst regards conceptions of

382 Problem Solving: Research, Method, and Theory

internal processing as dangerous; the information-processing theorist regards the search for S-R associations as sterile. Here, the precepts of each point of view can serve as healthy correctives for the excesses of proponents of the other. It is easy for behaviorists to generalize casually to complex phenomena on the basis of laboratory study of simple ones, invoking hypothetical reinforcement histories to account for particular observed behaviors. But these inferences are easier to make than to verify, and the instances thus "explained" are likely to be highly selected ones. An approach that confronts complex phenomena directly is more likely to discover events that are not explained neatly by a simple paradigm, and, if the approach is also concerned with empirical evidence, to demonstrate them. By the same token, the process approaches can profit from the hard-headed empiricism of the behaviorists. The sufficiency criterion can be an insidious one, since it provides reinforcement for the description of processes that are logically sound but not necessarily descriptive of the problem-solving processes of any organism. There is little doubt that much of the model building that has taken place describes the processes of no person other than the model builder, and does that with detours to comply with the exigencies of programming. These efforts may be useful for getting problems solved, but if they are to make contributions to psychology, their propositions must be subject to public demonstration. The contributions made by models to the understanding of human thought process will be enhanced if the theorists adopt some of the experimental techniques and much of the empirical attitude of the behaviorists. As mentors guiding the upbringing of a young science, the two approaches emphasize different character traits. The information-processing approach counsels courage, the behavioristic approach, honesty. Since a science needs to be both courageous and honest, psychology is probably fortunate, if momentarily nonplused, to have both sets of precepts.

References

Adamson, R. Inhibitory set in problem solving as related to reinforcement learning. J. exp. Psychol., 1959, 58, 280-282.

Adrian, E. D. The basis of sensations, the action of the sense organs. New York: W. W. Norton, 1928.

Anderson, R. C. & Ausubel, D. P. (Eds.) Readings in the psychology of cognition. New York: Holt, Rinehart & Winston, 1965.

Ayllon, T. & Azrin, N. H. Reinforcement and instructions with mental patients. J. exp. Anal. Behav., 1964, 7, 327-331.

Azrin, N. H. Some effects of noise on human behavior. J. exp. Anal. Behav., 1958, 1, 183-200.

Bahle, J. Zur Psychologie des musikalischen Gestaltens, eine Untersuchung über das Komponieren auf experimenteller und historischer Grundlage. Archiv für die gesamte Psychologie, 1930, 74, pp. 289-390.

Bahle, J. Der musikalische Schaffensprozess. Psychologie der schöpferischen Erlebnis und Antriebsformen. Leipzig: Hirzel, 1936.

Bahle, J. Eingebung und Tat im musikalischen Schaffen. Ein Beitrag zur Psychologie der Entwicklungs—und Schaffensgesetze schöpferischer Menschen. Leipzig: Hirzel, 1939.

Bandura, A. Social learning through imitation. In Marshall R. Jonex (Ed.) Nebraska Symposium on Motivation. Lincoln: University of Nebraska Press, 1962.

Baylor, G. W. Report on a mating combination program. Professional paper SP-2150, System Development Corporation, 2500 Colorado Avenue, Santa Monica, California, 1965.

Berlyne, D. E. Conflict, arousal and curiosity. New York: McGraw-Hill, 1960.

Berlyne, D. E. Motivational problems raised by exploratory and epistemic behavior. In S. Koch (Ed.) Psychology — A study of a science. Vol. 5. New York: McGraw-Hill, 1963.

Berlyne, D. E. Emotional aspects of learning. Annual Review of Psychology, 1964, 15, 115-142.

Berlyne, D. E. Structure and direction in thinking. New York: Wiley, 1965.

Berlyne, D. E. Laughter, humor and play. In G. Lindzey & E. Aronson (Eds.) Handbook of Social Psychology. (2nd ed.) Boston: Addison-Wesley, 1966.

Berryman, R., Cumming, W. N. & Nevin, J. A. Acquisition of delayed matching in the pigeon. J. exp. Anal. Behav., 1963, 6, 101-107.

Bloch, H. D. Learning in some simple nonbiological systems. American Scientist, 1965, 53, 59-79.

Bloomfield, L. Teaching children to read. In L. Bloomfield and C. L. Barnhart Let's read: A linguistic approach. Detroit: Wayne State Univ. Press, 1961.

Blough, D. Delayed matching in the pigeon. J. exp. Anal. Behav., 1959, 2, 151-160.

Bobrow, Daniel G. Natural language input for a computer problem solving system, MAC-TR-1, Project MAC, Massachusetts Institute of Technology, 1964a.

Bobrow, Daniel G. A question-answering system for high school algebra word problems, AFIPS Conference Proceedings. Vol. 26. Fall Joint Conference. Baltimore: Spartan Books, 1964b.

Bridgman, P. W. The way things are. Cambridge, Massachusetts, 1959.

Brown, R. Models of attitude change. In R. Brown, E. Galanter, E. H. Hess & G. Mandler New directions in psychology. New York: Holt, Rinehart & Winston, 1962.

Brown, R. & Fraser, C. The acquisition of syntax. In C. N. Cofer & B. S. Musgrave (Eds.) Verbal behavior and learning. New York: McGraw-Hill, 1963, pp. 158-196.

Bruner, J. S. The act of discovery. Harvard. educ. Rev., 1961, 31, 21-32.

Bruner, J. S., Goodnow, Jacqueline J., &. Austin, G. A. A study of thinking. New York: Wiley, 1956.

Bunderson, C. V. Personal communication, 1965.

Chomsky, N. Verbal behavior (a review of Skinner's book). Language, 1959, 35, 26-58.

Clark, J. H. Adaptive machines in psychiatry. In N. Wiener & J. P. Schadé (Eds.) Nerve, Brain and Memory Models. Amsterdam, 1963.

Cofer, C. N. Reasoning as an associative process: III. The role of verbal responses in problem solving. J. gen. Psychol., 1957, 57, 55-68.

Cohen, B. D., Kalish, H. I., Thurston, J. R. & Cohen, E. Experimental manipulation of verbal behavior. J. exp. Psychol., 1954, 46, 106-110.

Cohen, H. L. Behavioural architecture. Architectural Assn. J. (London) 1964, June, 7-12.

Cohen, H. L. G.S.C. 205 — Man's contemporary environment. Carbondale: Southern Illinois University, 1965.

Cohen, H. L., Kibler, R. J. & Miles, D. T. A preliminary report on a pilot study for educating low achievers. The Superior Student, 1964, 6, No. 2, 36-45.

Craig, R. C. The transfer value of guided learning. New York: Teacher's College, Columbia University, 1953.

Djakow, Petrowski & Rudik. Psychologie des Schachspiels. Berlin: Walter de Gruyter, 1927.

Dollard, J. & Miller, N. E. Personality and psychotherapy. New York: McGraw-Hill, 1950.

Duncan, C. P. Recent research on human problem solving. Psychol. Bull., 1959, 56, 397-429.

Duncker, K. On problem solving. Psychol. Monogr., 1945, 58(5), Whole No. 270.

Edfeldt, A. W. Silent speech and silent reading. Chicago: University of Chicago, 1960.

Feigenbaum, E. A. & Feldman, J. (Eds.) Computers and thought. New York: McGraw-Hill, 1963.

Feldman, J. Simulation of behavior in the binary choice experiment. Proceedings of the Western Joint Computer Conference, 1961, 19, 133-144.

Figurin, N. L. & Denisova, M. P. [Experimental investigation of the reaction to novelty]. In Voprosy geneticheskoi refleksologii (Questions of genetic reflexology). Leningrad, 1929.

Finley, J. R. & Staats, A. Evaluative meaning words as reinforcing stimuli. J. educ. Psychol., submitted.

Fuller, R. B. Personal communication, 1965.

Gagné, R. M. Problem solving and thinking. Annual Rev. Psychol., 1959, 10, 147-172.

Gagné, R. M. Problem solving. In A. W. Melton (Ed.) Categories of human learning. New York: Academic Press,
1964, pp. 293-317.

Gagné, R. M. The conditions of learning. New York: Holt,
Rinehart & Winston, 1965a.

Gagné, R. M. The analysis of instructional objectives for the
design of instruction. In R. Glaser (Ed.) Teaching machines and programed learning, II: Data and directions.
Washington, D.C.: National Education Association, 1965b.

Gagné, R. M. & Brown, L. T. Some factors in the programming of conceptual learning. J. exp. Psychol., 1961, 62,
313-321.

Garfinkel, Sylvia. Heuristic solution of first-year algebra
problems, Working Paper #11, Management Science Group,
Institute of Industrial Relations, University of California,
(Berkeley), February, 1960.

Gelernter, H. Realization of a geometry-theorem proving
machine. Proc. International Conference on Information
Processing, Paris. UNESCO House, 1959, 273-282. (Reprinted in Feigenbaum & Feldman, 1963.)

Gere, W. S., Jr. A heuristic approach to job shop scheduling.
Unpub. doctoral dissertation, Carnegie Institute of Technology, 1962.

Getzels, J. W. & Jackson, P. W. Creativity and intelligence.
New York: Wiley, 1962.

Goldiamond, I. Indicators of perception: I. Subliminal perception, subception, unconscious perception: an analysis in
terms of psychophysical indicator methodology. Psychol.
Bull., 1958, 55, 373-411.

Goldiamond, I. Visual signal detection, perception, and response variables as functions of development and mental
retardation. In Perceptual and Response Abilities of Mentally Retarded Children. Southern Illinois University, HEW
Cooperative Research Project No. 176 (6471), 1959.

Goldiamond, I. Perception. In A. J. Bachrach (Ed.) The experimental foundations of clinical psychology. New York:
Basic Books, 1962.

Goldiamond, I. Response bias in perceptual communication.
Disorders of Communication, Vol. XLII: Research Publi-
cations, A.R.N.M.D., 1964, 334-363.

Goldiamond, I. A research and demonstration procedure in stimulus control, abstraction, and environmental programming. J. exp. Anal. Behav., 1964, 7, 216.

Goldiamond, I. Justified and unjustified alarm over behavioral control. In O. Milton (Ed.) Behavior Disorders: Perspectives and Trends. Philadelphia: J. B. Lippincott Co.,1965a.

Goldiamond, I. Experimental studies of perceptual processes, Progress Report, NASA contract No. NsG-450, January 1965b.

Goldiamond, I. Stuttering and fluency as manipulable operant response classes. In L. Krasner and L. P. Ulmann (Eds.) Research in Behavior Modification. New York: Holt, Rinehart & Winston, 1965c.

Goldiamond, I., Dryud, J., & Miller, M. Practice as research in professional psychology. The Canadian Psychologist, January 1965.

Goldiamond, I., & Malpass, L. F. Locus of hypnotically induced changes in color vision responses. J. opt. Soc. Amer., 1958, 51, 1117-1121.

Goldiamond, I., & Pliskoff, S. S. Single-stage versus multistage methods in learning experiments: classical work as a limiting case (in preparation).

Goldiamond, I., & Pliskoff, S. S. Music education and the rationale underlying programmed instruction. Music Ed. J., 1965, 51, No. 4, 43-47, 190-195.

Green, B. F. Intelligence and computer simulation. Transactions of the New York Academy of Science, 1964 Ser. II, 27, 55-63.

Groot, A. D. de. Het Denken van den Schaker. Amsterdam, The Netherlands, 1946.

Groot, A. D. de. Thought and choice in chess. The Hague: Mouton & Co., 1965.

Gruber, H. E., Terrell, G., & Wertheimer, M. (Eds.) Contemporary approaches to creative thinking. New York: Atherton Press, 1962.

Guilford, J. P. Factorial angles to psychology. Psychol. Rev., 1961, 68, 1-20.

Guilford, J. P. Basic conceptual problems in the psychology of thinking. In E. Harms (Ed.) Fundamentals of psychology: The psychology of thinking. Annals of the New York Academy of Science, 1960, 91, Art. 1, pp. 6-21.

Guilford, J. P. Basic traits in intellectual performance. In
C. W. Taylor (Ed.) The second (1957) University of Utah
research conference on the identification of creative scientific talent. Salt Lake City: University of Utah Press,
1958.

Guilford, J. P. Personality. New York: McGraw-Hill, 1959.

Guilford, J. P., & Hoepfner, R. R. Current summary of struc-
ture-of-intellect factors and suggested tests. Rep. Psychol. Lab., No. 30. University of Southern California, Los
Angeles, December 1963.

Harman, H. H. Modern factor analysis. Chicago: University
of Chicago Press, 1960.

Hawkes, H. E., Luby, W. A., & Touton, F. C. New second
course in Algebra. (enlarged ed.) Boston: Ginn & Co., 1929.

Hayes, J. R. Problem topology and the solution process. J.
Verb. Learn. Verb. Behav.,1965, 4, 371-379.

Hebb, D. O. The American Revolution. Amer. Psychologist,
1960, 15, 735-745.

Herrnstein, R. J. & Loveland, D. H. Complex visual concept in
the pigeon. Science, 1964, 146.

Holland, J. G., & Skinner, B. F. The analysis of behavior.
New York: McGraw-Hill, 1961.

Hull, C. L. Quantitative aspects of the evolution of concepts.
Psychol. Monogr., 1920, No. 123.

Hull, C. L. Principles of behavior. New York: Appleton-
Century-Crofts, 1943.

Hunt, E. B. Concept learning: An information processing
problem. New York: Wiley, 1962.

Jenkins, J. J. Mediated associations: Paradigms and situations. In C. N. Cofer and B. S. Musgrave (Eds.) Verbal
behavior and learning. New York: McGraw-Hill, 1963.

Johnson, D. M. The psychology of thought and judgment. New
York: Harper, 1955.

Judson, A. J., Cofer, C. N., & Gelfand, S. Reasoning as an
associative process: II. "Direction" in problem solving as
a function of prior reinforcement of relevant responses.
Psychol. Reps., 1956, 2, 501-507.

Katona, G. Organizing and memorizing. New York: Columbia
University Press, 1940.

Keller, F. S., & Schoenfeld, W. N. Principles of psychology.
New York: Appleton-Century-Crofts, 1950.

Kendler, H. H., & Kendler, T. S. Vertical and horizontal processes in problem solving. Psychol. Rev., 1962, 69, 1-16.

Kendler, Tracy S. Development of mediating responses in
children. Monog. Society for Research in Child Develop.,
28(Whole No. 86), 33-48, 1963.
Koffka, K. Principles of Gestalt psychology. New York: Har-
court Brace, 1935.
Kohler, W. The mentality of apes. New York: Harcourt Brace, 1925.
Krasner, L. Studies of the conditioning of verbal behavior.
Psychol. Bull., 1958, 55, 148-170.
Krechevsky, I. The docile nature of "hypotheses." J. comp.
Psychol., 1933, 15, 429-443.
Laughery, K. R. An information processing analysis of prob-
lem solving behavior. Unpub. doctoral dissertation, Car-
negie Institute of Technology, Pittsburgh, Pa., 1961.
Laughery, K. R., & Gregg, L. W. Simulation of human problem-
solving behavior. Psychometrika, 1962, 27, p. 265-282.
Leibnitz, G. W. New essays concerning human understanding
(1765). New York: MacMillan, 1896.
Luce, R. D., Bush, R. R., & Galanter, E. Handbook of mathe-
matical psychology. Vols. I and II. New York: Wiley, 1963.
Luchins, A. S. Mechanization in problem solving. The effect
of Einstellung. Psychol. Monogr., 1942, 54 (Whole No. 248).
Mach, Ernst. The science of mechanics. Translated by T. J.
McCormack, Chicago, 1893.
Mackworth, N. H. Originality. Amer. Psychologist, 1965, 20, 51-66.
Maier, N. R. F. Reasoning in humans: I. On direction. J.
comp. Psychol., 1930, 10, 115-143.
Maier, N. R. F. Reasoning in humans: II. The solution of a
problem and its appearance in consciousness. J. comp.
Psychol., 1931, 12, 181-194.
Maier, N. R. F. The behavior mechanisms concerned with
problem solving. Psychol. Rev., 1940, 47, 43-58.
Maltzman, I., Brooks, L. O., Bogartz, W., & Summers, S. S.
The facilitation of problem solving by prior exposure to
uncommon responses. J. exp. Psychol., 1958, 56, 399-406.
Maltzman, I. Thinking: from a behavioristic point of view.
Psychol. Rev., 1955, 62, 275-286.
McNemar, Q. Lost: Our intelligence? Why? Amer. Psy-
chologist, 1964, 19, 871-882.
Millenson, J. R. On the Relationship Between Behavioristic
Stimulus-Response Notation and Flow Diagram Notation as
Representation of Algorithmic Problem Solving. Carnegie
Institute of Technology, Psychology Dept., Pittsburgh, Pa.
(CIP Paper #71) June 22, 1964. Ditto.

Miller, G. A. Foreword by a psychologist. In R. H. Weir: Language in the crib. The Hague: Mouton, 1962.

Miller, G. A. Some psychological studies of grammar. Amer. Psychol., 1962, 17, 748-762.

Miller, G. A. Some preliminaries to psycholinguistics. Amer. Psychol., 1965, 20, 15-20.

Miller, G. A., Galanter, E., & Pribram, K. H. Plans and the structure of behavior. New York: Holt, Rinehart & Winston, 1960.

Moore, E. F. (Ed.) Sequential Machines. Addison-Wesley,1964.

Moore, O. K., & Anderson, Scarvia B. Modern logic and tasks for experiments on problem solving behavior. J. Psychol., 1954, 38, 151-160.

Mowrer, O. H. The psychologist looks at language. Amer. Psychol., 1954, 9, 660-694.

Müller, G. E. Literaturbericht von Otto Selz's: Uber die Gesetze des geordneten Denkverlaufs. Z. Psychol., 1919, 82, pp. 102-120.

Neisser, U. The imitation of man by machine. Science, 1963, 139, 193-197.

Newell, A., Shaw, J. C., & Simon, H. A. Elements of a theory of human problem solving. Psychol. Rev., 1958, 65, 151-166.

Newell, A., Shaw, J. C., & Simon, H. A. Report on a general problem-solving program. The RAND Corporation, Paper P-1584, February, 1959.

Newell, A., & Simon, H. A. The simulation of human thought. In W. Dennis (Ed.) Current trends in psychological theory. Pittsburgh: Univ. of Pittsburgh Press, 1961.

Newell, A., & Simon, H. A. GPS, A program that simulates human thought. In E. A. Feigenbaum & J. Feldman (Eds.) Computers and thought. New York: McGraw-Hill, 1963.

Newell, A., & Simon, H. A. Computers in psychology, Chapter 7, pp. 361-428 in Luce, Bush, Galanter (Eds.) Handbook of Mathematical Psychology, Volume 1. New York: Wiley, 1963.

Newell, A., & Simon, H. A. An example of human chess play in the light of chess playing programs. In J. P. Schadé (Ed.) Progress in Biocybernetics. Amsterdam: Elsevier Publishing Co., 1965.

Osgood, C. E. Method and theory in experimental psychology. Oxford Univ. Press, 1953.

Osgood, C. E., & Suci, G. J. Factor analysis of meaning. J. exp. Psychol., 1955, 50, 325-338.

Piaget, J. Logique et Equilibre dans les comportements du sujet. In L. Apostel, B. Mandelbrot, & J. Piaget: Logique et équilibre. (Etudes d'Epistém. Génèt. II). Paris: Presses Universitaires de France, 1957.

Pliskoff, S. S., & Goldiamond, I. Some discriminative properties of ratio performance in the pigeon. J. exp. Anal. Behav., in press.

Polanyi, Michael. Personal Knowledge. University of Chicago Press, 1960.

Polanyi, Michael. The study of man. London, 1958.

Polya, G. How to solve it. New York: Doubleday, 1957.

Révész, G. Die Formenwelt des Tastsinnes I und II. The Hague: Martinus Nijhoff, 1938.

Russell, W. A., & Jenkins, J. J. The complete Minnesota norms for responses to 100 words from the Kent-Rosanoff word association test. Tech. Rep. No. 11. Contract No. N8 onr-66216 between the Office of Naval Research and University of Minnesota, 1954.

Russell, W. A., & Storms, L. H. Implicit verbal chaining in paired-associate learning. J. exp. Psychol., 1955, 49, 287-293.

Salaman, R. A. In A history of technology, Vol. 3, edited by Charles Singer, E. J. Holmyard, A. R. Hall, and Trevor I. Williams. London: 1957.

Salzinger, K. Experimental manipulation of verbal behavior: A review. J. gen. Psychol., 1959, 61, 65-94.

Scheerer, Constance (Ed.) Cognition: Theory, research, promise. New York: Harper & Row, 1964.

Schultz, R. W. Problem solving behavior and transfer. Harvard educ. Rev., 1960, 30, 61-77.

Sells, S. B. The atmosphere effect: An experimental study of reasoning. Arch. Psychol., 1936, Whole No. 200.

Selz, O. Uber die Gesetze des geordneten Denkverlaufs. Stuttgart: Spemann, 1913.

Selz, O. Zur Psychologie des produktiven Denkens und des Irrtums. Bonn: Friedrich Cohen, 1922.

Selz, O. Die Gesetze der produktiven und reproduktiven Geistestätigkeit, Kurzgefasste Darstellung. Bonn: Friedrich Cohen, 1924.

Selz, O. Versuche zur Hebung des Intelligenzniveaus. Ein Beitrag zur Theorie der Intelligenz und ihrer erziehlichen Beeinflüssung. Z. Psychol., 1935, 134, pp. 236-301.

Shepard, R. Review of E. A. Feigenbaum & J. Feldman (Eds.) Computers and thought, New York: McGraw-Hill, 1963. Behavioral Science, 1964, 9, 57-65.

Sherman, J. A. Use of reinforcement and imitation to reinstate verbal behavior in mute psychotics. J. abnorm. Psychol., 1965, in press.

Shute, W. G., Shirk, W. W., & Porter, G. F. Plane and solid geometry. New York: American Book, 1960.

Sidman, M. Tactics of scientific research. New York: Basic Books, 1960.

Sidman, M. Personal communication, 1965.

Simon, H. A. Administrative behavior. (2nd ed.) New York: MacMillan, 1957.

Simon, H. A., & Newell, A. Computer simulation of human thinking and problem solving. Datamation, 1961, 7, 18-20.

Simon, H. A., & Newell, A. Information processing in computer and man. Amer. Scientist, 1964, 52, 281-300.

Skinner, B. F. Are theories of learning necessary? Psychol. Rev., 1950, 57, 193-216.

Skinner, B. F. Verbal behavior. New York: Appleton-Century-Crofts, 1957.

Skinner, B. F. Pigeons in a pelican. Amer. Psychol., 1960, 15, 28-37.

Skinner, B. F. Teaching machines. Sci. Amer., 1961, 205, 90-102.

Skinner, B. F. Operant behavior. Amer. Psychol., 1963, 18, 503-515.

Spence, K. W. The nature of discrimination learning in animals. Psychol. Rev., 1936, 43, 427-449.

Staats, A. W. A behavioristic study of verbal and instrumental response-hierarchies and their relationship to human problem solving. Unpub. doctoral dissertation, University of California, Los Angeles, 1955.

Staats, A. W. Verbal and instrumental response-hierarchies and their relationship to problem solving. Amer. J. Psychol., 1957, 70, 442-446.

Staats, A. W. Verbal habit-families, concepts, and the operant conditioning of word classes. Psychol. Rev., 1961, 68, 190-204.

Staats, A. W. Comments on Professor Russell's paper. In C. N. Cofer & B. S. Musgrave (Eds.) Verbal behavior and learning. New York: McGraw-Hill, 1963.

Staats, A. W. Human learning. New York: Holt, Rinehart & Winston, 1964a.

Staats, A. W. Operant learning principles and communication. In A. W. Staats (Ed.) Human learning. New York: Holt, Rinehart & Winston, 1964c.

Staats, A. W. Conditioned stimuli, conditioned reinforcers, and word meaning. In A. W. Staats (Ed.) Human learning. New York: Holt, Rinehart & Winston, 1964d.

Staats, A. W., & Butterfield, W. Treatment of non-reading in a culturally-deprived delinquent child: An application of reinforcement principles. Child Developm., in press.

Staats, A. W., Finley, J. R., Minke, K. A., & Wolf, M. Reinforcement variables in the control of unit reading responses. J. exp. Anal. Behav.,1964, 7, 139-149.

Staats, A. W., Minke, K. A., Finley, J. R., Wolf, M., & Brooks, O. H. A reinforcer system and experimental procedure for the laboratory study of reading acquisition. Child Developm., 1964, 35, 209-231.

Staats, A. W., & Staats, C. K. Complex human behavior. New York: Holt, Rinehart & Winston, 1963.

Staats, A. W., Staats, C. K., Finley, J. R., & Minke, K. A. Mediating responses in the operant conditioning of word classes. Tech. Rep. No. 21. Contract No. 2794(02) between the Office of Naval Research and Arizona State University 1961a.

Staats, A. W., Staats, C. K., Minke, K. A., & Finley, J. R. Operant conditioning of a class of negative evaluative meaning words. Tech. Rep. No. 20. Contract No. 2794(02) between the Office of Naval Research and Arizona State University, 1961b.

Staats, A. W., Staats, C. K., Schutz, R. E., & Wolf, M. The conditioning of textual responses using "extrinsic" reinforcers. J. exp. Anal. Behav., 1962, 5, 33-40.

Swets, J. A., Tanner, W. P., Jr., & Birdsall, T. G. Decision processes in perception. Psychol. Rev., 1961, 68, 301-340.

Taube, Mortimer. Computers and Common Sense. New York, 1961.

Taylor, C. W. Some variables functioning in productivity and creativity. In C. W. Taylor (Ed.) The second (1957) University of Utah research conference on the identification of creative scientific talent. Salt Lake City: University of Utah Press, 1958.

Taylor, C. W. (Ed.) Creativity: Progress and potential. New York: McGraw-Hill, 1964.

Taylor, D. W. Thinking. In M. H. Marx (Ed.) Theories in Contemporary Psychology. New York: MacMillan, 1963, pp. 475-493.

Taylor, D. W. Decision making and problem solving. In J. G. March (Ed.) Handbook of organizations. Chicago: Rand McNally, 1965, pp. 48-86.

Taylor, D. W. Thinking and creativity. In E. Harms (Ed.) Fundamentals of psychology: The psychology of thinking. Annals of the New York Academy of Sciences, 1960, 91, Art. 1, pp. 108-127.

Terrace, H. S. Discrimination learning with and without "errors." J. exp. Anal. Behav., 1963, 6, 1-27.

Terrace, H. S. Errorless transfer of a discrimination across two continua. J. exp. Anal. Behav., 1963, 6, 223-232.

Thorndike, E. L. The fundamentals of learning. New York: Teachers College, 1932.

Tonge, F. M. A heuristic program for assembly line balancing. Englewood Cliffs, N. J.: Prentice-Hall, 1961.

Underwood, B. J. The representativeness of rote verbal learning. In A. W. Melton (Ed.) Categories of human learning. New York: Academic Press, 1964, pp. 48-78.

Underwood, B. J., & Schulz, R. W. Meaningfulness and verbal learning. Chicago: Lippincott, 1960.

Verhave, T. Recent developments in the experimental analysis of behavior. Proc. Eleventh Research Council. Amer. Meat Institution Foundation, Chicago, 1959, 113-136.

Verplanck, W. S. Unaware of where's awareness: Some verbal operants—notates, monents, and notants. In C. W. Eriksen (Ed.) Behavior and awareness. Durham: Duke Univ. Press, 1962.

Wertheimer, M. Productive thinking. New York: Harper & Row, 1945.

Wittrock, M. C. The learning by discovery hypothesis, 1965, in press.

Wundt, W. Uber Austrageexperimente und Über die Methoden zur Psychologie des Denkens. Psychol. Studien, 1907, 3, pp. 301-360.

Yntema, D. B., & Mueser, G. E. Remembering the present state of a number of variables. J. exp. Psychol., 1960, 60, 18-22.

Yntema, D. B., & Mueser, G. E. Keeping track of variables that have few or many states. J. exp. Psychol., 1962, 63, 391-395.

Zeigarnik, B. Über das Behalten von erledigten und einer-
   ledigten Handlungen. Psychol. Forsch., 1927, 9, 1-85.
Zimmerman, D. W. Durable secondary reinforcement: Method
   and theory. Psychol. Rev., 1957, 64, 373-383.

INDEX